W9-BNI-438

Murder

of a

Journalist

TRUE CRIME HISTORY SERIES

Murder

of a

Journalist

...

The True Story of the Death of Donald Ring Mellett

...

THOMAS CROWL

The Kent State University Press

Kent, Ohio

© 2009 by Thomas Crowl

ALL RIGHTS RESERVED

Library of Congress Catalog Card Number 2009005098

ISBN 978-1-60635-002-7

Manufactured in the United States of America

LIBRARY OF CONGRESS CATALOGING-IN-PUBLICATION DATA

Crowl, Thomas.

Murder of a journalist : the true story of the death of Donald Ring Mellett /
Thomas Crowl.

p.   cm. —   (True crime history series)

Includes bibliographical references and index.

ISBN 978-1-60635-002-7 (pbk. : alk. paper) ∞

1. Mellett, Donald Ring, 1891–1926.   2. Murder—Ohio—Canton.
3. Murder victims—Ohio—Canton.   4. Trials (Murder)—Ohio—Canton.   I. Title.

HV6534.C282C76 2009

364.152'3092—dc22

2009005098

British Library Cataloging-in-Publication data are available.

13 12 11 10 09   5 4 3 2 1

This book is dedicated with love to my daughters,
Jennifer and Laura

Contents

Preface

The late-nineteenth-century press lord and father of journalism's highest award, Joseph Pulitzer, wrote in 1904, "Our republic and its press will rise or fall together. An able, disinterested public spirited press, with trained intelligence to know right, and courage to do it, can preserve that public virtue without which popular government is a sham and a mockery."

Pulitzer knew something about journalism as a profession and the role of the press in a free society, having himself become rich crusading against public and private corruption. Pulitzer introduced a populist appeal to newspapers, asking the public to accept them as a champion of the little guy. His splashy investigative articles and editorial crusades worked. Circulation went up and with it profits and influence. Every successful publisher of the day would have to follow some version of Pulitzer's model. There were critics, and charges of yellow journalism, but the industrialization of newspapers by large corporations seeking profit ensured that Pulitzer's template would endure. Despite this new aggressiveness by the press, violence against journalists was very unusual.

The 1926 murder of Donald Ring Mellett was an exception—a rare act of retribution against a journalist for what he advocated in print.

The 1920s are remembered today for bootleggers and gangsters who organized crime syndicates that were far more sophisticated than most city law agencies and who operated across the lines of legal jurisdiction. A newspaper editor murdered for his editorial stance would be shocking today. But in the 1920s—the Roaring Twenties—at the height of Prohibition, it was seen not as a killing but an assassination, with the victim becoming a martyr. The Eighteenth Amendment was adopted to bring about a better world, one free of the social ills associated with alcoholic excess. Instead, Prohibition resulted in a rise in crime, rich and powerful bootleggers, gangland violence, and widespread corruption. Prohibition could not have arrived at a worse time. The country was in a buoyant mood. A world war had just been won, and the United States was an emerging world power. The stock market was in a seemingly endless climb, fueled by borrowed money. And then there were the flappers wearing eye-popping short skirts, smoking, listening to the new jazz, and dancing the Charleston. Prohibition was seen by many Americans as spoiling the party and was ignored in the pursuit of a good time. Reasoned voices in America, especially in the press, decried the decline in accepted mores and increasing disregard for the law. Their editorial protests generally lacked a focal point, however, and did not succeed in sparking national outrage.

But, for a brief time, the slaying of Don Mellett did provide the focus needed to bring the issue of corruption and chaos to national attention. While calling for the speedy apprehension and punishment of Mellett's slayers, many editors could not resist the opportunity afforded by the murder to attack what they saw as an epidemic of lawlessness that an apathetic American public seemed willing to tolerate. Press giant William Randolph Hearst wrote in the trade journal *Editor and Publisher* that the assassination was "a crime against human life, a crime against freedom of the press, a crime against the safety of the public."[1] Journalists saw Mellett's death as an assault by powerful criminal forces on their most cherished ideal: the freedom of the press. For many in the newspaper world, nothing less than the fate of the republic was at stake.

Don Mellett was not your typical 1920s journalist. A college-educated, temperate, and God-fearing man, Mellett came from a family of newspapermen in Indiana that believed it was the duty of the press to work for the public good. He married his high school sweetheart and was father to four young children. As the sixth of seven sons born to a small-town publisher, Mellett was, not surprisingly, highly competitive. His much-traveled career included stints as the editor of a pro-Prohibition paper and of his own failed daily in Indiana. At age thirty-three, Mellett landed in Canton, Ohio, and in less than a year became editor and publisher of the *Canton Daily News*, one of several papers owned by former Ohio governor James Cox and the number-two paper in a two-newspaper town. Mellett, who came to the job feeling he was a failure, was determined to achieve the professional success that had thus far eluded him.

Canton, nicknamed "Little Chicago," was a typical midsized northern industrial city with a large immigrant population and more than its share of crime and corruption.[2] Robert T. Small of the *Daily News* wrote, "Canton is not the wickedest city in America. It is but a way station . . . on the national highway of crime."[3] Here Mellett found fertile ground for a crusading journalist bent on boosting circulation. He set out to reform Canton, whether or not Canton wanted to be reformed. He approached the task with a zeal that bordered on recklessness. Mellett was not only going to make the hapless *Daily News* profitable, but he was going to make it a force to be reckoned with in the region.

Don Mellett never doubted that his vision for Canton was right. He expected to step on toes, in high and low places, as he hung Canton's dirty laundry out for everyone to see. Occasionally, he pushed the limits of journalistic ethics to make his point. Yet to him, attacking crime bosses and public officials in print was his job. It sold newspapers, and it was for the public good. However, this proved to be a fatal miscalculation. Nothing in Mellett's small-town Indiana experience prepared him for the ruthless men he encountered in Canton. He failed to appreciate that while he did not consider his editorial crusades personal attacks, his targets did. Mellett's dogged pursuit of what he believed right while failing to realize he was making dangerous enemies ultimately led to his death at the hands of an unholy alliance of boot-leggers and corrupt cops.

When newspapers were the primary media of the day, report-ers strove to be both factual and entertaining. They sensationalized crime stories, and readers loved it. An assassinated editor was front-page news. Mellett's murder rose rapidly to national prominence. Ohio governor Vic Donahey told reporters, "It [Mellett's murder] was one of the most atrocious crimes in the history of Ohio."[4] Henry Tim-kin, Canton's wealthiest citizen and former owner of the *News*, told a reporter that the murder was "a crime against society itself . . . an intellectual problem requiring thinking."[5] For this reason, Mellett's slaying stands apart from thousands of other gangland killings in the Prohibition era.

The unfolding saga of the murder investigation and manhunt, en-livened by periodic discoveries and revelations, did hold the atten-tion of the man, and woman, on the street. So much so, in fact, that assembling juries of Stark Countians without firm opinions on the crime proved difficult. And the trials were anything but anticlimactic. Prosecutors saw the trials, which received national newspaper cover-age, as Canton's chance to live down its Little Chicago image and re-deem itself by demonstrating that it did have a collective conscience. Unfortunately, their success turned redemption into vengeance and produced one conviction too many.

This is Don Mellett's story. It is a good Ohio murder tale set in the era of flappers and bathtub gin. It is an inspiring story of one journal-ist's single-minded pursuit of what was right. At the same time it is a tragic example of the lawlessness that marked Prohibition and con-tributed to its failure. Don Mellett's peers in the press remembered him for a generation after the *Canton Daily News* was awarded the Pulitzer Prize in 1927 for his work. But today, even in Canton, he is an obscure figure, the passage of time dimming the memory of his sacrifice. His story deserves to be reintroduced not just as a piece of Ohio true crime history but, in this time of multimedia news sources and amid discussion of journalistic ethics, as a shining example of what journalists aspired to in the days when newspapers were king and editorials could change lives.

. . .

No work of this nature could have been contemplated or completed without the assistance of reference librarians. I want to especially thank the staff at the Columbiana Public Library, the Stark County District Library in Canton, the Cleveland Public Library Photograph Collection, and the University of Akron Archives. In addition, I want to express my gratitude to Janet Metzger at the William McKinley Presidential Library for her invaluable assistance, as well as the Nanty Glo Historical Society.

I am indebted to the family of William Dean Krahling for making his voluminous papers on Don Mellett available to researchers and to the work of other scholars who were captivated by Don Mellett and that era of Canton's history: Jerry Updegraff, Glenn Himebaugh, and Elizabeth Greiner.

Last, but not least, I want to thank Joanna Hildebrand Craig, Mary Young, and the staff at the Kent State University Press, without whose invaluable assistance this story might never have been published.

And, of course, I am indebted to Don Mellett, gone eighty years now, without whose courage and determination there would be no story.

1

The Newspaperman

Who was Donald Ring Mellett that by virtue of his death he achieved overnight nationwide fame and recognition? The Mellett name was French. A distant relative and the first governor of South Dakota, Arthur Calvin Mellette, wrote proudly of those who bore the Mellett name: "They are a law abiding, industrious, temperate Christian family. . . . The men are patriotic and brave." While the governor may have been engaging in some political hyperbole, the description was accurate and extended to subsequent generations.[1]

Don came by his journalistic skills and principles honestly. Born September 26, 1891, he was the sixth of seven sons born to Jesse and Margaret Ring Mellett in Ellwood, Indiana, where Jesse was a former schoolteacher turned publisher of the daily *Ellwood Free Press*. In an era when most newspapers identified with a political party, the *Free Press* was unabashedly Democratic. Yet Jesse Mellett was not an unprincipled party hack. Though Grover Cleveland was the only Democrat elected to the White House between 1860 and 1912, the elder Mellett refused to support Cleveland's attempt at a second term in 1892. Jesse's endorsement of Cleveland would have secured him the lucrative Ellwood postmastership and at least four years of prosperity for the Melletts. However, this failure to endorse the eventual winner on a matter of principle (one no one in the family could later recall) meant the family had to continue to scrape by on the meager profits of the *Free Press*. The episode left the Mellett boys to contemplate the real personal cost that can accompany a principled stand. The *Free Press* eventually failed and forced the family to leave Ellwood in 1900.[2]

From Ellwood, the family moved to Muncie, where, around 1900, Jesse briefly published another unsuccessful newspaper. Next stop was a short stay in Anderson, Indiana, before they finally settled in Indianapolis. It was in the state capital that Don attended Shortridge High School, where he was known for his amiability and thoughtfulness. While attending Shortridge, Don met classmate Florence Mae Evans, an orphan living with an aunt and uncle. Petite, brunette, barely five feet tall, with large, captivating dark eyes, she was as smitten with the brown-haired, gray-eyed Don as he was with her. On graduation day in 1909, they became engaged.

That fall, Don entered Indiana University at Bloomington, and there he renewed his childhood acquaintance with another son of Ellwood, Indiana, Wendell Willkie, who was studying law. Don was determined to follow his father and four of his five older brothers into what was now the family profession: journalism. Don's older brother Lowell, who had a bright career that would include the editorship of the *Washington Star* and membership in Franklin Roosevelt's circle of "Brain Trust" advisers, articulated the Mellett family philosophy regarding the press: "Newspapers should be free agents of public service." Of Don, Lowell later wrote, "(Don) took public issues personally. The public's fight was his fight, always."

At Indiana University, Don was a member of the press club and the cross country team. He also worked as a student reporter for the *Indianapolis News*. On Christmas Eve 1913, he married Florence, and during the spring term of 1914, he took over the editorial reins of the *Indiana Student* newspaper, published six days a week. It was a position his elder brother John once held. "Print the truth, the whole truth and nothing but the truth. . . . Legitimate publicity is the cure for almost all evils," he wrote at the beginning of his tenure as editor.[3] As the *Student*'s editor, Don Mellett wrote forty editorials, some high-minded and some preachy. He campaigned for reform of the Greek system at the university, for improvements to the Bloomington municipal water supply, and against the use of profanity and tobacco by students (some of those editorials did not endear him to his fellow collegians). He also oversaw the first issue of the *Indiana Student* written entirely by women.

Don Mellett's last day as editor of the student newspaper also marked the end of his college career. Acknowledging that he had taken some unpopular stands with sometimes preachy editorials, he said of the criticism he had received, "It hurts."[4] Overseeing thirty-one staffers, writing editorials, and being newly married left him exhausted and brought on a new flare-up of nephritis, a condition that had plagued him a few years earlier. Don withdrew from the university that spring of 1914, never to return. He was a single term shy of graduation.

The strain of Don's last year of college was so great that he turned his back on journalism. The young couple moved to the country, Brown County, Indiana, where they purchased a seventy-seven-acre orchard with a two-story log home using money Florence had inherited from her parents. Don knew little about farming, but under the tutelage of a kindly neighbor, Dale Bessie, he gamely planted a thousand new apple trees and produced a large quantity of grape juice—but no wine. On January 24, 1915, the Melletts' first child, Evan Ring Mellett, was born.

A local newspaper quoted Don as being "much pleased with farm life" after a year and a half, but friends recalled more candidly that he talked all the time about getting back into the newspaper business. With an abundant apple crop larger than he could pick or sell, a tired but healthy Don sold the orchard in the fall of 1915, and the Melletts headed for Indianapolis.[5]

In December 1915 Don was hired as managing editor of the *National Enquirer*, a paper based in Indianapolis and owned by former Indiana Republican governor J. Frank Hanly. As governor, Hanly was known for his honesty, for his integrity in prosecuting members of his own administration for theft, and for his prohibitionist zealotry. Some rival Prohibition leaders rightly accused Hanly of starting the paper just to promote the prohibition of alcohol and to advance his own political ambitions. Indeed, Hanly used Mellett as a front man to give the paper legitimacy. While saying that "the paper will hereafter be in his charge," Hanly remained editor-in-chief. While Don attempted to broaden the *Enquirer*'s public appeal and enliven its dull, lecturing tone, Hanly insisted that it carry the full text of his prolific speeches. And Don dutifully covered the 1916 Prohibition Party Convention that nominated Hanly for president. Circulation, however, remained at around 12,000. Hanly lost the election, and by the spring of 1917, Mellett was replaced as editor. Although the Mellett family did not use alcohol, they were not ardent prohibitionists. The *Enquirer* disappeared a short time later, merging with another prohibitionist newspaper.

In the spring of 1917, Don was reduced to working as a salesman for his brother Roland's printing company in Indianapolis. When the United States entered the war in Europe, the newspapers were full of bravado. The Yanks were coming, they warned the world. But one Yank who was not headed off to war was Mellett, who received an exemption from military service based on his value to his family, which now included a daughter, Jean, born in September 1916. By late 1917, Don was ready to become an editor again. Moving again, this time to Columbus, Indiana, Don assumed the editorship of the *Columbus Ledger*, a solidly Democratic daily in a city of 11,000 about forty miles south of Indianapolis. He and Florence liked Columbus, and their family grew with the births of Betty Lou in 1920 and Mary Jane in 1922.

The two-year-old *Ledger* was the product of a business plan promoted by Paul Poynter and partially funded by the Democratic Party to start newspapers in small towns and then sell a one-third interest to energetic young men for a share in the profits. Mellett jumped right in and set about trying to boost circulation, the gold standard for a newspaper's success. Unfortunately, Columbus already had a strong daily backed by the Republican Party. Don tried everything to compete—publishing wire service news and commodity market reports and emphasizing Democratic politics. To increase his profile in the community, he helped found a Kiwanis club, joined the Moose and Elks lodges and the chamber of commerce, taught Sunday school at the Presbyterian church, and promoted the Boy Scouts. And he wrote editorials—pointed ones, such as his attack on a Columbus department store for deceptive advertising, and more general ones, as in his railing against the evils of patent medicine. Yet even the catchy new slogan "Covers the county like dew" wasn't enough to make the paper a roaring success, and the *Ledger* remained number two, never breaking 3,000 in circulation.

Financially, the *Ledger* was failing. A poor farm economy made even a paper that cost less than two cents a copy a tough sell. Creditors forced Poynter out in January 1922, giving Don half-ownership of the paper; unfortunately, the other half was held by local businessmen who did not understand the newspaper business. After several months of acrimony, Don allowed himself to be bought out. He resigned on June 24, 1923. On Don's departure, the Democratic newspaper in nearby Shelbyville wrote, "You published a dandy good paper."[6] Eventually, the owners sold the *Ledger* to its cross-town rival in August 1924. Don had seen firsthand how difficult it was to make money with a newspaper. Yet this would not be the last time Don Mellett would face an uphill battle in a two-newspaper town.

Following the advice he gave a *Ledger* staffer in 1920—"When you are going down the street . . . just for a cup of coffee, act like you are going some place, like you are busy"—Don left the *Ledger* with his head high. He let it be known around Columbus that he was passing up several good newspaper job offers to stay in town and rest up a while. But when he finally did go back to work, the position he took was a major step down. In July 1923, he accepted the job of advertising manager at the *Akron Press*, a Scripps-Howard property located some 300 miles east in Ohio. Those close to Mellett said it was his old college pal Willkie, now a corporate lawyer in Akron, who was instrumental in bringing Don to the *Press*. Don had initially jumped at the offer, but he quickly discovered that the *Press* was a loser, a third-string daily in a city with three newspapers. Furthermore, selling advertising was difficult, and it wasn't journalism. Even before his family arrived in Akron, Don wrote Florence, admitting, "Think I have landed in the middle of the hardest job in the entire Scripps circuit."[7] So not long after moving his young family to Ohio, Don Mellett began looking for yet another newspaper job, this time one that would realize his journalistic ambition.

· · ·

Canton in the 1920s was typical of the industrial cities across the Midwest and Northeast. Founded in 1805 when the settling of northeast Ohio began in earnest, Canton, the seat of Stark County, was a midsized northern industrial city. The estimated population in 1926 was 110,000, about 20 percent greater than the official 1920 census. A fifth of that population was foreign born, with more immigrants arriving by the hour on the nearly 150 trains that stopped in Canton each day. Heavy industry and manufacturing were the backbone of the city's economy, producing steel, ball bearings, vacuum cleaners, bank vaults, and paving bricks.

Canton's place in history—long before the arrival of professional football—was secured by its favorite son, William McKinley, a Civil War veteran, Republican congressman, Ohio governor, and U.S. president.

Like all rapidly growing cities of the day, Canton had its seamy underside. The immigrant wage earners, ignored and unwelcomed by Canton society, were a magnet for crime. Beginning in the late 1880s, gambling and prostitution flourished in the city. The red light district, which grew up around the first railroad depot, was southeast of the city center. South Cherry Street became the most notorious thoroughfare, and the district around it became known in the twenties as "the Jungle." This crowded warren of narrow streets was home to saloons, gambling dens, and brothels and yet was only a stone's throw from the courthouse and city hall. Just behind the courthouse, South Court Avenue, known to the locals as "Whiskey Alley," was the town's gambling center. County prosecutors, who through open windows could hear the dice rolling and chips rattling, "solved" the gambling problem by keeping their office windows closed.[8]

In September 1905, *Cleveland Plain Dealer* reporter William S. Couch opined, "For a lurid little city, commend me to Canton." Yet, he observed, while Canton had plenty of vice, it had not yet reached the depths of municipal corruption seen in other Ohio cities, like Cincinnati. "If any city in Ohio has an interest in checking a spread of this system [of graft] before it gets further," he wrote, "that city is Canton."[9] His advice went unheeded, however. And by the 1920s the South Cherry Street area was responsible for giving Canton its new nickname, "Little Chicago."

Adding to the mix was noble experiment of Prohibition. National Prohibition, which began by constitutional amendment in January 1920, was sold to the American public as a means to reduce crime and corruption, solve social problems, reduce taxes needed for police and prisons, and improve public health. The ardent evangelist preacher Billy Sunday, himself an occasional visitor to Canton, predicted an end to sin. "Hell will be forever for rent," he crowed, thanks to the prohibition of alcohol. But it didn't work out that way. By all accounts, Prohibition was a dismal failure. Although enough Americans supported it to pass the Eighteenth Amendment, the vote was a classic urban versus rural divide. Most city dwellers were lukewarm to Prohibition at best, and a significant number were downright unwilling to give up their booze, a vice that had been legal one day and, with the stroke of a pen, illegal the next. Some crimes were obviously morally wrong— murder, robbery, rape. But, people asked, was having a drink in that same category? Congress and state legislatures, unwilling to boldly back a policy whose support began to erode as soon as it became law, were increasingly reluctant to pass forceful laws to police it. During the 1920s alcohol consumption in the United States actually increased,[10] and unintended, and unforeseen, consequences abounded: drinkers experimented with harder drugs when alcohol was unavailable; bootlegging and moonshining exploded vastly, thereby increasing the cost of law enforcement; and all that illicit money in the hands of criminals made public corruption inevitable and rampant.[11] George Remus, the lawyer who became the "King of the Bootleggers" and who operated the largest illegal liquor enterprise in the country from his Cincinnati base, estimated that fully half of his $40 million annual gross went to pay off police and public officials. In Chicago, Al Capone preferred other forms of vice to bootlegging, because bootlegging required him to bribe so many people—"Too many overheads," he joked.[12]

Canton was no exception. Just below the city's veneer of respectability, crime and corruption was a growth industry. For much of the first three decades of the twentieth century, the city's vice lord was James "Jumbo" Crowley, the nickname a jab at his short stature. Crowley was a dapper, surprisingly well-read man who was fond of hunting, fishing, and boxing. His residence was an unpretentious house on

North Cherry Street.[13] As early as 1906, before the Great War, Jumbo ran a tavern that was known nationally as being a "gun joint," a place where fugitives could hide out for a fee and the promise of good behavior, a way station on the highway of crime. During Prohibition he claimed to be the owner of a second-hand store and auto garage. The inventory of the former was mostly stolen, however, and most of the cars in the latter belonged to him, including a prewar nine-passenger armored touring car known around Canton as "the box car." Jumbo had been arrested twice, once for disorderly conduct and then for a liquor law violation, for which he was fined and released.[14] Jumbo didn't drink, though, and was heard saying, "Liquor isn't made to drink, it's made to sell." His entourage was composed of a group of thugs, called "yeggs" in 1920s slang, who rode around in the box car.[15] He survived, according to a *New York Times* reporter, by always keeping someone else between him and the law. Crowley and his colorful crew made good newspaper copy. Crowley and his lieutenants ran a tight ship. Protection was their primary service. They kept the lid on petty crime in Canton, a questionable public service, for which in return only out-of-towners and those behind in their protection payments got arrested. For the right candidate, Jumbo could deliver the Jungle vote. Former prosecutor and common pleas court judge H. C. Pontius said, "Jumbo Crowley has done more to corrupt the public officials in this community who are corruptible than any other man who has lived here."[16] To his credit, by the 1920s Crowley had turned away from using murder in his business. He called it "the poorest sort of work." Nevertheless, he made an attractive symbol for the national press intent on illustrating Canton's corruption and lawlessness.[17]

One of Crowley's protected vices was prostitution. As was the case in most industrial cities, prostitution had a long history in Canton. Beginning in the 1880s, this oldest profession was centered in the area around the old Pennsylvania Railroad depot on the city's southeast side. The depot later relocated, but "the District," as it became known, stayed, resisting efforts to close it down. The city's Third, Fourth, and Fifth streets southeast and Rex, Cherry, and Walnut avenues southeast bordered Canton's red light district. The brothels were run by madams, and the real estate was owned by vice lords. The women ran the profession, and pimps were not welcome. In general, prostitution was tolerated in Canton. From 1906 to 1913 there were only 231 prostitution arrests, and one-third of those were customers. When the purveyors were arrested, usually it was the madams who were charged, not the working girls. In the early 1920s, one Saturday each month police arrested some of the girls, the chief of police explaining to the unlucky ones, "It's your turn. We have to do it for the record."[18] Jail time was rare, and fines ranged from $1 to $50. An effort by clergymen in 1900 to rid the city of prostitution ended abruptly when the mayor asked what he should do with all these sinners who would be homeless if he padlocked their brothels. Perhaps, he suggested, each minister could take one or two home. They didn't, and by July 1926 there were more than 100 brothels in the Jungle.[19]

For vice to flourish in Canton, somebody—corrupt politicians and police—had to look the other way. In 1909, the *Daily News* predecessor, the *Stark County Democrat*, spearheaded a brief campaign against lax law enforcement by city police. In 1912 a reformed-minded Socialist, Harry Schilling, was elected mayor by two votes in an election decided by the appellate court sitting in nearby Youngstown. Schilling promptly fired the police chief, Billy Smith, for corruption, drunkenness, and dereliction of duty. The new mayor appointed forty-five-year-old Socialist police patrolman Saranus A. "Ed" Lengel as chief with orders to clean up the Jungle. Lengel did curtail prostitution in the city, but the civil service commission restored Billy Smith to duty, and Schilling's reform movement died in early 1913.[20] Over the next eleven years, Canton's reputation had the attention of Columbus. Three city officials were removed from office by two different Ohio governors, and Mayor Charles Poorman was sacked by Governor James M. Cox for failure to protect life and property during a 1919 steel strike, because, as Cox explained, "I asked him to do his duty, and he paid no attention to the defense of property and life."[21]

In April 1924 Governor Victor "Veto Vic" Donahey, a Democrat and no friend of Prohibition, removed Canton's popular second-term Republican mayor, Charles C. Curtis, for malfeasance. Called "one of the more colorful and controversial persons to have served as mayor," Curtis, an attorney, was removed, Donahey said, "to provide a free hand for a probe of vice conditions in Canton." It was said that Jumbo Crowley provided 500 votes from the Jungle to elect Curtis in the first place and that the mayor's brother, Ed, who held the part-time position of safety director, supplemented his income by taking bribe money from Jumbo Crowley and his lieutenants. Officially, five police officers filed a complaint citing a $50 bribe Ed Curtis took from bootleggers. The charge brought about the safety director's eventual conviction and imprisonment. It was rumored that Ed Curtis had failed to notify Crowley of a pending liquor raid that cost Jumbo $5,000. The policemen's formal complaint was said to be Crowley's revenge, and Jumbo even went so far as to provide evidence against Ed Curtis. Police officers filing the complaint were police chief Saranus Lengel, who was reappointed chief by Charles Curtis in 1922, as well as Sergeant Daniel J. Van Gunten, Captain Ben Clarke, and Detectives Floyd Streitenberger and Homer Moore. (All would become targets of Don Mellett.) By the time Charles Curtis was out of office and brother Ed in prison, the damage was done, and Canton had a national reputation as a city wide open for prostitution, narcotics, gambling, and bootlegging and was living up to its "Little Chicago" nickname.[22]

Cantonians kept up with the crime and corruption news in the two daily newspapers, the *Canton Evening Repository* and the *Canton Daily News*. The *Repository* was the oldest and more widely circulated of the two dailies. Established in 1815 as a weekly, it has been published daily since the late 1870s. In the 1920s the *Repository* was a conservative, don't-rock-the-boat paper closely aligned with the Republican Party. This was not surprising, since the paper's founder, John Saxton's daughter, Ida, was married to William McKinley. In 1926 the *Evening Repository* was owned by the Brush-Moore newspaper syndicate.

Canton's other daily had a more checkered past. The *Canton Daily News* began in 1833 as the *Stark County Democrat*. It was purchased in 1848 by Archibald MacGregor, a staunch Democrat who was fiercely anti-Lincoln. Union Army recruits, unhappy with the paper's editorial position, raided the paper in August 1861 and burned it. The unrepentant MacGregor himself was arrested in October 1862 and was held until he took the oath of allegiance to the Union. The *Democrat* survived to become a morning daily in 1878. The paper survived several owners in the next two decades.[23] Henry H. Timkin purchased the *Democrat* in 1912 after years of neglect and decline. Timkin was arguably Canton's wealthiest citizen. He owned Timkin Roller Bearing Company, which produced those tiny steel balls so vital to America's industrial machine. In 1924, Timkin's income was estimated at $5 million, one of the ten highest in the nation. Timkin had no newspaper experience, but he bought the dying *Democrat* as a civic gesture because he felt Canton needed two newspapers. No Democrat, Timkin, who belonged to the progressive wing of the Republican Party, changed the name to the *Daily News* and made it an afternoon paper. After installing a new editor, Timkin had the good sense to leave the management of the paper to professionals. He limited himself to Saturday visits to tend to whatever business matters needed a publisher's attention. This hands-off management style coupled with Timkin's golden touch increased circulation from 8,000 to 20,000 readers per day by 1923, competing with the *Evening Repository*'s 27,000 circulation.

Timkin sold the *Daily News* to the News League syndicate in May 1923, its fourteenth publisher. Timkin no doubt profited handsomely from the sale, but he had other reasons, too. A candid interview with *Forbes* magazine in November 1924 quoted Timkin as saying, "No man can honestly and effectively run two or three different kinds of businesses which are not allied. . . . You can always do your work better by sticking to one job."[24] The News League was owned by James M. Cox, who began his press empire by purchasing his first newspaper, the *Dayton Daily News*, in 1898 at age twenty-eight. Cox made the Dayton paper a success by following a subdued version of Joseph Pulitzer's aggressive model. Editorial crusades, sales promotions, wire service news, innovative advertising, and professional staff all figured into Cox's business plan. In 1905 Cox acquired the *Springfield (Ohio) Daily News* and the News League was born.[25] Cox's tactics were not without controversy, however, and a rash of legal actions resulted. Cox won most of these and explained his philosophy in his 1946 autobiography: "I could not dismiss the conviction that it was the duty of our newspaper to stand by the community regardless of the consequences. And incidentally, any newspaper in time of stress which does not recognize its duty to a community is not deserving of

Donald Ring Mellett, circa 1925. Stark County Historical Society

the name. There is nothing worse than an invertebrate publisher. He does neither the public nor his profession any good."[26]

Cox was elected to Congress in 1908 as a Democrat and to Ohio's governorship in 1912. A mildly progressive and reform-minded Democrat, Cox built on his success in Ohio to secure his party's 1920 presidential nomination in an all-Ohio presidential campaign against the Republican nominee, small-town newspaper publisher and Ohio senator Warren G. Harding. Cox campaigned hard, but after a world war and eight years of a Democratic presidency, the country embraced Harding's "Back to Normalcy" message. Cox was defeated in a landslide and retired from politics. His presidential bid is best remembered as the national debut of his vice presidential running mate, Franklin Roosevelt.[27]

By 1924, Harding was dead, and Cox had turned his full attention to his newspaper business, which now owned papers in Dayton and Springfield, Ohio, and Miami, Florida, where Cox wintered. Why Cox purchased the *Canton Daily News* is not clear.[28] It didn't take long for

Cox to realize that northern Ohio industrial cities were not like those downstate in southwest Ohio. "This city [Canton] was very different from others in which we operated," Cox wrote in his autobiography.[29] The former governor should have known that the state's northeastern cities, with their large immigrant populations and racial and ethnic turmoil, had different problems and politics than those of southwest Ohio. Moreover, Henry Timkin drove a hard bargain when he sold the *Daily News*, leaving Cox with a heavy financial burden, and, worse still, the *Repository* actually widened its daily circulation lead by 2,000 readers in Cox's first year of ownership. All this left Cox less than pleased with his purchase: "On mature consideration, I was not very keen about our investment."[30]

But Cox was a stubborn competitor. He extolled the *Daily News* staff to develop a unique image for the paper, arouse the interests of potential readers overlooked by the competition, promote new business ventures, feature more blue-collar sports stories, write more local editorials, and, of course, give full coverage to Democratic politics. And like all successful executives, Jim Cox was always on the lookout for good young talent.

Cox met Don Mellett late in 1924 at a statewide press gathering in Columbus, Mellett there in his role as advertising manager for the *Akron Press*. Both men shared an enthusiastic interest in Democratic politics and held similar ideas about how to run a newspaper. Cox decided that Mellett was "a go-getter and probably could manage the [*Daily News*] at the same time" and hired him, sending Don to the *Canton Daily News* in January 1925.[31] His new editor, Cox said, was "full of ambition. . . . His love of the newspaper profession and his ideas as to the responsibility of any journal to the community which it fosters were inherent."[32] So with high hopes and enthusiasm, Don Mellett headed to Canton.

Mellett in Canton

D on Mellett went to Canton feeling that it might be his last chance in the newspaper business. At this point in life, he considered himself a failure. He had not finished college and had failed twice as a newspaper editor. Competitor that he was, Mellett wanted a successful career in journalism. He couldn't be blamed for comparing himself to his brothers, who were in the same profession. Two had press jobs in Washington, one owned a successful printing company, and even Lloyd, four years younger, was a wire service reporter in Indianapolis. Failure might mean going back to Indianapolis and that salesman's job in his brother's printing company. Don Mellett *had* to succeed in Canton.[1]

The new job Jim Cox offered at the *Canton Daily News* was an indication of what the publisher must have seen as Mellett's forte: his experience on the business side of a daily paper. Cox hired Don to be the paper's business manager, not a journalist. He wanted the *Daily News* to be profitable and saw in his new business manager someone who might be able to achieve this goal. Cox's approach to selling newspapers was not as extreme as those of Joseph Pulitzer. He didn't buy into the screaming headlines or oversized photographs and didn't advocate any real changes in layout or typography.

Don Mellett believed in and practiced "new" journalism, where the business office assumed increased importance. This coincided with the industrialization of newspapers and the rise of corporate ownership whereby several properties were owned by large syndicates, like Cox's News League. Previously, the industry had been fractured, each paper often a reflection of the publisher's individual partisan and sometimes quirky views. Anyone who could write could be a reporter. Profits were often razor thin or nonexistent. That changed with corporate management. Newspaper publishing became a business and was no longer a Jeffersonian passion. Its main objective was to secure as much advertising revenue as possible. And as profit became a driving force, business managers assumed a greater role in determining a paper's content. Don had seen his father's and his own papers fail financially and clearly understood the importance of employing sound business practices. He understood his job: "Jim Cox sent me in here to get his paper out of the red, and I'm going to do it." Cox did set limits, however. He wrote to Timkin in October 1925 explaining what he was trying to give Canton: "We are trying to give you a decent newspaper. We might have made . . . a yellow sheet out of it, but I will not run that kind of paper."[2]

This new business model coincided with new attitudes among journalists regarding the press's social responsibilities. Reporters of the 1890s were told to keep their opinions out of their stories, but by the 1920s editors began to advocate interpretive reporting to help readers understand complex issues. To separate fact from opinion, editors made bylines commonplace, allowing readers to decide for themselves which reporters provided the right mix of fact and opinion. However, what was good for a newspaper's bottom line was easily confused with what it considered to be the public good.[3] So those on the sharp end of an editorial or exposé were not enthusiastic supporters of this new brand of journalism.

The January 1, 1925, edition greeted the new year with a guest editorial written by Canton mayor Charles M. Ball, a Republican, who had ascended to the office from the city council when Mayor Curtis was removed by the governor. Ball wrote, "The efforts to clean the city of vice and crime will be continued, and every effort made to make Canton the best place to live," thereby setting the tone and mission for the *Daily News*.

Don, who had an outgoing, salesman's personality, wasted no time in becoming an active participant in the city's civic, social, and political scene. He moved his family into a rented home on the corner of Broad Avenue NW and Crown Place. He and Florence became active in the largest Presbyterian congregation in Canton, where Don taught a Sunday school class and they were among the thirty-five young adults who attended the special Centennial Class. It was to this group that Don revealed that it was necessary to throw the spotlight on corruption in Canton to make it a better place to live, but he feared that some morning the class might read that he had been killed.

Don was also active in the Kiwanis Club, Democratic politics, and the University Club, a group of about 250 men who had attended college. And on discovering "a lack of willingness on the part of many persons to recognize or admit new blood into the community, especially when the new blood is of a highly competitive nature,"[4] Don organized the Molly Stark Club for newcomers to Canton. The name was adopted from the *Daily News*'s personal advice column, "Molly Stark, Her Personal Column," written by Jeanne Potter. This would not be the first time Mellett would take a shot at the "old guard" in Canton.

For "relaxation," Don played tennis, golf, and bridge. He hated to lose, his friends said, and sometimes was even a "hard loser." One Saturday morning, for example, he and frequent doubles partner Walter Vail lost a hard fought tennis match. Not satisfied, Don roused Vail from a nap later that afternoon for a return to the courts for a rematch. This time they won. Don loved good literature, an easy passion to satisfy in the era of Hemingway and Fitzgerald. He also loved to sing and play the piano. He and Florence were fond of the popular music of the 1920s. His favorite tune was "I'll Be Loving You Always."[5] Friends, too, were important to the Melletts, and none more so than Walter and Carrie Vail, who owned a nursery in town. Similar in age, the Vails had three children, and rarely was there a Sunday the two families didn't get together for picnics in the country, ice cream sodas, or long drives.

As quickly as the couple became assimilated into Canton socially, Indiana still had a strong pull for the Melletts. While the family was active in Canton's First Presbyterian Church, they never joined, preferring to remain members of their old church in Columbus, Indiana, evidence of the Melletts' reluctance to abandon their deep Indiana roots. Every couple of months, the family made the long drive west to Indianapolis to visit family and friends, especially Don's aged mother. While Don's motives in his civic involvements in Canton were sincere, they were also business.

Indeed, Don came to Canton to make the *Daily News* profitable, and that meant selling more papers and advertising—maybe even more than the rival *Evening Repository*. Within weeks of his hiring, more expensive boxed and highlighted classified ads began to appear. The newspaper began to promote itself by sponsoring lectures on health and wellness. It sponsored an annual school picnic in June that would see attendance reach 30,000. Yet Mellett's name didn't even appear in print until April 5, 1925, when he was listed as business manager. In fact, he was so unknown in the newsroom that when his name did appear in an April 24 article, it was misspelled.

What was later called "a turning point in newspaper journalism in Canton" took place on Sunday, May 17, when the *Daily News* published an editorial entitled "What the News Stands For." This was essentially a platform marking the beginning of a more aggressive and controversial editorial policy that promoted the paper's view of improvements Canton needed. What the *Daily News* advocated would make any twentieth-century politician proud: mass transit, smoke abatement, better roads, soft water, and better schools. A fairly nonpartisan, nonconfrontational list, it made no mention of crime or corruption. The first real editorial stand, its first genuine crusade, began in July with an editorial under Don Mellett's byline. A prominent local real estate developer, T. K. Harris, proposed a citywide ban on new construction until all vacant properties were leased. Harris no doubt had his own unleased space in mind. The paper was highly critical of the scheme. Under the lead "Canton Leaders Have Faith in Growth of City," Mellett advocated more construction in Canton, not less. This outraged Harris, who was, by coincidence, married to the daughter of a former owner of the *Repository* and not accustomed to the press opposing his ideas. Harris's plan died for many good reasons other than the editorial crusade, but the reverberations in the local business and press community cost the *Daily News* the support of the *Repository* in its future crusades.

Mellett was by nature a pious, conservative man of strong opinions. His old paper in Indiana, the *Ledger*, described Mellett as being "of the militant school of journalists, one who struck straight from the shoulder as he saw it." He was the sort of guy who married his high school sweetheart, campaigned against profanity in college, edited a Prohibition newspaper, and taught Sunday school. There was plenty for him to rail against in a city with a crime-riddled neighborhood nicknamed the Jungle and a prosperous red light district referred to as "the Tenderloin."

At the *Daily News*, Don faced many of the same frustrations he had encountered in Akron, only this time he was in a much better position to deal with them. By the summer of 1925, he was the de facto publisher, filling the void created by Cox's hands-off, absentee ownership. While few staffers voiced any opinions of Mellett during this time, there was, no doubt, resentment against this upstart business manager who assumed so much authority. Don was instrumental that summer and fall in forcing out two editors, Herve Miner and Norval Luxon, as he consolidated his power.

Cox, satisfied that he made the right decision and that Mellett had "met the trial," promoted him to publisher on October 1, 1925.[6] Just the week before, Don's brother Lloyd, a quiet, hard-working man who adored his older brother, arrived at the *Daily News* to become city editor. Given the brothers' closeness, Lloyd was the natural choice to put the final polish on Don's ideas and get them into print. The younger Mellett's credentials as a working journalist and writer were as good or better than his older brother's. And what has often been overlooked in the story of Don Mellett is that while Don was the front man and lightning rod, Lloyd played a very significant role at the paper. As city editor, he had final say over what was printed in the *Daily News*.

One of the first things the Melletts changed was the way police and court news was reported. Instead of presenting a mere summary of the police blotter, whole stories were now developed around a newsworthy event. Reporters were instructed to turn their notes and copy in at the city desk where it was rewritten into a printable story by one of the staff writers. In the case of crime or corruption news, Lloyd Mellett personally directed or rewrote those articles, and wrote the lead. And it was Lloyd who actually wrote the editorials that were associated with Don.[7]

Another move Don made as publisher was to emphasize home delivery subscriptions over newsstand sales. This was done at a time when conventional wisdom said that street sales were of prime importance. Former *Repository* editor John G. Green said that in the 1920s "every minute up at city square, beating the opposition, meant selling a hundred papers."[8] Mellett made changes in the *Daily News* delivery system to make it more reliable and subscriber friendly, which attracted national attention. Known as the "mother system," it placed a married woman in charge of each distribution area to ride herd on the sometimes rowdy newsboys and carriers. Don also priced the paper competitively: seven days of home delivery was just 10 cents, while on the streets the Sunday edition alone was 10 cents. He felt that it was better for the paper's long-term growth to have happy subscribers than erratic street sales.

During the summer of 1925, one of the first stories to land on the new city editor's desk also provided the Melletts with a close look at how organized crime operated in Canton. Nick Magiros, a small-time proprietor of an illegal gambling joint, filed a lawsuit in county court against Jumbo Crowley to recover money he had paid Crowley for protection. Magiros claimed he paid $200 a week to keep the Canton Police Department from closing him down. When the word went out to vice operators to close down before the August primary election, in order to make the Republican incumbent, Charles Ball, appear to be tough on crime, Magiros complied. When he reopened, he claimed, all he could afford was $125. Two days later police raided his establishment. Crowley then turned the gambling concession over to the Spiros brothers. The affair was settled in an out-of-court shootout in which Magiros's brother, Pete, was wounded and arrested. The Spiros brothers continued with their gambling operation.[9] Further implications involved senior police officers, including Chief Lengel and Captain Ben Clarke, who were overheard discussing the need to loosen up on vice arrests during the election campaign to secure votes in the Jungle for Mayor Ball.

But it was a much less political incident that really galvanized Don Mellett to go after bootlegging corruption in Canton. According to Walter Vail, one evening in the fall of 1925, the Melletts and Vails were dining in a local restaurant when four intoxicated teenagers entered. Don knew one of them was from a prominent family and announced, incensed, "I am going to start tomorrow and find out where they are getting this from. There must be something wrong here in Canton." He later told Florence that Canton was not a fit place to raise children.[10] Don took his personal feelings to the editorial page on October 30. "Just where those young folks acquired their liquor might be an interesting question for the proper city officials to look into. . . . And yet a shrug of the shoulders, perhaps a mild protest and Canton goes her way . . . yet until public conscience awakens to the seriousness of lax law enforcement . . . conditions in Canton will not improve."

That fall, Democratic challenger Stanford Swarts, a Spanish-American War veteran, ran a folksy campaign against Mayor Ball that did not need to focus on law and order—the *Daily News* did that for him. According to Lloyd Mellett, the paper campaigned for Swarts because he pledged to "go all the way with the *News*" in bettering Canton. It was a campaign promise the Melletts bought and one Swarts later regretted. On Friday, October 30, the *Daily News* took law enforcement in Canton to task, as well as the public apathy that tolerated corruption. "It would seem the people of Canton are a bit blasé in their attitude towards law enforcement," the editorial accused, going on to chide city officials for their indifference and civic leaders for their poor example in obeying the law, especially regarding Prohibition and gambling. "Our city officials by their indifference, and many of our prominent citizens by their example, in the matter of enforcement of prohibition and gambling laws, are sowing the seeds of anarchy and red socialism." And a pre-election editorial focused on issues of law and order: "The voters of Canton know that law enforcement has been lax. It knows that bootlegging and gambling has gone on, more or less unmolested, for many months. It knows that whether the mayor and his staff knew these things or not, they should have known them, and should have stopped them. It knows that lax law enforcement has brought about an alarming condition for the young men and women of Canton—a condition that must be corrected if a real menace to their futures is to be removed."[11]

The day after the November general election, the *Daily News* headline proclaimed, "Swarts for a Greater Canton," announcing that the Democrat had won by the largest majority ever in Canton, by almost 5,000 votes. Swarts owed his victory less to the *Daily News* than he did to a divided Republican party in which the primary loser, ousted mayor Charles Curtis, threw his considerable support behind Swarts. Even the Cox News League recognized this and reported on the statewide wire that "it is no secret in Canton that Curtis forces aided materially in the election of Swarts." Nevertheless, the Melletts were pleased with the outcome and saw this as a sign that Canton's public conscience was at last awakening. The *Daily News*'s only other success was the election of two school board members it had endorsed as a result of a scandal over missing athletic funds. Importantly, however, the rival *Evening Repository* headline crowed, "GOP Wins All but Mayorality." The Republicans' win of all city offices but mayor condemned Canton to a divided government.

The Mellett brothers were willing to try anything to stir up interest in their law-and-order campaign. Perhaps the most bizarre move was introduced on November 8 in the form of William LaSalle, "the Marvel Man," who was a supposed lip-reader hired by the paper to hang around downtown and report on the hushed conversations of Canton's bootleggers, pimps, and dope dealers. The short-lived Marvel Man feature began as a publicity stunt, with the tag line "be careful of your conversations from now on," but it soon turned serious as LaSalle began to pick up real intelligence on narcotics trafficking. How he accomplished this would later be questioned, but his information did prompt a two-hour meeting that included the Mellett brothers, LaSalle, and ranking officers of the Canton police force. The *Daily News* offered to work with the department to clean up the narcotics trade, but the police were lukewarm and nothing came of it. Though they blamed Captain Ben Clarke for this failure, it may have been that the Melletts were asking too much of a law enforcement agency to let the press play an active role in its investigations. However, when another informant fingered Clarke as an active player in the narcotics trade, the Melletts were ready to print the accusation. Fortunately for them, before they ran the story, the informant was arrested on federal narcotics charges. Still, the Melletts continued to believe Clarke was corrupt.[12] This marked the beginning of Mellett's vice and corruption campaign that began in deadly earnest that November.[13]

Crime was not all that made news in Canton. When the board of directors of Aultman Hospital, the oldest hospital in Stark County, made some unpopular and arbitrary staff changes, the *Daily News* jumped into the fray. Most of the hospital staff disliked the new medical and nursing directors, and the fact that impending personnel changes were leaked to the paper before they were made public was an indication of how quickly Mellett had established himself in town as someone willing to take sides. The leak angered the hospital board, which was composed of many influential citizens, and the trustees accused the paper of irresponsibility, ignoring the age-old advice to never argue with a man who buys ink by the barrel. The paper was blunt in its response: "For printing the news, the *News* has no apology."

Critics accused Mellett of starting an editorial crusade by publishing seventeen editorials in two months on the Aultman controversy. (It was standard practice for newspapers to publish several editorials each day. The *Daily News* gave important editorials front-page exposure.) But there may have been more to it. Lloyd Mellett told investigators that the brothers were made aware (likely through their newfound sources among the disgruntled hospital staff) that the new medical director might be involved in illegal trafficking of the hospital's narcotics supply. However, there was never enough evidence to print this accusation or bring legal charges.[14] The hospital resolved the staffing dispute internally, and Mellett's interest turned elsewhere.[15]

There were side issues, but Don Mellett focused the *Daily News* squarely on law enforcement beginning in the fall of 1925. Every issue featured front-page crime news, either local or drawn from the wire services. Conditions in Canton had become a matter of personal outrage for Don, and he embarked on a one-man crusade to clean up Canton—whether Canton wanted cleaning up or not. In anticipation of a meaningless grand jury report on crime, he editorialized on November 20: "The *News* is sick of hearing about the workings of the bootlegging ring, the gambling ring, protection operators, the dopers, etc. and would like to see the whole crowd run out of Canton." And the paper's first editorial to question the integrity of the police department appeared on November 29. Not mincing words it suggested that "sometimes a good shakeup and clean out of one's own house is imperatively necessary."

The campaign was no secret. Former Republican campaign manager Samuel Holliday, who was about to be named the city's interim safety director, went to see the Melletts in late November. Holliday was not playing political games; he was genuinely moved by the newsmen's efforts. "I saw Don was interested in cleaning up the town, and was big enough to back it up with his newspaper."[16] He offered, "If you folks are sincere . . . I am ready to go all the way helping you."[17] Holliday then toured Canton incognito with a part-time state Prohibition agent, Jack Campbell. In just one evening, the pair located thirty-one brothels and a bootlegging wholesaler and witnessed widespread gambling.

Stung, Chief of Police Saranus A. "Ed" Lengel personally led a raid on a local strip show on West Tuscarawas on December 10. Eighty-eight men and four women present were arrested. However, Mellett supporter police sergeant John "Jiggs" Wise, liquor agent Jack Campbell, and a *Daily News* photographer were already there to record the raid when the chief's entourage arrived with sirens blaring. Lengel had been upstaged and was furious. He was reported as having said, "I wish I had the editor of the *Canton Daily News* here. I'd blacken his blankety-blank eyes." Harsh words from Canton's top lawman. The *Repository* reported December 11 that the chief believed that Wise and the *Daily News* tried to "frame him by making it appear he was not on the job." The thin-skinned Lengel a few days later told the strip show's promoter (who likely paid protection money to prevent police raids) to blame Holliday, Wise, and Mellett.[18]

It was well known that Wise and Lengel had different views of law enforcement. Holliday, as safety director, and the Melletts came to depend on Wise, an honest cop who had the frustrating task of liquor law enforcement. Wise provided Mellett with intelligence on police department activities. But not everyone was dissatisfied with Lengel. When federal narcotics agents conducted a December 13 raid in Canton, they praised the chief for his assistance. Even the *Daily News* gave in a little: "This is real work and the department is to be commended. But there should be no let up."[19]

As 1925 drew to a close, and with it Don Mellett's first year, the *Daily News* was printing three times as many editorials on local affairs as the *Repository*. Mellett had been unafraid to challenge the city's power structure by wading into the Aultman Hospital dispute, school board issues, and real estate plans and by attacking the city police force. But the *Evening Repository* still held a three to two edge in circulation at year's end. Much of Canton's power elite and many in the middle class felt Mellett was unnecessarily running Canton down by exaggerating the crime situation to sell papers. Thanks in part to a well-oiled vice machine and well-bought police force, most of white middle-class Canton experienced little crime.[20]

Glenn Himebaugh, who researched Mellett extensively, speculated that "Mellett's willingness to ruffle feathers of such leading citizens as T. K. Harris, school board officials and hospital trustees may have contributed to some degree, to the lack of general support his efforts received from a majority of the community's established power structure."[21] Wendell Willkie had warned Mellett that sensational crusading would produce revulsion among the "best people."[22] Many ordinary citizens were similarly put off by Mellett's attacks. Don's own neighbor, plumber Leo Schumacher, a longtime reader of the *Daily News*, said that "Don was slurring our [police] force a little bit too much."[23] And not to be discounted was that Mellett was less believable because he was a Democrat publishing a newspaper owned by a former Democratic governor—both outsiders in a clannish and predominantly Republican town. Many in Canton seemed willing to accept the wisdom that while men like Chief Lengel were less than honest, maybe even crooks, at least they were *our* crooks.

On Christmas Eve 1925, the *Daily News* began a series of investigative reports on the bootleg liquor trade. The articles were purportedly written by wordsmith Lloyd from information gathered by Don.

The very first article challenged police to arrest Mrs. Jennie Meadows, whom the paper crowned "queen of the bootleggers." In its reporting, the paper named bootleggers. Harry Bouklias was described as "clever and ruthless," and generous giving each city police officer a turkey for Christmas that year,[24] and it accused police detective Joseph "Fats" Metzger of selling perfume to bawdy houses when he was off duty. It charged that when the law was enforced, it was only selectively enforced and suggested that "regularly a little show of cleaning up is put on. This makes a good impression. . . . [But] a select few operate without fear of any actual interference."

Then, on December 27, Canton's well-oiled crime machine slipped off the tracks. Officer Walter "Tiny" Guthrie, the largest man on the police force, arrested bootlegger A. H. Harris with a load of Canadian whiskey. This was a mistake on Tiny's part, since Harris wasn't supposed to be arrested because he worked for well-known and well-connected crooks Carl Studer and Louis Mazer. Studer and Mazer came to Harris's rescue and purportedly bribed the assistant city solicitor, Norman Clark, who served as police prosecutor. Clark suggested a light fine of $100 while at the same time concealing Harris's previous arrest record. Judge Bowman accepted the recommendation, and Harris never even appeared in court. When the story later broke, the judge lamely claimed he had been duped by the prosecutor. Officer Guthrie was later reassigned for his "mistake."[25]

Harris's arrest and prosecution was the subject of a December 29 editorial. The *Daily News* reported that a meeting was held the previous day, December 28, in Chief Lengel's office that included Lengel, Detective Metzger, and Louis Mazer, who expressed anger over his man's arrest, which he had paid protection money to avoid. The alleged participants denied the meeting. Mazer, upset over this publicity, sought Lengel's counsel. The police chief told him to complain to the *Daily News*, which he did, along with Carl Studer and Morris Rudner, whose brother, Ben, was rumored to be deeply involved in bootlegging in Canton. At the *Daily News* offices they met with Lloyd Mellett and berated him for poor reporting. (The paper reported, among other things, that Mazer had owned the padlocked Canton House brothel. Actually, Studer's parents had owned it, and a check of property records by the *Daily News* would have confirmed that fact.) The tense meeting ended with Lloyd suggesting Mazer come back later so they could talk more. But all Mazer wanted was a retraction, or "we know how to take care of guys like you."[26] After this episode, Mazer was occasionally seen parked at the Elks Club across from the *Daily News* building watching Mellett's office. Chief Lengel added his weight to the demand for a retraction, and the editors admitted the error but didn't retract the whole story.[27]

The arrest of Harris produced an invaluable informant. A. H. "Iani" Harris was an alias used by J. E. Wing, who in mid-April 1925 began running bootleg liquor for Studer and Mazer, whose pool hall front in the Jungle was known variously as the Lyceum Pool Room or the Lincoln Billiard Parlor. Wing claimed that these two bootleggers were the only ones in Canton who handled bonded whiskey, spirits certified by a regulatory agency to indicate consistent quality. The quality of liquor varied considerably during Prohibition, and bonded spirits were highly desirable, since they were certified and sealed to indicate consistent quality. Bonded whiskey came from Canada or Europe or was stolen from pre-Prohibition inventory locked in warehouses. This top-of-the-line whiskey commanded a higher price—so high that some bootleggers engaged in "cutting," which involved removing the bottoms of bonded bottles, sparing the seals and labels, and refilling the bottles with lower-quality distillate and then replacing the bottoms and selling the product as bonded. For the less affluent, Canton's premier bootleggers also dealt in grain alcohol or moonshine.[28] Wing told the Melletts that he was directed by his bosses on occasion to supply liquor to various police officers, and he provided a list of eight names. Included on the list were Detective Floyd Streitenberger and Elmer E. Clark, who was Chief Lengel's executive clerk. In that position, Clark handled all arrest reports and shuttled information between the chief's office and prosecutors—which included his brother, police prosecutor Norman Clark.

Clearly, Wing's employers were not worried about the city police. But they did warn him to be careful handling the liquor so as to avoid arrest by state liquor agents, although a friendly agent identified only as "Meltzer" usually tipped off Mazer and Studer when state agents were in Canton. Nevertheless, Wing was arrested three times while acting as their runner. Each time he escaped with only a fine, thanks to an arrangement between the attorneys and the bootleggers. Even Wing's arrest records were changed so that he could plead guilty under one of a number of aliases—W. E. Wink, S. A. Winski, or Iani Harris—which allowed him to circumvent Ohio law that required anyone thrice convicted of liquor law violations to be considered a felon and face jail time.[29]

The *Daily News* ended 1925 observing that "Canton enjoys the reputation in the larger cities of the country of having, for its size, one of the most highly developed underworlds in the country. Full realization of local conditions have not yet dawned upon the public, but it is coming." The end of the year saw the *Repository* still holding its circulation lead of 10,000 readers,[30] but the *Daily News* was gaining ground and attention. Governor Cox sent a congratulatory message to the entire staff.

In the new year the Mellett brothers continued to hammer Chief Lengel. And their efforts were now showing some effect. When Lengel asked the city council to approve the hiring of twenty-five new patrolmen in late December, the council had refused. The Melletts lauded this decision: "The city council acted wisely last week when it tabled the request of the Chief of Police Lengel for twenty five additional patrolmen. . . . There is no need at this time for an additional twenty five patrolmen. Neither would it be wise to add that number of men to the force under the present Chief Lengel . . . an additional twenty five members would do little more than fill the club rooms at the headquarters."[31]

Of all the editorials Don Mellett was responsible for in his career, the most memorable appeared on January 2, 1926. Carried on the front page so that no one could miss it, it made crystal clear the *Daily News*'s position on the police department. "That the public may not misunderstand the attitude of the *News* towards Chief Lengel in his official capacity, it should be stated very openly that Canton needs a stronger hand at the helm of its law enforcement department. . . . Frankly," Don wrote, "the *News* has little faith in Chief Lengel's ability or desire to cleanup Canton. . . . It does not challenge his integrity nor his motives. . . . If he can't do the job, no matter how good his intentions, he should resign or be removed. . . . Thus, Mr. Lengel, do we extend our New Years greetings! Get busy or get out!"

Considering Mellett's ties to the new Democratic mayor, Lengel should have taken this as something akin to an official warning. But he did not. Instead, on January 3 he enacted a policy of censorship regarding police news. All contacts with the press would now go through the detective bureau, and reporters were barred from riding along on emergency calls—a press privilege the *Daily News* called "universal." Nothing got a journalist's attention like censorship. On January 5 the paper ran an editorial that reaffirmed the Melletts' philosophy: "All the people have not the time to examine (public) records. They expect newspapers to do it for them, and beyond a corrupt officialdom, there is nothing (more) contemptible than a conniving press."

By this time it was no secret that members of the department who were in agreement with the Melletts were acting as informants, and these leaks rarely favored the chief. In fact, by early 1926 the *Daily News* editors were seeing a steady stream of informants parading through their office doors. The Melletts regularly met with the city safety director, mayor, Prohibition agents, common criminals, and police officers. The newspaper's knowledge of what went on in the police department was extraordinary. One key source came from illegally bugged conference rooms at police headquarters. Unknown to prisoners, defendants, or their lawyers, the police hired stenographers to listen and transcribe all that was said during these candid conversations. One stenographer, Mildred "Mickey" Haag, said this was how Sergeant Wise got much of the material he gave the *Daily News*.[32]

On Sunday, January 17, the *Daily News* called for the removal of Lengel, Ben Clarke, Ed Swope, and Fred Metzger, and, in a January 29 editorial, reiterated the call flatly: "Eventually Lengel and others will have to go." January's reporting stepped up the pressure and included exposés on overcrowding and miserable conditions at the county workhouse and rum-running in Canton. When approached privately by the safety director about stepping down, Lengel vowed to fight, an obstinance no doubt motivated by the eighteen months of service he needed to draw a pension. More creative thinking on the part of the city administration regarding Lengel's financial needs might have solved more than just the police chief's problems.[33]

Also in January the *Daily News* closely followed the arrests of Harry Turner and Harry Bouklias, recognized kingpins in the illegal booze business. Both men were on probation for their part in the 1924 E. E. Curtis bribery scandal and had avoided prison by turning state's evidence. On January 23, police sergeant Wise led a liquor raid that netted Mary Kizman, wife of small-time retailer Paul Kizman. This angered the Kizmans, who were paying $50 a month for protection. The *Daily News* paid $200 of Mary's $750 fine and, in return, got the Kizmans to talk about the Turner/Bouklias bootlegging ring, which was moving about a thousand gallons of liquor a week. Just prior to the early February trial, while Bouklias was out of jail on $6,000 bond, Paul Kizman received an offer from a Bouklias operative, a man named Martin Unger, to forgive everything if he would decline to testify against Bouklias. Smelling a setup, Kizman contacted the *Daily News*, which in turn sent him to the new safety director, James A. Rice.[34]

Together the *Daily News* and the safety director set up a sting. Paul and Mary Kizman were to appear to accept Bouklias's offer and not testify against him. But when the Bouklias man, Unger, arrived with a fresh stock of whiskey, liquor agents would be waiting. A delivery was set for the evening of the first day of Bouklias's trial. At the appointed hour, 8:00 P.M., liquor agent Jack Campbell and Sergeant Wise were hiding in the Kizman house. Unger arrived with the liquor, closely followed by none other than Ben Clarke and Homer Moore of the city police. Wise and Campbell arrested Unger. Clarke claimed that he and Moore had received a tip through Chief Lengel about the whiskey delivery. This may have been true, but the Melletts were certain that Clarke was part of the original frame-up designed to undermine Kizman's credibility.

In the end, Stark County Common Pleas Court judge A. W. Angler sentenced Bouklias and Turner to prison for eighteen months to ten years for violating their paroles. Don Mellett bragged to Governor Donahey that he was responsible for Turner's and Bouklias's trip to the Ohio Penitentiary. But it was county prosecutor Charles McClintock who received the most acclaim for his role in the whole affair when the *Daily News* said that he had "accomplished what the entire Canton police force could not or would not do" in getting the paroles revoked.[35] The employment of informants and private detectives would be the method used by McClintock to later solve the Mellett murder. As for the Kizmans, their final reward was to have their house burned to the ground by unknown arsonists on February 25, an act the Mellets called "a reign of terror."[36]

Some accused the Melletts of framing Bouklias and Turner. Bouklias's attorney certainly did. As author William Dean Krahling wrote in his study of Mellett, "The situation serves well to illustrate the tight rope the crusader often walks. The propriety of his actions is often thinly determined by whose means for what ends. The predicament was one obviously faced by Mellett and the *Daily News.*" So were they making the news or reporting it? The *Daily News* denied setting up the bootleggers. Calling framing "an evil practice," the paper pointed out that it was often used by corrupt police departments. Answering charges that private detective H. B. Burton, who occasionally worked for the *Daily News*, might have entrapped Turner by soliciting liquor from him, the editors deflected this criticism by decrying the use of legal technicalities by defense lawyers to get "notorious underworld characters" off. In a final odd twist, the well-off bootleggers succeeded in getting the county to pay for their defense.[37]

In early February, the Marvel Man was arrested by Detective Floyd Streitenberger for impersonating a federal officer, and a search of his hotel room turned up badges from several different law enforcement agencies. LaSalle was sentenced to ninety days in the county workhouse. This was not LaSalle's first brush with the law in Canton. At one point he was said to have jumped out of a hotel room window to avoid arrest during a liquor raid. The *Repository* made an issue of the arrest, claiming that LaSalle was attempting to entrap police officers by offering to sell them liquor. In a sarcastic editorial on the 11th, the Melletts addressed the rival paper's approach to the issue: "Our worthy contemporary should be commended for its splendid exploitation of the police feat in nabbing LaSalle." The *Daily News* defended LaSalle, saying he had performed his lip-reading service for other newspapers. Lloyd Mellett called him a newspaper stunt writer, who, regardless of his faults, was a marvel as a lip-reader: "The man's work and effectiveness in a newspaper feature way speaks volumes for him." The arrest was unfortunate, according to the *Daily News*, but, always on the lookout for a chance to attack Lengel, it claimed that police ignored the Marvel Man's impersonation of a lawman for weeks. For good measure, the *Daily News* attempted to link the *Evening Repository* to Chief Lengel and crime conditions in Canton.[38] Streitenberger would later claim, after Mellett was dead, that the Marvel Man's former employer offered the detective a bribe to let the lip-reader off on the charge of impersonation.[39]

Throughout the winter of 1926, the *Canton Daily News*, in stories and editorials, continued to attack Lengel, whom they had begun referring to as "the Old Man" and who served as the lightning rod for the city's compromised law enforcement. The paper accused the police department of tipping-off favored vice operators in advance of raids by local, state, or federal agents and of making occasional local arrests strictly for show. It made clear that it didn't condone the "joke" made of law enforcement by the Canton police department. The *Daily News*'s relentless editorial campaign was getting the attention of Canton's best people. When Mellett's University Club friends began calling him a "crusader," he forcefully rejected the title because of its association with yellow journalism.[40]

The weak city council made a fumbling attempt at curbing gambling by prohibiting public card playing. The Democratic mayor vetoed the ordinance, but the Republican council overrode the veto. The *Daily News* editorialized that "the ordinance passed has too much the appearance of class legislation and class legislation is contrary to the point of American government." A municipal judge ruled the law unconstitutional in June.[41]

The *Daily News* and Don Mellett had painted Mayor Swarts into a corner, where Lengel was concerned. Swarts's ardor for reform may have cooled since the election, but Mellett's editorials had made it uncomfortable for the mayor not to be doing *something*. The police chief had civil service protection in Canton in the 1920s and could not just be summarily dismissed. Nor would he agree to quietly resign. So Swarts was forced to fire him and face a civil service hearing by a commission appointed by the mayor's Republican predecessors, who had the ultimate authority over Lengel's future. This he did on February 23, citing "incompetency, inefficiency and neglect of duty." The *Daily News* was pleased and said the mayor was to be "complimented." The *Repository* labeled the dismissal "political." Swarts appointed easygoing police officer Charles Martin interim chief.

It took Lengel just two days to request a hearing and specification of the charges against him. At the same time he filed a $50,000 libel suit against the *Daily News*, claiming the paper published "false, malicious and defamatory articles" aimed purely at "getting" him. What angered him most were the rum-running articles that accused him of tipping-off favored bootleggers to planned police raids. On March 1 Lengel's attorney, J. L. Amerman, deposed Mellett in the presence of the *Daily News* council, former judge H. C. Pontius. Amerman's questions were directed at trying to find out what solid evidence the publisher might have regarding Lengel's alleged ties to Canton's vice lords. While it is not uncommon for defendants giving sworn depositions to be vague and evasive, Mellett gave Amerman almost no specifics to back up his editorial claims that Lengel was lax in enforcing the law.[42] While Mellett certainly had some evidence, it also appears that, at least in part, some of the paper's accusations were based on rumor and tips supplied by informants with varying degrees of credibility. Nevertheless, there was general agreement in Canton that Chief Lengel was a poor administrator, and Lengel's firing was inevitable. This marked the high point of Don Mellett's career.

Emboldened by his success, Mellett wrote an article, under his own byline, claiming that "Canton's cleanup of vice conditions has only just started."[43] Under the category of nefarious operators, he said vice lord Jumbo Crowley and smaller fry like Studer, Mazer, Meadows, and Bouklias should be put out of business. With them should go some members of the police department: two captains (including Clarke), one lieutenant, four detectives (Swope, Streitenberger, Metzger, and Moore). When asked why he decided to sign this article, making it clear that Lloyd or another staff writer wasn't the author, Don said, "Well, they said they were going to 'get' the guy doing all this." According to Florence, this was when the threatening calls began. And shortly thereafter was when Don told his Sunday school class he feared he might be killed.[44]

Lengel's civil service hearing began March 15 before a packed city council chamber. Canton's legal and political community considered Lengel to be an intelligent man totally lacking executive ability. Within the police department he was seen as an easygoing but inefficient chief who could be stolen blind. He let the likes of Louis Mazer, Ben Rudner, and crooked bail bondsmen like Teddy Abbey hang around headquarters, even on occasion providing them with fatherly advice. It was Lengel who sent Mazer to see Mellett about unflattering *Daily News* articles.[45]

The three-member civil service commission was composed of Price Jansen, John Burris, and James Allardice, all of whom were political appointees of previous mayors. Only Allardice was considered sympathetic to Mayor Swarts's removal of Lengel. To the *Repository*, the issue was who was the real chief of police at the moment, Lengel or his interim successor?

The city's witnesses were, for the most part, a parade of underworld characters and dismissed police officers. The most important witness, Paul Kizman, was arrested after testifying on a complaint of perjury filed by Lengel himself. Even the testimony of one good cop, John "Jiggs" Wise, was considered by the *Repository* to be more beneficial to Lengel than detrimental.[46] Lengel's defense featured W. K. Powell, chief of police in nearby Youngstown, who credited Lengel with running a very efficient department. Powell noted that in Youngstown he had more than 100 officers, while Lengel had only seventy for a city of comparable size. Powell was followed by a Youngstown police detective and a Massillon insurance investigator. Captain Ben Clarke, currently suspended for thirty days for misconduct, also came to Lengel's aid. Lastly, Valentine Schreiber, regional director of the Anti-Saloon League, testified on Lengel's behalf.[47]

Lengel was his own best and last witness. He listed his accomplishments as chief: retirement of horse patrols, the introduction of traffic controls, and, more ominously, the stockpiling of teargas and high-powered rifles. Lengel wasn't bashful about laying blame for his predicament. When asked if he believed he was a victim of a conspiracy headed by the *Daily News*, he replied, "I absolutely do." The chief's attorney, W. Bernard Rogers, told the commission that "this case has a commercial aspect set up by the Canton *Daily News* for the lone and sole purpose of increasing circulation." After two weeks, seventy witnesses, and 400,000 words, the three commissioners agreed they required time to weigh Lengel's fate, and adjourned to deliberate.[48]

Two spectators at the hearing were police detective Floyd Streitenberger, Lengel's favorite detective, and Louis Mazer. The two men were unlikely acquaintances. Streitenberger, thirty-four, from rural southern Ohio, was tall and gangly, had a toothy grin, and spoke with a Kentucky accent. A former army top sergeant, he had joined the force in 1920. Mazer, Jewish and from Canton, was short and compact and, though a natty dresser, preferred to keep a low profile. Streitenberger claimed to have arrested Mazer once, but nothing came of it because Mazer was too smart to have a long criminal record. Despite Mazer's lower social status, it seemed that Streitenberger needed him more than Mazer needed the detective. In recent months, Streitenberger had taken to calling Mazer when he needed some good beer for a party, and Mazer would personally deliver it in his Hudson automobile.[49] Mazer gave Streitenberger $200 he collected for Lengel's defense fund, some of which was coming from Canton's leading criminals.[50] Mazer possibly had another reason to want Mellett to back off. The rumor was that he and ex–federal convict and bootlegger Ben Rudner were planning to open a speakeasy that featured the best smuggled bonded spirits but that Lengel was refusing to protect it as long as Mellett was stirring things up in Canton.[51]

The commission chairman in charge of the deliberations was prominent Canton attorney Price Jansen, who had graduated at the top of his law school class at Ohio State in 1917 and was no fool. But he was arrogant and opinionated. He considered Lengel honest but "of just ordinary ability, and he was a stubborn man." He later commented on the pressure commission members received, claiming that Don Mellett telephoned him and bluntly told him, "I have you in an awkward position. I have a newspaper, and you haven't." Jansen and Mellett only spoke this once, but Jansen's dislike of Mellett remained undiminished for the rest of his life. There is no doubt the men talked; what exactly was said, however, is an open question.[52]

With Jansen and John Burris voting in favor, the civil service commission reinstated Lengel as chief of police on April 7. The majority wrote that it found that most of the charges levied against him to be "wholly unfounded" and that Canton was no worse than hundreds of other cities. Yes, there was vice and crime, they wrote, but the problems in Canton were societal, aggravated by Prohibition—a lukewarm endorsement of the city police department. Testimony regarding corruption in the police department just wasn't credible, Jansen said. And the *Repository* said that the "only direct evidence against the Chief . . . was that he used profanity at times."[53] Writing as a minority of one, commission member James Allardice was direct: "If the civil service commission . . . had deliberately sought to establish a low standard of efficiency, I can conceive of no better illustration."[54] The *Daily News* tried to put a good face on the setback by praising Mayor Swarts for a "splendid public victory" against vice and corruption despite the loss. The Melletts had come to suspect they would lose. It was rumored that Jansen's law partner held an interest in a bank that catered to vice lords. Rumors aside, what was known for certain was that the commission's secretary was Clyde Hovis, managing editor of the *Repository*. This just was not a fight the *Daily News* could win—this time.[55]

During the excitement of Lengel's civil service hearing, Don Mellett quietly slipped out of town and made the trip to Cleveland to testify in a federal investigation of three Canton men charged with narcotics violations. While there, he told the United States district attorney that he had been receiving death threats. Mellett was later quoted in an Associated Press article as saying, "Canton police threatened to get me if I testified in this [narcotics] case."[56] At about the same time police informants picked up intelligence that someone in Canton hired two out-of-town thugs to blow up Don Mellett's home. However, word on the street was that the would-be bombers took the money and skipped town without lighting a fuse. But the Don Mellett family did receive a bomb threat in late March. Don and Lloyd carefully searched the premises but found nothing.

The abortive Lengel firing marked the high and low points for Don Mellett in Canton. He had succeeded in getting a Democrat elected mayor, who in turn, and reluctantly, had fired the chief. Mellett could take comfort in the fact that Lengel's dismissal was a direct result of his editorial crusade. Unfortunately, the civil service hearing and reinstatement of Lengel demonstrated Mellett's lack of support in Canton among those who held most of the power. The hearing had been a parade of unsavory characters who offered less than creditable tales of Canton's seamy underside. The city's most influential newspaper, the *Repository*, regarded the whole affair as a mere act of political retribution. Lengel and his supporters were not shy in painting Mellett as a newcomer trying to sell newspapers. It was no wonder that many city residents found the episode distasteful and unnecessarily damaging to Canton's reputation and viewed Mellett and the *Daily News* in an unfavorable light.

Some of Mellett's faults as an editor were also on display. Mellett's bull-in-the-china-shop approach to Canton's problems was costing him support he needed to achieve true reform. A more deft touch and subtle approach might have yielded more lasting results. Mellett's lack of patience was hurting him and the *Daily News* in the court of public opinion. He needed a new tack in Canton. Finally he began to realize this, and so did Jim Cox.

Though Jim Cox employed a hands-off style of management, this did not mean he was unaware of what was going on in Canton. Copies of all Cox newspapers were sent to him in Dayton every day. And purportedly an unnamed person went to see the former governor in Florida that winter concerning Mellett's escalating editorial campaign. Former judge Pontius, the *Daily News*'s legal counsel and a Mellett friend, wrote to Cox in Florida on March 29 concerning the course Mellett was pursuing in Canton. Cox's reply was a qualified endorsement: "Mellett has some fine qualities. He became imbued just a little too much with the spirit of the crusader. The government of a place ordinarily will be just as good as the public wants it, no better. If our papers can fix in the mind of a community a higher standard, then a real service will have been given."[57] A *Daily News* reporter, Dennis R. Smith, also sent weekly reports, with Mellett's knowledge, to Dayton.

The News League editor-in-chief, Cox's former personal secretary and Mellett's successor, Charles E. Morris, often visited Canton and consulted with Mellett. Morris tried to discourage crusading, but Don took his case directly to Cox apparently without rebuke.

Sometime in the spring of 1926, Cox and Mellett met. Cox reminded Mellett, like he had Pontius, that the affairs of a community cannot be made any better than the citizens want them to be and extensively questioned him about what he was doing in Canton. Mellett asked if this meant Cox had lost confidence in him. Not at all, Cox told him; he only wanted to help Mellett avoid mistakes he had made when he was younger, possibly referring to all those lawsuits Cox had endured in his early years as a publisher. Mellett showed his boss an improving financial picture and got Cox's rather reluctant approval to stay the course in Canton. Nevertheless, Cox warned Mellett, "I admire your courage, but I am sure you must realize you are in great danger."[58]

The *Daily News* labeled Lengel's full reinstatement on May 3 "a public disgrace." But this setback in the campaign against police corruption did not dampen the paper's editorial rhetoric, and it called for an investigation of affairs in Canton by the U.S. Justice Department. Yet during most of May, the mayor and new safety director, James A. Rice, assumed the lead in attempting to reform the police department. Rice's moves to make personnel changes, regulate vacation time, and increase the power of the safety director within the police department—all the while bypassing Lengel—failed, frustrated by a Republican city council, the civil service commission, and the courts.

The *Daily News* launched a month-long campaign of civic boosterism that culminated on May 30 with the aptly named "industrial" edition, a massive three-pound tome that detailed Canton's history, industry, business, and culture. This special edition was delivered free to all of Canton's 27,000 homes and was sent to major libraries across the country. Presented to Cantonians as a means to "stimulate and accelerate [the city's] future growth and development," it received high marks from the Chamber of Commerce, of which Don Mellett was publicity chairman.

In June, and in "the best interests of the city of Canton," the *Daily News* once again turned its focus on law enforcement. The unsuccessful

Rice was replaced with another new safety director, Earl A. Hexamer, a veteran and a former police motorcycle lieutenant. Both the *News* and *Repository* found him a well-qualified choice—"an excellent selection" in the opinion of the *News*. For his part, Hexamer promised that all newspapers would receive equal treatment.[59]

If the city police were ignoring vice activities, county prosecutor Charles McClintock was not. In mid-June McClintock recommended a raid on Doll Carey's house. Carey, Louis Mazer's girlfriend, ran a brothel on Walnut Avenue that was, coincidently, also Mazer's residence. The prosecutor had sent the note to Chief Lengel, who had passed it to Detective Streitenberger. The bootlegger and the policeman, who had formed a mutually beneficial friendship, met on June 17 and agreed to keep the proposed raid a secret yet minimize the number of arrests. Doll Carey's brothel had a secret room under the stairs where girls could hide if necessary, so the two arranged the raid so that only one girl, Thelma Harris, a former shop girl, was arrested.

Chief Lengel's selective enforcement of gambling laws had led to the cancellation of the harness races during the 1925 county fair. Lengel and Hexamer agreed to prohibit betting on the races at the 1926 fair also, which again resulted in the event being cancelled. The *Repository* deemed the move "consistent with the police department's effort to stop gambling," but the *Daily News* lamented the loss of a fine old sport so that the chief could protect his future pension and pointed out that baseball pool betting was widespread and unchecked in Canton.

The *Daily News* was delighted when Sergeant Jiggs Wise's liquor enforcement squad carried out a series of raids on June 26 and praised it as the "finest liquor haul of the season." Well-known bootlegger Carl Studer and an associate named Naugle were caught in the net, but, like all the others, they wriggled out after only paying fines. The evidence, locked in a wooden cabinet at police headquarters, had mysteriously disappeared. Chief Lengel and Captain Clarke both examined the cabinet and stated emphatically that it had not been tampered with.[60] This was not the first time booze had mysteriously disappeared from the police evidence cabinet.

The Fourth of July fell on a Sunday in 1926, making it a three-day weekend. As was their custom, the Melletts drove to Indianapolis to see family, stopping along the way in Dayton to see Jim Cox. Elder brother John Mellett recalled seeing a revolver in Don's car. A private detective the *Daily News* employed, probably Burton, had insisted he have it, but Don admitted to his brother that he didn't know how to use it. The brothers discussed an offer Don had received from a Cleveland newspaper to become their business manager at a better salary. John urged Don to take the offer, but Don refused, saying he felt committed to Cox. Perhaps at year's end, he said, when the *Daily News* had a year in the black, he would go. This was the same reply he had given Florence. Don admitted to John that some advertisers in Canton had shunned the paper because of his editorial crusade, but he stuck with it because it "increased circulation, and then, finally, boosted ad revenue."[61]

While Don was away, Lloyd received a visit from former mayor C. C. Curtis. Curtis wanted Lloyd to help get his brother, Ed, paroled from prison. The parole was in the bag, Curtis said, if the *Daily News* would agree not to criticize Governor Donahey for the release. Lloyd declined to speak for Don. Curtis pressed harder, telling Lloyd that all he had to do was agree—since he and Don were both Melletts, what difference did it make who gave the okay. When Lloyd finally reached Don in Indianapolis, the elder Mellett went immediately to Columbus on July 7 and urged Governor Donahey not to pardon Ed Curtis or Turner and Bouklias for their good behavior while in prison. (The governor had already received some criticism for the soft jobs Turner and Bouklias had been given in prison, Bouklias a greenhouse job and Turner chief operator of the phone system.) But so worried was Donahey about the *Daily News*'s reaction should he pardon the men that he already had decided to postpone the Curtis parole. The power of Mellett's pen had touched Columbus.[62]

Don Mellett was not done with the civil service commission. Lengel's hearing had revealed that the commission's records were neglected, that it rarely held formal meetings, and that more than twenty serving police officers were hired without examination. The *Daily News* further suggested that problems within the police department were actually due to an inattentive civil service commission. "Very often a sore cannot be cured until its source is found," it editorialized on June 27. As a good example it pointed to the case of Sergeant Daniel J. Van Gunten, who had once bodily thrown a *Daily News* reporter out of police headquarters. The lawman was restored to duty on March 16 without a hearing after being removed on charges of bribery and brutality.

The Melletts also felt they had evidence of criminal ties by members of the civil service commission but not enough to print the accusation. Instead, Canton police officer George Beresford, a Mellett supporter, filed a complaint with Mayor Swarts against two civil service commission members, Jansen and Burris, using the *Daily News* information. The complaint alleged neglect of duty and inefficiency in the reinstatement of Chief Lengel. Taking his cue from the *Daily News*, Beresford stated, "The civil service commission itself is the root of the trouble."[63] Removing Jansen and Burris would clear the way for the mayor to appoint members more sympathetic to his own views. This was not a partisan move. After all, Jansen was a Democrat and a future candidate for Ohio's lieutenant governor. Swarts either believed the commissioners needed to go or he felt pressure from the *Daily News*, which insinuated that Jansen and Burris had to reinstate Lengel to cover their own inefficiency. The mayor set July 14 as the date for hearing the charges.

The two embattled civil service commission members managed to get the hearing postponed. Jansen blamed Beresford's complaint on a conspiracy of two: Mellett and Swarts. Then Jansen did a stupid thing. He issued a long, rambling personal statement attacking Mellett. Jansen said, in part that "Mr. Mellett . . . brought to Canton a mouthing, slobbering overworked, oversized jawbone and . . . blackguarding, muckraking tactics [that have] caused Canton immeasurable harm." Jansen went on to suggest that in a less civilized time Mellett would have been ridden out of town on a rail. Don Mellett knew a gift when he saw it and wanted to print the entire Jansen statement on page one in the July 12 issue. But Lloyd thought it too inflammatory and, fearing for his brother's safety, was opposed. An embarrassed *Repository*, whose editor was the commission's clerk, declined to print the full statement. Don overruled Lloyd and ordered the statement printed without telling him. He tried to lessen the tension the next day when the editorial took the high road, saying the paper had only the "kindest of feelings" for Jansen.

During this episode, Chief Lengel suspended Sergeant Wise for ninety days for being under the influence when involved in an automobile accident. Wise and a friend were in a one car accident at 5:20 A.M., Tuesday, July 13, three miles north of the city. A nearby farmer claimed the two men were drunk. Wise denied it. The *Daily News* supported Wise, one of the Melletts' favorite officers, and recognized him as being Lengel's "much disliked officer" whose pursuit of bootleggers has been "entirely too intense . . . to please the bootleggers and their friends."[64] The *Daily News* pointed out that Wise didn't drink, was only late to work by ten minutes, and still completed a full day's work. Hexamer reinstated Wise on July 16, saying only that Lengel was "misinformed."[65]

In the days to come, being misinformed would be the least of Lengel's problems.

The Murder

During a golf outing on Sunday, July 11, Don Mellett told his partner, Vic Merson, who was on the *Daily News*'s advertising staff, about the now-frequent threats against his life.[1] Increasing the pressure was Don's revelation that he had discovered who killed Paul "Mooney" Kitzig in August 1921. Friends and family knew that if Don did solve the Kitzig murder, it could be very dangerous for him.[2] The deeper Mellett got into Canton's underworld, the more dangerous it was for him, whether he printed what he uncovered or not. It was very risky for the vice lords to have a journalist closely examining their relationship with the police.

The Kitzig murder was one of Canton's important unsolved murders. On his arrest, Kitzig, a low-level driver for bootleggers running liquor from Pittsburgh to Canton and Cleveland, had been easily persuaded to turn state's evidence. His testimony helped convict Ben Rudner, son of a wealthy Canton hardware merchant, on federal liquor law violations.[3] Rudner had a criminal record beginning at age eighteen, when he hit an old man over the head with a pipe and robbed him of $200.[4] Years later he was free, pending appeal of his liquor convictions, when Kitzig was found shot in the back of the head at very close range.[5] John Mellett revealed that Don had discovered that a "hophead" (1920s slang for a drug addict) had killed Kitzig for $25. Then the killer himself was bumped off. The insinuation was that Ben Rudner was behind it, but Don couldn't print this accusation because his only source was an addict.[6] (Occasionally, Mellett had an unfortunate tendency to take informants at their word. This may have been one of those times, for the murder was not amateurish; it had a professional air to it.) That same Sunday evening, July 11, Ben Rudner, who bore a passing resemblance to Al Capone in features and build, was involved in a fender bender with a contractor named D. D. Zell. There were no injuries, but Zell insisted they go to Canton police headquarters to report the damage. Ben's unusual influence with the Canton police was highlighted when a patrolman told Zell, "Your car isn't hurt worth talking about, and you'd better let it drop or Rudner is likely to knock you down."[7]

No one in Mellett's circle knew how seriously to take the threats he was receiving. Don honestly believed that his law-and-order campaign was based on principle, and he professed no personal enmity toward any individual. Yet in reality, the *Daily News* had named names, identified criminals to prosecute and policemen to be fired. Suggesting someone be fired or arrested was more serious than castigating fraternity boys for profanity, as Don had done in the college newspaper. But the Mellett brothers did not see the difference. They did not truly appreciate that bootleggers and gamblers played by different rules.

Rumors about threats against Mellett were abundant in the summer of 1926. Many were not credible, one reason Don seemed unfazed by them. And some he never knew about. A local attorney told Chief Lengel that Rocco Ferruccio, the local Black Hand leader, had showed him a gun and said he wanted to shoot Mellett.[8] (The Black Hand was a particularly violent crime organization often confused with the Mafia. Secretive and poorly understood by American lawmen, the Black Hand was especially brutal and ruthless. Blowing up property and people was their specialty.)

But the most credible threat came on Saturday night, July 10. Don and Florence had gone out for the evening, leaving the four children with the teenaged babysitter, Helen Koons. While they were out, Helen took a strange telephone call. The caller, who refused to identify himself, wanted to speak to Don Mellett. Eleven-year-old Evan saw the distressed look on Helen's face and snatched the phone from her. But he could not understand the caller's muffled voice. The next evening, Sunday, July 11, at 10:30 P.M., while sitting on the front porch with Florence, the Vails, and Lloyd and his wife, Frances, Don received an anonymous telephone call: "There are three men at your garage, and they have been there several nights." The caller emphasized "three" and identified himself as "somebody who is opposed to your enemies." Don, Lloyd, and Walter Vail made a fruitless search of the entire premises, looking primarily for a bomb. The three men then spent the night on guard in the Mellett parlor armed with a single pistol (borrowed from liquor agent Jack Campbell) and baseball bats. Florence and the children refused to leave. Walter Vail later said, "That was the first time I ever saw that he was sort of afraid."[9]

That same day, Don had secured the services of a sympathetic police officer, George Beresford, to guard his home. Beresford, who was on a ten-day unpaid leave after clashing with his superiors, was a close Mellett ally and was the officer who filed the complaint against the civil service commission. At the Mellett residence, he kept watch at night, usually sitting in the garage or walking the neighborhood. The next day, Monday, Don spoke with a friend in the clergy, Reverend W. H. Longsworth, and in discussing the threats he was receiving said, "I have more than a premonition. It comes in the form of a warning that is almost direct."[10]

Wednesday evening the Mellett brothers and their wives went to the Meyer's Lake ballroom, a popular entertainment spot, to see a show. (Don had recently favorably reviewed another show in a paid *Daily News* advertisement.) On the way home they were caught in a speed trap on Broad Avenue. Don was driving too fast, Lloyd later admitted, but he also claimed that the officer inflated the speed on the ticket by twenty mph when he saw the driver was Don Mellett. Lloyd later complained that the *Evening Repository* made an issue of Don's arrest, but in reality the rival paper only listed Don among the twenty other speeders caught that night. However, the police report listed Don's speed at fifty-three miles per hour, the fastest of the speeders that night, so perhaps the arresting officer did inflate it. Lloyd and his family stayed at Don's house Wednesday night.

After three uneventful nights, and with Beresford's reassurance that he had little to worry about, Don thanked the officer and sent him home on Thursday, July 15. Beresford, who was less confident than he let on, offered to come back that evening and stay until the last streetcar of the night. Florence felt they needed protection, but Don didn't want to keep Beresford from his family. This was a mistake. It had been a week when three murders had occurred in the Jungle. Circulation manager Charles Gaston and press foreman Walter Streby both warned Mellett to be "very careful," because some of these hoodlums "would stop at nothing."[11]

Thursday morning at police headquarters, Floyd Streitenberger stopped by Ben Clarke's office and asked him if he knew Don Mellett had moved. Clarke wrote down the new Tuscarawas address on a scrap of paper and handed it to the detective. Being helpful, Clarke added that there were two trees in front of the place making it easy to identify. Clarke didn't ask why Streitenberger wanted to know.

That same morning, the most recent circulation figures were available, and they should have given Don a boost. The *Daily News* had been steadily gaining on the *Repository* and was now only 6,000 paid subscribers behind.[12] In a promotional ad in that day's edition, the paper crowed, "To the *News* [our] constantly and rapidly growing circulation is an evidence of a reader confidence in the *News*' policy of printing all the news fairly and without favor." The circulation figures were on track to meet Mellett's goal of equaling the *Repository* by year's end.

Don spent three hours that afternoon with Henry Roemer, manager of Canton's minor league baseball team, the Canton Coal Hoppers. Jim Cox had suggested the paper feature more local sports, and Mellett had enthusiastically supported the local team. The *Daily News* had recently underwritten an exhibition game with the St. Louis Americans. This afternoon, Don, working his contacts, had raised $2,000 so the team could complete the season. The grateful Roemer later recalled that Don was "somewhat nervous" during the afternoon.[13]

Don arrived home at 6:30, a little later than usual. He told a worried Florence that he had stopped on his way to deliver an electric fan to a sick child.[14] After dinner, the Melletts sat on the front porch of their newly rented home on the corner of Tuscarawas and Claremont avenues, located in Canton's better northwest side and where they'd moved in the spring. They could hear the festivities of the first night of a military mardi gras at the county fairgrounds just two blocks north. Sponsored by the Canton National Guard unit, the affair advertised a battle reenactment in which $10,000 munitions would be expended, including 45,000 rounds of machine gun ammunition. Don was not interested in the mardi gras, but he had consented to let the older children go down the street to watch the military parade. Typical of Don, he was too restless that evening to sit around. He decided that Florence should put down her sewing and call the Vails. They should get a babysitter and all go to the Molly Stark Club anniversary dance.[15]

That evening at the fairgrounds with his family, Lloyd Mellett saw a trusted member of the police department and told him about the week's threatening calls. The unidentified officer said that it sounded like the work of Captain Ben Clarke, whose dismissal the Melletts were advocating. Later that evening, Lloyd ran into Clarke. Clarke asked about Lloyd's health, saying he didn't look well. Clarke also asked other odd, seemingly irrelevant questions that disconcerted and baffled Lloyd.

Once Helen arrived, shortly after 9:30, the Melletts and Vails went out. It was Don's habit to do the driving, but this evening Don didn't argue when Walter Vail insisted he drive, which left Don's big blue Rickenbacher in the driveway behind the house.[16] Later this would be interpreted as a safety measure, given the threats. However, Don more likely felt chastised for receiving a speeding ticket the previous evening.

The Molly Stark Club met in a large room above Schlabach's drugstore. The Melletts and Vails only stayed for two dances, leaving around 11:00 to go downstairs to the drugstore for chocolate sodas.[17] Sipping his soda, Don's competitive streak surfaced, and he started a good-natured debate over which drugstore in Canton made the best soda, Schlabach's or Bierys. With Carrie Vail siding with Don against their spouses, there appeared to be no way to resolve the issue short of going out Cleveland Avenue to Bierys for a second soda—which they did, only to discover that Bierys was closed for the evening. The argument unresolved, the two couples headed back to the Mellett home.

A few miles west of Canton, in Massillon, Ben Rudner was enjoying a private gathering with a few close friends at the Fessler residence. Ben supposedly worked for his father in the family's hardware–auto parts store in Massillon. He was paid as a regular clerk and worked a scheduled shift, but most people knew he was mixed up in bootlegging. Ben enjoyed the notoriety and didn't discourage the rumors. Rudner attended the party not in the company of his wife but with an unidentified woman. No one questioned this arrangement; Ben's hot temper was well-known. The party lasted until the early hours of Friday morning, when Ben insisted a handful of tired guests accompany him on a meandering car drive around Stark County. Ben was the picture of health that night, clearly recovered from the severely infected finger he suffered the week before.

At about 11:30 P.M., Floyd and Kate Streitenberger were also hosting an impromptu post–mardi gras party at their home on Sixth Street.[18] They invited their neighbors Walter and Emma Craft, Mrs. Craft's aunt, the Duff Youngs, and the Carl Gussetts and their two children. The primary draw was beer—which was legal during Prohibition, provided you brewed it yourself—that Detective Streitenberger had received from Louis Mazer. The guests knew better than to ask too many questions about the beer's pedigree. A nattily dressed man came to the door at about midnight, and Floyd left with him a short time later. The party broke up about 12:30 A.M.

The Melletts and Vails returned home from the dance at about 11:40. Walter parked his car on Tuscarawas, right in front of the house. Carrie and Florence waited on the front porch, which faced the street, while the men went around to the back door, which was just a few steps from where the Melletts' Rickenbacher was parked. The back porch light was on, and both men were clearly visible from a vacant lot across Claremont Avenue as they unlocked the back door. (For $65 a month rent, the Melletts only got keys to the back door.) The foursome sat for a while on the brick front porch talking. The Kitzig killing came up. Don said he had different informants come into his office and that he had solved the case. The *Daily News* might publish the killer's name, he told them.[19]

All was quiet now, the festivities at the fairgrounds concluding earlier in the evening. Like the evenings before, it was cool. Walter was sleepy and wanted to call it an evening. But the Melletts jokingly reminded him that they had stayed later on their last visit to the Vail home. Florence insisted on making some coffee to keep them awake. When the Vails tried to beg off, Don teased about ending their friendship if they did. As usual, Don won out, and the Vails agreed to stay.

It was about 12:20 when Florence and Don went to the kitchen at the back of the house, which had two large double-hung windows that overlooked the garage. They had to rummage around the kitchen looking for some sugar to serve with the coffee. The Vails called their babysitter to alert her to the change of plans. Preoccupied with making the coffee, Florence barely acknowledged Don saying he was going to put the car in the garage. She had made it a point not to let Don go outside at night alone. The oldest Mellett daughter, Jean, age nine, awake in an upstairs bedroom at the back of the house, heard her father say he was going to put the car away.[20] Walter joined Florence in the kitchen while Carrie brought the hats and purses left on the porch into the front room.

The night was dark, but Don was silhouetted by the porch light as he descended the back stairs and walked over to the Rickenbacher and got in. The single-story, two-car garage and driveway were just steps from the door, and Claremont Avenue was only a few paces to the left. Across Claremont was a vacant lot overgrown with brush and weeds; a slight earthen embankment paralleled the street. Don pulled the car into the garage bay closest to the house. The garage doors were hinged, carriage house style. Don stepped out of the car and closed the left door.

From the kitchen window, Florence saw a flash between the branches of a syringa bush beside the house. Then they heard a shot or two, then a volley of gunshots, six or perhaps ten (there was never agreement on exactly how many). Moving toward the back door, Florence saw dull muzzle flashes come from in front of tall bushes in the northwest corner of the vacant lot, the flashes coming in rapid succession from close but different points of fire. A bullet smashed through the window, spewing glass shards into her hair and missing Walter's head by mere inches before slamming into the wood trim of a window on the east side of the kitchen.

The firing stopped as abruptly as it began. Florence looked out and saw her husband slumped in the driveway next to the open right garage door. She screamed, "I believe they got Don!" She then dropped to her hands and knees and crawled to the stairs, instinctively thinking of the children.

Upstairs in the back bedroom, young Jean heard loud noises and saw flashes of light outside. She jumped out of bed and ran to sit at the top of the stairs. Helen, the babysitter, was also in bed upstairs. When she heard the shots she first thought of the battle reenactment at the fairgrounds. But that had ended at 11:30. She put on her robe and ran downstairs. Florence instructed her to confine the children upstairs. The Vails, Walter in the lead, went out the back door and rushed to Don, who was on the cement, his back against the open garage door. Neither of them saw any of the assailants. Walter yelled for someone to call a doctor. Carrie was too shaken to find the number, so Florence took the phone book and made the call.

Leo Schumacher, a self-employed plumber who lived a half-block north of the Melletts, was returning home, driving south on Claremont and turning west into the alley, Glenn Place. With him was Bessie Zimmer, the wife of a fellow plumber and the ailing Mrs. Schumacher's nurse.[21] As Schumacher made the turn, the car's bright lights panned the vacant lot, and the pair saw nothing amiss. Rolling just 100 feet west on Glenn Place, Schumacher then turned left and pulled up to his garage a few feet from the street. Just before the car came to a stop, its lights reflecting off the garage door, they heard a rapid succession of shots, seven or eight possibly, certainly more than three, close by. Schumacher thought the shots came so fast that an automatic pistol was used. They froze in the car, thinking they were being robbed, but there were no demands for valuables. Leo then thought it was boys shooting over at the fairgrounds, but then they heard footsteps running west on Glenn Place, behind their car, one or two men. But they didn't see anyone, nor did they hear a car start nearby. Leo locked his car and garage doors, and sent Bessie upstairs to his wife, who was confined to bed with a nervous condition. The gunfire outside her bedroom window had awakened Mrs. Schumacher, who looked at her bedside clock. It was between 12:20 and 12:25 A.M.

They all heard Florence Mellett screaming and calling for Don, although at the time they didn't know who the new neighbors were in the old Mike McKinney home. Only a few minutes elapsed before Leo ran over to the Melletts', a distance of only sixty yards or so. He arrived as the Vails were struggling to carry a lifeless Don up the rear porch steps, momentarily startling the Vails and Florence. Walter, his light summer suit covered with blood, had Don under the arms. Schumacher relieved Carrie Vail, who was struggling with Don's legs. Florence kept asking, "Do you think he is dead?" The two men carried Don into the parlor and laid him on the sofa. Schumacher placed a pillow under Don's head. He felt for a pulse. Nothing. Asked again by Florence if he thought Don was dead, Schumacher hedged by suggesting they wait for a doctor. Florence got a basin of water and some towels. She opened Don's collar and made a vain attempt to help her husband.

Walter Vail rushed out and drove the ten blocks to Columbus Avenue where Lloyd Mellett lived. Lloyd had gone to bed an hour earlier, so Vail woke him by pounding on his apartment door, yelling, "Come quick, they have shot Don. They have got Don, they have killed him!" Lloyd was so shaken that Vail had to help him get dressed.

Alone with the women, Schumacher suggested calling the police. Florence objected and said she feared the police might be involved in the shooting. But she relented when Schumacher pointed out that at least they could administer first aid. He telephoned the police from the Melletts' parlor. Minutes later, Mellett family physician and Sunday school class friend Dr. Guy Maxwell arrived. His brief exam revealed a bullet entry wound on the left side of the head above the ear. The right side of the skull was distorted by the energy of the bullet, but he found no exit wound. Dr. Maxwell pronounced Don Mellett dead just before 1:00 A.M., Friday morning, July 16, 1926.

At police headquarters, a desk officer took Leo Schumacher's call that a man had been shot at the corner of Tuscarawas and Claremont. That officer was slow passing the information on to Laura Hardy, the night operator of the police signal system. Like most cities in the era before radio communication, Canton had a system of police call boxes, referred to as a recall system, special telephones strategically located around the city. Once activated, sirens and flashing lights on the boxes alerted patrolmen walking a beat to call headquarters. The nearest Canton policeman to the Mellett home was normally stationed several blocks east, closer to the city's high-crime areas. In addition to foot patrols, two motorized units were on duty, one of those assigned exclusively to the vice-ridden Jungle on the southeast side of town. Although the efficient Miss Hardy put the urgent Mellett call out at 12:50 A.M., no patrol officer answered for over twenty minutes. In her experience, this was an unusually slow response. Also odd was the disappearance of police Sergeant Daniel J. "Van" Van Gunten, who was supposed to be the officer in charge at police headquarters that night. The new safety director, Earl Hexamer, had just that previous afternoon issued an order requiring a lieutenant to be in charge of each shift, but as of yet it was not implemented. Still, Schumacher thought the police "made good time coming out," less than ten minutes, he thought, driving so fast they missed the house and skidded to a stop a ways down the street.

Patrolmen Harry Jacobs and W. H. Ritz arrived at the murder scene at just about the same time. Lloyd Mellett appeared moments later. The *Daily News* once mistakenly accused Jacobs of wrongdoing, but had retracted it. Ritz, however, had physically ejected one of the paper's reporters from police headquarters. There was no love lost between the two policemen and the younger Mellett.[22] Patrolman Clarence Pollack arrived just after Lloyd. The three officers faced the wrath of a distraught Florence and belligerent Lloyd Mellett. Blaming the police for Don's murder, Florence told them, "We know who killed him. . . . Get hold of Chief Lengel or Captain Clarke. They can tell you who killed him."[23] Then Sergeant Van Gunten, who had been out riding with a patrolman when he should have been at police headquarters, arrived.[24]

Van Gunten had only been on the force for five years, but in a department where loyalty and connections trumped professionalism, it was enough experience to warrant being left in charge at night.

He was yet another officer the Melletts thought should be dismissed. Lloyd, furious, confronted the officers, calling them "blackhearted" and "assassinating." He ordered Van Gunten out of the house.[25] The lawmen backed Lloyd against the wall, and Jacobs threatened to handcuff him.[26] One of the officers called headquarters from the Mellett parlor and reported that Don Mellett was shot. It wasn't long before almost a dozen lawmen were present. (It was then that Leo Schumacher learned that the murder victim was the editor of his daily newspaper.[27]) Defiantly, Florence asked the police milling around in her parlor, "Why don't you get out and do something?" The police eventually persuaded her to go upstairs and rest.[28]

Just after 1:00 A.M., Stark County coroner T. C. McQuate, a ten-year veteran, was roused from his bed in Massillon and hurried to the scene. McQuate took charge of the body and removed the bullet lodged in the wood trim in the kitchen.[29] Five slugs were eventually recovered: one by Captain Clarke from the yard behind the house and two by McQuate, one from the body and another, which had barely missed Walter Vail, from the woodwork in the Mellett house. All five bullets were later rushed by McQuate himself, in Henry Timkin's personal chauffeured automobile, to a ballistics engineer at Winchester Repeating Arms Company in New Haven, Connecticut.[30] At 1:30 McQuate called Stark County prosecutor Charles B. McClintock, who came straight to the murder scene. At about this same time Chief Lengel was called. However, the police chief did not go to the murder scene but went straight to police headquarters, where he called out all the force's detectives and telephoned every large city police department within 100 miles to be on the lookout for nobody knew what. Lengel didn't go anywhere near the scene of Canton's highest profile murder in decades. He later lamely claimed that McQuate and McClintock advised him not to go because of the family's hostility.

Meanwhile, at about 2:00 A.M., Sergeant Van Gunten drove to police captain Ben Clarke's home. "Ben, get up. Don Mellett got shot!" Van Gunten banged on the door.[31] As the department's Bertillon officer, Clarke was in charge of the physical characteristics and photographs kept on every arrestee as a means of identification at this time before fingerprints were widely used. He wasn't accustomed to being called out in the middle of the night. On his way to Mellett's, Clarke drove over to detective Floyd Streitenberger's home to roust him out of bed too.[32]

Eventually, Chief of Detectives Ed Swope arrived to conduct an investigation.[33] Lloyd felt somewhat better about Swope than Clarke, although the *Daily News* had also suggested his dismissal. Aware of the Melletts' animosity, Clarke never went into the house when he arrived at the scene. Clarke and Swope searched around the house, using a flashlight to check windows for bullet holes and the yard for tracks. Two other detectives checked around the weedy lot and Schumacher's house. On the whole the police were content to keep onlookers and the curious at bay.

Their "investigation" amounted to interviewing one neighbor and speculating about bullet trajectories by examining the holes in the garage and house. They spoke with Bessie Zimmer, but no one went up the alley in the direction she told them she'd heard men running. Swope explained that "anyone in a machine would have had plenty of time to get away before now."[34] No one interviewed Mrs. Schumacher, whose bedroom window overlooked the vacant lot and who earlier in the evening had heard someone in the bushes outside.[35] And though a neighbor, Mr. Gerber, had also heard shots from the vacant lot, he was not interviewed by police either. Interestingly, however, when Bessie Zimmer asked if there had been a robbery, Swope answered, "No, revenge."[36]

Florence Mellett refused to talk to Captain Clarke.[37] She eventually did give a statement to Judge Wise.[38] Five shots were all that could be accounted for, according to the police, based on the holes found in the garage doors and the back of the house.[39] The house directly east of the Melletts' was only six to ten feet away. Based on the angle of the gunshots, it would have been impossible for a shot fired at the victim—even a wild one—to not have hit something—a house, a tree, the sidewalk. But, even in daylight, the police did not undertake a thorough examination of the area to look for bullet holes. On the whole, the police work lacked direction and coordination, evidenced by the number of policemen milling around and bumping into one another.[40] The next day's *Repository* credited Chief Lengel with being in charge. The paper did not reveal that he was never at the scene.

The detectives made no attempt to secure the crime scene on Tuscarawas Avenue. And as dawn approached and the police drifted away, Jean Mellett, peeking through drawn curtains, saw curious onlookers surrounding the house and garage. Some fingered the bullet holes, others gawked at the blood-stained driveway. A few daubed at the blood with handkerchiefs.[41] The police did nothing to keep people off the lawn where additional spent bullets might have been found in daylight.

Meanwhile, at police headquarters, Chief Lengel was receiving an early-morning visitor. Sometime before 6:00 A.M., Ben Rudner showed up and went right in to see the chief. Rudner had heard of the murder from his sometime bodyguard, merchant policeman[42] J. W. "Smitty" Smith, in Massillon when Ben returned from his joyride at about 4:00 and immediately called Lengel. He had been to police headquarters just the evening before, supposedly to discuss vandalism at one of the Rudners' hardware stores in Canton, and he and Lengel had a hushed conference on the sidewalk outside the building. Now he was back again with questions about Canton's most recent murder. Apparently Lengel didn't consider all this attention from Ben Rudner, whom he had known since his juvenile delinquent days, unusual.[43]

After sunrise, a sleepy and haggard McQuate dropped off his coroner's report at police headquarters. As he was leaving he bumped into Ben Rudner, also departing. The always-helpful Rudner offered the tired McQuate a ride home to Massillon, where they both lived. Rudner had Smitty Smith along as a driver, which meant that Rudner could devote his full attention to finding out what he could from McQuate about Mellett's killing. But McQuate, exhausted, dozed off on the trip west. He jerked awake when he heard Ben open the glove box and saw him extract a .45 caliber semi-automatic pistol. Smiling, Ben said that he wanted the coroner to know what kind of gun Ben Rudner carried. By 10:00 A.M. that same morning, Ben Rudner was seen back in Canton having breakfast with Louis Mazer at the popular D&E Sandwich Shop.

When the news broke that Friday morning, the motive was known to everyone in Canton who read the *Daily News*. The question was who was bold enough to kill a journalist to silence him? A motive of revenge only narrowed the list of suspects down to the dozens of corrupt police officers, bootleggers, dopers, gamblers, and madams Mellett had named in his editorials. And so a conspiracy was suspected from day one.

The murder of the young crusading newspaper publisher shocked the city of Canton, Ohio, and the nation. The *Repository* called Mellett's killing a "cowardly assassination," and other newspapers took up the cry. The story remained front-page news in the *New York Times* for five consecutive days. After all, Don Mellett was a member of the press. He had been murdered in the line of duty, and the newspaper world was demanding justice. An editorial on the front page of the *Daily News* on July 16 likened its slain publisher to a "captain in battle" and called him "a born fighter." "He has been laid upon the altar, a martyr," it eulogized. "His ideals are emblazoned brighter than ever on his escutcheon." The tribute closed with, "His passing does not mean the end of the battle. The *Daily News* will carry on."

Whether Lloyd wrote this is not known, but he did author an "Appeal for Justice" that appeared in the paper. Disavowing any thoughts of revenge, the younger Mellett stated emphatically, "I want justice done." He concluded by writing what everyone in Canton was already thinking: "I do not know who did this deed. I do know it was hired, planned and premeditated." Of Don, brother Lowell later wrote, "he took public issues personally. The public's fight was his fight, always."[44] The *Repository* became an overnight convert to the crusade for law and order, predicting that Mellett's "untimely murder will arouse a public sentiment that will demand the apprehension and conviction of his assassins, and stamp out the evil forces that have brought about this calamity. There can be no middle ground in such a crisis. A point has been reached where the community must decide whether law and order or the gunman shall control."[45]

Don Mellett's funeral was scheduled for Saturday afternoon, July 17, at his home. On that Saturday morning, for reasons he never explained,

Chief Lengel sent four workhouse prisoners, under the supervision of a turnkey named Fred "Fritz" Graub, to clear the vacant lot of brush and cut the grass. Graub, who spoke with a heavy German accent, was only a jail guard, not a detective, but Lengel told him Friday afternoon, "You go out there and cut the weeds, and mark it for inspection and look for guns." The workhouse crew arrived at about 9:00 A.M. and cleared the lot across from the Mellett garage. Then they did the same thing to a vacant lot north of the garage. The conveniently timed cleanup destroyed any chance future investigators had of finding anything useful in the very area where all the witnesses agreed the shots had come from. Perhaps Lengel was cleaning up the lot before Mellett's Saturday afternoon funeral as a gesture of condolence and respect, but he should have known better, and forever after he would be accused of having more sinister motives.[46] As the Saturday cleanup was under way on Claremont, an alert photographer hanging around police headquarters snapped a photo of Chief Lengel laughing with a crony, a copy of the *Daily News*, its murder headline clearly visible, under his arm.[47] The picture became front-page news.

Former sheriff C. W. Kirk called Mellett's killing the "worst murder in the history of Canton." Mayor Swarts, who was a lukewarm reformer, but owed his election in large part to Don Mellett, told reporters, "The frightful murder has doubtless brought to the attention of the people the terrible conditions that have existed in Canton." Governor Donahey, who had met with Mellett less than ten days ago regarding Turner and Bouklias, said, "He died in a battle for right, a battle to make his city a better place to live in."[48]

At the small Canton funeral Don Mellett was eulogized by the Reverend Birchard F. Brundase as having joined "the battalion of martyrs." After the brief service, the Mellett brothers, Florence, and the children escorted the body back to Indianapolis for another, more public funeral at brother Roland's home on July 19, an event attended by journalists from all over Ohio and Indiana.[49] Jim Cox spoke at length of his slain publisher: "It is unfortunate . . . that such a thing must occur to cause the American public to realize that similar danger hangs over the people of most industrialized cities unless the crime situation is placed under control." He said of Mellett, "I never knew a finer moral courage."[50] Cox's remarks were reprinted in their entirety on the front page of all Cox newspapers.[51]

But Cox did not go to Canton after the murder, for which some criticized him. In a private letter to the *Daily News* attorney, H. C. Pontius, the former governor claimed that he was in constant communication with the *Daily News* beginning at 3:00 A.M. that fateful Friday, but he chose not to go to Canton to avoid the "melodramatics" the "affair" had produced.[52] He further excused himself on account of a kidney stone attack the week before. Cox went on to praise Mellett, whom he called a "splendid boy," and wrote, "Sometimes it requires a terrible sacrifice to bring a community to a consciousness of conditions which the average citizen is not apt to notice. This underworld development is right now one of the most serious phases in our American life. The clean-up in Canton just must be completed. It will not only be helpful there, but all over the country." He said that he was sending "a very excellent man" to take over the *Daily News*.[53]

Don Mellett's murder was a national sensation in a time when every newspaper in America carried numerous local and national crime stories every day. What was a local crime and an immense family tragedy came to be seen as an attack on the freedom of the press. According to Glenn Himebaugh, "If Mellett's crusade fell short of stamping out the evils it sought to eradicate, that is not to say that it was fought in vain, for his death resulted in a national newspaper outcry, and a campaign to awaken Americans everywhere of the dangers of criminal influence in local government."[54]

Newsmen from all around the country descended on Canton in the days after the shooting. They filed 276,000 words of copy through the Western Union telegraph office in the nine days after the crime. Newspapers and periodicals from all across the nation eulogized Don Mellett and editorialized about an apathetic public willing to tolerate crime and corruption that drew much of its sustenance from increasingly unpopular Prohibition. In the eyes of many journalists, Don Mellett's murder was a direct attack on the First Amendment, and one that would not be soon forgotten.[55]

The *Pittsburgh Press* declared, "Mellett is a martyr to public service."[56] The *Albuquerque State Tribune* asserted, "Society is the loser by the death of such men as Mellett. The world needs fighters for civic righteousness. They are all too scarce." The *New York World* said, "He died gloriously. His end was a flaming tribute to militant journalism which even death cannot dim." Robert Scripps of the Scripps-Howard newspaper chain observed, "The assassination of Editor Mellett for printing the truth about thuggery and crookedness in Canton must come home to every newspaperman. . . . To seek justice in the Mellett case must be made the personal business of all of us." The *Raleigh News and Observer* pointed out, "In the matter of the assassination of Editor Mellett, every newspaperman in America has a deep concern." "The courageous, uninfluenced newspapers of America must meet the challenge of the men who killed Don R. Mellett in Canton," the *Brooklyn Eagle* demanded. "This merely emphasizes the duty and responsibility of American journalism." The *Wall Street Journal* opined, "In unnumbered communities, the question may well be asked whether the police department and the municipal administration generally is any stronger than the appallingly weak one unmasked by the cowardly shooting of D. R. Mellett." William Randolph Hearst concluded, "The assassination of Mellett is more than a murder. It is an attempt to suppress by crime and violence the activities of the public service press."[57]

Don Mellett was buried in Crown Hill Cemetery in Indianapolis. A posthumous tribute of sorts came when the final circulation figures for July 1926 were released showing the gap between the *Daily News* and the *Evening Repository* to be 37,000.[58] Mellett's law-and-order crusade had indeed increased circulation, but at a terrible cost. John Barlow Martin, writing in *Harper's* twenty years after the murder, said, "The unequal struggle, in Canton and in the nation at large, between public conscience and public officials, both corrupted by Prohibition and a cynical materialism after the 1914–1918 war, had been reduced to just this . . . a bullet fired into an editor's brain on a sultry night."[59]

Above: The rear of the Mellett home and garage as seen from across Claremont Avenue NW on the day of Don Mellett's Canton funeral, July 17, 1926. Cleveland Public Library

Right: A Canton police officer points to a bullet hole in the garage door at the murder scene. Cleveland Public Library

Above: View of the murder scene from Claremont Avenue NW. Cleveland Public Library

Right: Florence Mellett, Walter Vail, and a Mellett daughter the day of Don Mellett's Canton funeral. They are standing on the spot where Mellett was slain. Cleveland Public Library

Above: Canton police officers: Detective Floyd Streitenberger (third from left), Chief S. A. Lengel (fourth from left), and Captain Ben Clarke (second from right). Cleveland Public Library

Below: Five of the six surviving Mellett brothers (from left to right): Lloyd, Lowell, Hickman, Roland, and John. Cleveland Public Library

4

Unraveling the Conspiracy

I t would not be an easy crime to solve. But perhaps a substantial reward would loosen a few tongues in Canton's underworld, or lure some reluctant witnesses out of the shadows. Whether the idea for a reward was prosecutor Charles McClintock's, former judge and Mellett friend H. C. Pontius's, or the *Daily News*'s isn't clear. Nevertheless, within hours of the murder, Pontius provided the first $1,000 followed immediately by Henry Timkin's $5,000. The reward fund eventually grew to $27,000, including major contributions of $5,000 from Scripps-Howard newspapers, $5,000 from Cox's News League, $1,000 from the *Evening Repository*, and $2,000 from the county commissioners (who would also have to foot the bill to bring the perpetrators to justice). Almost all of the reward was provided by Canton's civic and business leaders and Ohio newspapers.[1]

Not unexpectedly, the money attracted an army of amateur and professional sleuths who arrived in Canton in the days following the crime to join the contingent of journalists already covering the story. In 1926, $27,000 was a substantial sum, worth nearly $250,000 today, and a frugal man might retire on a payday of that size. Crime was also paying off in legitimate ways for the city's hotels, boardinghouses, restaurants, and telegraph services as the hordes of reward seekers took up residence and the newsmen filed 276,000 words of copy through the telegraph offices.[2] The *Repository*, perhaps whistling past the graveyard, noted on July 19 that "newspapermen assembled here to cover the story [of Mellett's murder] agreed there was little to warrant the assertion that vice is rampant and open."

There were other possible rewards not counted in cold cash. Public officials could not profit monetarily, but the political gain could be significant. That politics would play a role in the pursuit of justice was almost a given. Both the county prosecutor and his assistant were running for higher office, and even the governor had a political stake in the outcome. Don Mellett, partisan that he was, was no stranger to politics or the motives of politicians. Nor had he been above attempting to use political pressure to achieve his goals in his law-and-order crusade. He would not have been at all surprised that politics played a role in investigating his murder and in trying his killers. Even defense attorneys stood to gain should they succeed in getting a defendant acquitted in this high-profile case.

The Canton police department, under Chief Lengel's guidance, had already exhausted its leads by the time Mellett was laid to rest in Indianapolis on July 19. After stumbling around the crime scene the night of the shooting, detectives were sent that Friday to check car rental agencies, haul in strangers found on the city's streets, and bring in twenty or so of the leading vice purveyors for some not-very-hard questioning by Lengel, Swope, and Clarke. All were released within three hours. Mellett supporters decried the fact that many of those questioned were notable for testifying against Lengel at his civil service hearing.[3] Not surprisingly, no one admitted to knowing anything. Lengel then completed his bumbling investigation by dispatching the workhouse crew to clean up the vacant lot on Saturday morning.[4] Lengel concluded that the murder was an outside professional job, a "Black Handed" affair, he said, and the work of Pittsburgh Italians, many a police department's prime suspects for unsolved murders.

Yet no one offered a motive for why Italian thugs would want to kill Mellett. The Black Hand was generally nothing more than local Italian gangs who made their living extorting money from other

Italians in return for not blowing up their homes or businesses. The *Daily News* paid the Black Hand scant attention. In fact, the paper reached out to Canton's ethnic communities in ways few other newspapers did. In November 1925, Mellett had hired Theodore Andrica, a Romanian, to edit and report news from the immigrant neighborhoods. While this cost $35 a week, it made the paper the first in Ohio to publish this type of news and engendered considerable goodwill.[5]

With no leads, Lengel was groping for an answer and may have recalled that earlier warning about a Black Hand plot against the editor. In Pittsburgh, George "the Greek" Psialias (not George "the Italian") was questioned about the murder but later released.[6] (Privately, Captain Ben Clarke told a police informant the same thing: Black Handers were to blame.[7]) By Sunday evening, July 18, police were reduced to checking license plate numbers of cars seen by witnesses in the vicinity of Tuscarawas and Claremont late Thursday night, and Lengel admitted to the *Repository* that "this method of obtaining information is a long shot." The crucial first forty-eight hours passed without any suspects, let alone arrests.

At this time, becoming a police officer often required little more than knowing the right people. Basic civil service testing was haphazard, training happened on the job, and promotions were rife with politics. Lengel was a good example of the system. He left primary school at age ten to work in the Pennsylvania coal fields. He apprenticed as a baker in his teens and stayed at it for more than twenty years, not becoming a cop until age thirty-nine. In just five years, he jumped from patrolman to chief (because he supported the sitting mayor, Socialist Harry Schilling). When the civil service commission returned the former chief to duty, Lengel went back to patrol. Ten years later, he was chief again.[8] Price Jansen, one of the members of the civil service commission who voted to keep Lengel in his job, called him "a Dutch baker who got on the police force," and James M. Aungst, police prosecutor from 1921 to 1922, said of Lengel, it was "difficult to teach an old dog new tricks."[9] So no one really expected the Canton police, led by Lengel, to solve this crime—perhaps least of all the police themselves.

Lack of faith in Canton police to keep the peace and solve Mellett's murder was felt as far away as Columbus. Governor Donahey received an unfavorable report on conditions in Canton from his aide, C. H. Sisson, and sent private detective Joseph D. Cleary to look around. Lieutenant General Frank D. Henderson ordered National Guardsmen to Canton to guard the homes of investigators.[10] This produced an episode of gunfire on August 6 when a car with three men aboard slowed down while passing the home of prosecutor McClintock. A guardsman jumped on the car's running board only to be pushed off by the occupants. In return, he fired his rifle at the car, but missed.[11] Aside from that tense evening, little else occurred in the city. The guardsmen were withdrawn after a few weeks, and the federal government was represented by postal inspectors who were dispatched to check for threatening letters.

The federal government, specifically the Department of Justice, felt it had no jurisdiction in local crimes like murder. The Federal Bureau of Investigation would lead the fight against organized crime in the late 1920s and 1930s, but in 1926 it had yet to carve out a niche for itself and was mainly restricted to stopping white slavers and looking for stolen cars. Furthermore, Ohio had no state police, which had proven effective against organized crime in Pennsylvania. The county sheriffs' lobby effectively blocked any legislation that threatened the power of local sheriffs.

Since the Canton police department lacked the leadership and training to launch a serious investigation into Mellett's murder, the real investigatory work was left to the reporters and private detectives. Perhaps the best reporter assigned to the case was William Tugman of the *Cleveland Plain Dealer*, who arrived in Canton the afternoon of July 16. After checking in with the local press as a courtesy, Tugman registered at the Courtland Hotel, and by late afternoon was knocking on doors around the Mellett neighborhood. He talked to twenty residents and found only one who was interviewed by the police. The *Plain Dealer*, who had employed Tugman since 1919, assigned him more or less permanently to the Mellett murder, and he stayed in Canton until the end of the year. Tugman was able to use his connections in Cleveland to provide valuable intelligence to investigators in Canton as well as his own paper.[12]

Both the *Daily News* and the county prosecutor's office employed private detectives to assist in routine investigations. One such sleuth was a part-time detective named Jack Campbell, who held the generic title of "special investigator" but who later became a Prohibition enforcement officer. H. B. Burton, a private detective from Columbus, was paid by the prosecutor, but he also gave copies of his reports to Lloyd Mellett (eventually he worked for the *Daily News*).[13] The Mellett family's attorney, H. C. Pontius, retained Hutchison and Smith Detective Bureau from Akron to investigate, and their work at the murder scene was far more thorough than the city police.[14] Mellett's former employer in Akron, Scripps-Howard, which had made the slaying a crusade of its own, hired Ora Slater of the Cal Crim Detective Agency in Cincinnati. An ace investigator of unquestioned integrity, Slater had already solved one high-profile crime in Ohio that year by obtaining the confession of Jake Nesbitt in a sensational murder case in Troy.

Ora Major Slater was not your stereotypical private eye. Of medium build and height, with thinning gray hair and gray eyes,[15] the fifty-one-year-old Slater looked more like somebody's quiet grandfather. Looks could be deceiving, for Slater was not lacking in guile and courage. He began to develop an interest in the law when, in his teens, he became engrossed in a killing in his hometown of Lawrenceburg, Indiana. He became a railroad detective and was best remembered for single-handedly arresting thirty-eight disgruntled workers who threatened to derail a train in a pay dispute. "Follow me boys, and you'll get your pay," Slater is said to have told the men as he led them into custody. Slater was elected sheriff of Dearborn County, Indiana, in 1910 and served two terms. During the war, he worked for the U.S. Justice Department's Bureau of Investigation as a special agent in Cincinnati. While in federal service, he participated in the 1919 "Black Sox" investigation of the fixed World Series. But mostly at this time the Bureau concentrated on rounding up radicals and "Reds," recovering stolen cars, and enforcing the Mann Act against white slavery. In 1922 he left the government to join the Cal Crim Detective Agency, founded by two former Cincinnati police detectives. A shrewd interrogator and sharp observer, Slater eschewed the violence all too common among lawmen of the day. He liked to claim he never shot a man and rarely carried a gun.[16]

On Saturday evening, July 17, just thirty-six hours after Don Mellett's murder, Ora Slater was in Canton. He met straightaway with Earl Hexamer, the safety director, and during the two-hour meeting, Slater was introduced to Chief Lengel and Detective Streitenberger, who was just back from following up on an empty lead in Steubenville. Slater would later recall in a moment of convenient hindsight the detective as being hostile. At the time, though, Slater was not surprised that the local cops didn't welcome him. Slater and Hexamer also visited the crime scene that morning, but little useful evidence was left to find. Slater later bitterly complained that Lengel's yard work in the vacant lot made it impossible to find any clues about where the shots were fired or how many shooters there were. The chief's orders to clear the vacant lot were beginning to make him look more than just incompetent. The seeds sown in investigators' minds regarding Lengel's motives would grow into allegations more serious than "the Old Man" could have imagined that July.[17]

Accompanying Slater to Canton was Thomas Freeman representing Scripps-Howard, who was paying Slater's fee. That evening Slater and Freeman met with county prosecutor Charles B. McClintock to discuss the case. In his second two-year term as prosecutor, the diminutive McClintock, a native of Wayne County, Ohio, and a former schoolteacher, was trying to follow in William McKinley's footsteps and make the leap from prosecutor to U.S. Congress, running on the Republican ticket against a popular Democratic incumbent.[18] Known to pass downtime in court working complex algebraic problems, he possessed a talented, analytical mind. He usually wore a poker face that only rarely broke into a flash of a smile, and in court he was intense, combative, and every bit as competitive as Don Mellett. He built his cases slowly and methodically. But in Canton in the days following the murder, time was a luxury McClintock didn't have. He was feeling pressure from the Mellett family, Henry Timkin, and the community.[19]

Appreciating that the Canton police would be no help at all—or, if the family's suspicions were valid, an obstacle—McClintock realized he needed investigative help. Earlier that day, Cox's right-hand man, Charles Morris, called the prosecutor when he learned Slater was on the case and suggested acquiring the detective's services. So McClintock, Slater, and Scripps-Howard made a deal, backed with $5,000 from the county, and by Sunday morning Ora Slater was officially working for the Stark County prosecutor's office. It proved to be a fortunate arrangement.[20]

Slater's first real break in the investigation presented itself Sunday afternoon in the form of Bill and Eva Bitzler. The Bitzlers had first gone to see McClintock. The prosecutor, overwhelmed by tipsters, thanks to the reward, sent the couple along to Slater without hearing their story. Although Slater had been in town less than two days and already heard lots of theories, he couldn't know who had valuable information, so he listened. "I'll tell you who I think done it," offered the loquacious Bill. The Bitzlers told him that on Sunday evening, July 11, the couple was window shopping along Market Avenue South when Bill caught sight of a familiar face from back home in the Pennsylvania coal fields. Patrick "Red" McDermott had traveled with Bill to Hoboken, New Jersey, in 1920 looking for work. The Bitzlers moved frequently, just ahead of persistent creditors, and had just recently arrived in Canton from Akron. The last Bill had heard of Red, he was in federal prison. They told Slater that after exchanging the usual pleasantries, Pat bragged that he was in Canton working for the "high muckety mucks." During the course of the brief conversation, Pat, who had always been well-turned-out, noticed that Bill's clothes were worn. He had recently come into some extra clothing—gifts from female admirers, he told the Bitzlers, and offered them to his old pal. Bill accepted, and Pat said he would stop by their home the next evening to drop them off.[21]

Promptly at 5:30 P.M. Monday, July 12, Pat McDermott appeared at the Bitzlers' door on Patterson Avenue SW and suggested he and Bill go back to Pat's Cleveland Avenue boardinghouse for the clothes. On the streetcar ride, Bill showed Pat the best places to get a drink, which they did, more than once. Arriving at Pat's room—where he was registered under the alias Charles Thompson—McDermott made a big show of reaching under the pillow and extracting a large revolver, which he unloaded. "Some gun ain't it?" he boasted, handing

it to Bill. Duly impressed, Bill told Pat, "It looks like a cannon to me."
Pat stuck the revolver in his vest and handed Bill the clothes, which
included a coat, a vest, five shirts, three pairs of pants, and some silk
ties. They left the boardinghouse together and then parted company.

The next night, Tuesday, McDermott dropped by the Bitzler home
again. This time the men sat on the porch, Pat regaling his old friend
with the story of a party he attended the previous night with all the
"high muckety mucks" of Canton. He also bragged about his rich
friend in Massillon who had an expensive house in the tony Meyer's
Lake neighborhood. "I'm in solid here," he told Bill. "I can go down
the street and tell the cops to go jump in the lake, and no cop would
do anything about it." With that statement and claiming pressing business elsewhere, Pat hurried off into the night. Eva heard every word of
it through the screen door.

Late afternoon on Wednesday, Pat showed up at Canton Drop
Forge, where Bill worked as a low-level electrician. He told Bill he had
spent the afternoon with his wealthy Massillon friend. He then asked
Bitzler to ride along with him while he shadowed a guy. Bill declined,
fearing that Pat was driving a stolen car. McDermott denied this and
promised to have Bill home by 8:30. Bill held fast. Pat left but returned
at quitting time. The joyride was off, he said. Instead he had a job
transporting a load of liquor to Cleveland for $25 in a nice Hudson
motorcar. The two men then shared a bottle of wine Pat procured as
they wandered toward Pat's rooming house, where they parted.[22]

On Thursday evening, July 15, Bill and Pat bought some wine
on 11th Street and went to Canton Drop Forge to drink it, though
Pat didn't drink any of it, saying he had a big job that night. He
produced a five-dollar bill he said he received from the rich friend
with the expensive house on Meyer's Lake and boasted that he could
easily get more money—"I'll have $200 tomorrow." Pat went on to
complain about the *Daily News* maligning his new friends in Canton. Brandishing a copy of the paper and pointing to a picture, he
told Bill, "There's the guy I'm mixed up with." Pat then said that he
might have to leave town but promised to call if he did.[23]

Bill Bitzler learned of the murder Friday from the cries of newsboys. His knowledge weighed heavily on him. The more he thought

about it, the more worried he became. What if Pat McDermott was involved? Plenty of people had seen him with McDermott. What if the police identified Pat as a suspect and thought he was an accomplice? At noon, Bitzler nervously left work at the forge and went home to tell Eva his suspicions. Bill decided to check the boardinghouse. Not finding Pat there, he asked the proprietress about Charles Thompson. Hattie Gearhart told him that he received a telegram around noon telling him to return to his home office or go to the Massillon store. He told Hattie he was going to Massillon. Bitzler was now convinced Pat had a part in the murder.

Slater had the Bitzlers repeat their story for Hexamer. Bill appeared sincere when he told Slater and Hexamer that he was less interested in the reward than avoiding trouble. He told them about his creditor problems in Canton and truthfully detailed his arrest record: Johnstown, Pennsylvania, in 1916 for bastardy (a common charge for fathering illegitimate children) and again in 1921 in Ebensberg, Pennsylvania, for stealing a valise, which resulted in nine months in prison. Slater and Hexamer were satisfied that the Bitzlers' story was genuine. Slater took extensive notes and cautioned the couple to go home and keep quiet lest they alert McDermott.

First thing Monday morning, Hexamer and Slater paid a visit to Hattie Gearhart's boardinghouse on Cleveland Avenue. Gearhart was a large middle-aged woman who had difficulty walking. She confirmed that Charles Thompson was a boarder whom she had never seen before he arrived a week ago Saturday. She told them that Thompson left Friday after receiving a telegram. The two investigators checked the room and found only an empty Western Union envelope.[24]

Slater and Hexamer checked with Western Union and were told that a telegram to Charles Thompson was sent from Massillon on July 16. In the Massillon telegraph office, fewer than ten miles west of Canton, they located the original message written in longhand: "Take Massillon store or report to home office at once. R. L. Strang." All the clerk could recall was that it was sent by a man he did not recognize.[25] Slater was unable to find an R. L. Strang in Massillon and put out feelers to his numerous contacts in Ohio and Pennsylvania providing the few details he had on McDermott.

Not all of the examinations of the murder scene were as shoddy as the one conducted by the Canton police. A few days after the crime, assistant county prosecutor Henry Harter, former judge Pontius, and two assistants inspected the Mellett garage and house and the recently mowed vacant lot. Their search was followed up by Ray Bechtol, an assistant county engineer, who used surveying equipment to try to trace the trajectory of some of the bullets that were fired through the kitchen window and garage door. Four rounds could be accounted for this way: two passed through the open garage door, one struck Mellett, and one went above the back door and struck the house. The crude results estimated that the firing points were four feet apart and made from a crouched position and standing upright, advancing forward as the shots were fired. Potential firing points in the vacant lot included a telephone pole, a scrap-metal pile, and a small embankment screened by a tree trunk and brush. The range was estimated at 100 to 200 feet from Mellett as he closed the garage door. Given all this, observers had difficulty believing that one shooter could be responsible for all the shots fired.[26]

M. A. Robinson, the Winchester ballistics engineer, reported his findings in a letter dated July 24. He felt that the three bullets he examined were fired from two or three weapons. All bullets recovered were .38 caliber and were fired from revolvers, not semi-automatic pistols or submachine guns. The fatal bullet and the one removed from the woodwork in the house were fired from handguns in which the rifling in the barrel had a right-hand twist. The bullet recovered from the ground, supposedly after it had hit the brick house, had a metal jacket and was fired from a revolver with a left-hand twist to the rifling. Smith and Wesson revolvers were produced with right-hand twist rifling; Colt revolvers were manufactured with a left-hand twist. Robinson estimated that the condition of the barrels varied from "poor" to "like new." He also made a completely subjective guess that all were fired at a range of less than fifty feet.[27] The most salient aspect of this expert's report was that it was impossible for all three bullets recovered at the scene of the shooting to be fired from the same weapon. With this report, the investigators had to decide if they were looking for a lone assassin with two or more handguns or for multiple gunmen.

. . .

While many in Canton suspected that the police investigation into
Don Mellett's murder was a sham, Chief of Police Lengel did little
to allay those concerns. Four days after the murder, after questioning fifty people and holding none, Lengel pronounced himself satisfied that the murder was an out-of-town job. Such a declaration was
meant to absolve local authorities of any expectation that they should
solve the crime.[28]

There was considerable finger-pointing in Canton that July. Civic
and business leaders were rightly concerned that all this negative
publicity would be bad for business. The out-of-town press wasn't
flattering. In a July 26 article titled "Stench," *Time* magazine called
Canton an "ugly industrial town at best" and a "stagnant backwater
of the Midwest underground." The mayor formed a citizens' committee to look into the sorry state of law enforcement in Canton,
but the committee was paralyzed by partisan bickering.[29] Committee
member Henry Timkin, the closest Canton came to having a civic
conscience, fumed over the indifference of Cantonians to their city's
plight and threatened to "get some damn action or resign,"[30] and the
Daily News attacked the members' inertia. When the group finally
made some recommendations to the mayor, he rejected them as in-
consequential. Within three weeks of the murder, the citizens' committee folded, having accomplished nothing.[31]

Mayor Swarts decided he'd had enough of Chief Lengel and took
command of his city on July 24, once again suspending the chief for
thirty days. Swarts cited "lack of control of the police department" and
told him that "contact of members of your department with known violators, permitted by you, has made it impossible for said department
to successfully enforce the laws." Prosecutors had not been bashful in
suggesting that Lengel's police department did not have clean hands
and had not mounted much of an investigation into the murder of
Don Mellett. Lengel took the suspension in stride, joking that when
his wife saw him coming up the walk with his umbrella and overshoes
under his arm, she would know he'd been suspended again.[32] The
mayor named Earl Hexamer acting chief. As chief, Hexamer tried to

put an end to crooks making themselves at home at headquarters and promoted Patrolman Beresford to detective. His appointment also put the city's underworld on notice and, conveniently, gave Ora Slater access to the resources of the Canton police department.[33]

In late July, in front of the Courtland Hotel, Ora Slater and Ben Rudner met face to face. Slater recognized Rudner when Ben, who considered it his business to know men like Slater, introduced himself to the detective. In fact, he offered Slater a car ride so the two of them could talk. Each attempted to obtain valuable information about the murder from the other. Neither got much. When Ben asked Slater how he had made Jake Nesbitt (the Troy murderer) confess, Slater could not resist telling Ben that it was "just like this"—by talking with him. The odd encounter with Rudner only served to point Slater's antennae in the direction of the ex-con who ran bootlegging in Canton, or so some said. He knew by now that Ben had visited Chief Lengel the evening before the crime and that the two held a private conference on the sidewalk outside the police station. Furthermore, Rudner was in Lengel's office at 5:00 or 6:00 on the morning of July 16.[34] And this erstwhile hardware merchant from Massillon was showing exaggerated curiosity in the investigation of Mellett's killing.

It took little effort for Slater, with his federal connections made during his wartime service with the U.S. Justice Department, to discover that Pat McDermott and Ben Rudner were in the federal penitentiary in Atlanta at the same time. McDermott was from a small coal mining town in central Pennsylvania, Nanty Glo. Pat was from a well-known Irish family that operated a coal mine, a hotel, and a pool hall in Cambria County, Pennsylvania. McDermott tried working in the mines as an electrician, which may have been how he met electrician Bill Bitzler, but he soon abandoned the mines for a career as a poolroom hanger-on. Drafted, McDermott couldn't help coveting all that war material and was suspected in the robbery of an army warehouse and then convicted in a general court martial, arriving at Atlanta's federal prison on February 1, 1922. Ben Rudner was sentenced to the federal prison in Atlanta for liquor law violations, arriving there on December 6, 1922. In the prison hierarchy, Rudner was housed with other well-heeled prisoners who could use bribery to secure extra privileges like private cells, unlimited telephone calls, and conjugal visits from wives or girlfriends. The smooth-talking McDermott managed to get himself assigned as a barber on "millionaires' row," which gave him plenty of opportunity to get acquainted with Rudner.[35]

Slater learned more valuable information from Norman Clark, who until January 1 had been an assistant city solicitor serving as police prosecutor. Clark now had a private law practice, and some of his clients had appeared as defendants in police court. He had been involved in the Harris/Wing plea deal, which, on the surface, looked fixed, as well as other questionable plea deals that included falsifying arrest records; and two of his more important clients were Louis Mazer and Carl Studer.[36] Clark told Slater that when he was trying to decide whether to talk to investigators about two weeks after the murder, he received a preemptive visit from Mazer. The bootlegger told Clark to shut up or risk getting "the same dose Mellett got." Clark's pregnant wife heard this threat, became hysterical, and required a doctor. Thereafter Clark went straight to Slater, who then sent him to federal district attorney A. E. Bernstein in Cleveland.[37]

The most important break in the case arrived in Canton from Cleveland on Friday morning, July 23. Steven Frank Kascholk went to the free Cleveland Legal Aid Society in the Fidelity Mortgage Building on Thursday, July 22, and met with a volunteer staff attorney, Paul Welker. He told Welker that he and Pat McDermott had traveled to Canton a week before the murder of Don Mellett. Welker recognized the significance of Steve's tale and went to the federal district attorney. Bernstein told Welker to take Kascholk to Canton to see the county prosecutor. So with the Justice Department providing the contacts and the Legal Aid Society paying the train fare, Paul Welker, with Steve Kascholk in tow, arrived at McClintock's office in Canton and told the prosecutor a story that meshed with Bitzler's and filled in many of the blanks confronting Slater and McClintock. McClintock sent Kascholk and Welker to Slater's temporary office in the *Daily News* building at 400 Second Street NW. When Steve dropped the name Pat McDermott, Slater knew they had hit pay dirt: "The name struck me like a bolt of lightning." After all, only a handful of people knew that the investigators were looking for Pat McDermott, and Steve Kascholk wasn't one of them. Slater extracted Steve's story in a process the master interrogator politely said "plodded along."

Kascholk had been jailed in Pennsylvania from November 25, 1925, to May 3, 1926, for failure to support his wife and young child. On release from jail, he went to Cleveland, where he had relatives, in search of work and to escape his domestic situation. On July 8 he bumped into Pat McDermott, an old acquaintance from Nanty Glo, on a Cleveland streetcar. Pat told Steve that he was just hanging around town, living off his relatives. Since prison, he had worked as a barber in Toledo and a sign painter in Boston, where he acquired the nickname "Boston Red." Steve told Pat that he wanted to go to Detroit to look for steady work, but McDermott had another idea. Pat told him that in his cruising of Cleveland's pool halls and barbershops he had learned of a good job in Canton. On Steve's dime, Pat tried to call a friend in Massillon about the job but failed to reach him. He then talked Steve into going with him to Massillon. Pat was broke, so Steve used part of his last $10 to buy tickets on the Pennsylvania Railroad to Massillon, via Alliance.

Once in Massillon later that day, the two men checked their meager baggage at the station and found a restaurant for dinner. After Pat had a haircut, according to Steve, the men registered at Sailors Hotel under the aliases John Glover and Pete McDonald (Steve was paranoid about his child-support payments, which he was behind on again). Pat, still unable to reach his friend by phone, recalled that his friend's father was in the hardware business and set off to look for local stores. Steve decided to make the rounds of local factories to look for a job. The two met later at the hotel, where Steve told Pat he had a job prospect at Central Steel. McDermott said he had made contact with his friend and was going to see him that evening. When Pat returned at about 11:00 P.M., he told Steve, "This here Rudner wants us to do a job. We'll go out and slug a guy."

In the morning a man introduced to Steve as "Smitty" picked them up in a Hudson coupe in front of Rudner's hardware store and drove them to Canton. Steve sat in the back with the luggage, some bootleg liquor, and a police dog. He couldn't hear what the two men up front talked about and only spoke once, to ask the make of the car. Once in Canton, they stopped at Smitty's place to drop off the dog before going to the New Barnett Hotel, where reservations had been made for Pat and Steve. In Canton's red light district, the New Barnett was commonly known to be used as a bootlegger hideout.[38]

On the evening of July 9, Pat took Steve to reconnoiter the Broad Avenue home of the guy they were to "slug." To get there they rode a streetcar to its junction and walked the rest of the way. During this trip, Pat showed Steve a gun, a large black and blue pistol eight to ten inches long, which Steve guessed was a .45. After checking out the neighborhood, they returned to their hotel room, where they discovered a trunk under the bed that contained men's clothing and a half-pint of whiskey.[39] While drinking the whiskey, they contemplated what to do with their find. Pat said that he would sell the clothes on a trip to Chicago that he and Rudner were planning. The two then went to a nearby drugstore to buy cigarettes. There Steve brought up the "slugging." He told Pat that he only wanted honest work because of his "family" (which also happened to include his girlfriend and their two young, illegitimate children) and asked Pat what he was going to do with the gun. Pat told him, "I'm going right up to the door and stick the gun in his ribs. Then I can take him out in the backyard and beat hell out of him there." (Pat claimed to have been an amateur boxer.) He then advised Steve, "You stick with me and you won't have to work. You will make enough money on this one job that you won't have to work for a month. But you've weakened all right. You're yellow."[40] The next day, July 10, the two moved to less expensive lodging in town, Hattie Gearhart's boardinghouse. That evening McDermott left again, and Steve, who decided he wanted no part of what Pat was planning, quietly slipped out and took the streetcar to Cleveland. He stayed that night with his cousin Joe Kascholk.[41]

Slater had to determine if Kascholk's story was completely truthful or a self-serving half-truth designed to deflect suspicion from a coconspirator. His alibi seemed solid. Several of his Cleveland kin vouched that from July 11 on, Kascholk remained in Cleveland. His brother, Andrew, gave him $7.50 on the 11th and a bank draft for $20 on the 15th and also helped Steve try to find a job. The week of the 11th Steve stayed with his cousin Steve Novak and his wife, who confirmed that Steve was with them on July 15, 17, and 18. Joe Kascholk also stated that Steve was at his home the evening of the 15th until 9:30. It appeared unlikely to Slater that Steve could get to Canton by 12:30 A.M., when Mellett was murdered.[42]

Steve Kascholk proved to be an invaluable witness, but not an entirely reliable fellow and one who was easily led astray. So when Steve expressed concern for his safety, Prosecutor McClintock solved the problem by placing him in the county workhouse under protective custody. McClintock also advanced Steve the money he needed for his child support and saw to it that he was paid the standard workhouse rate of $1 a day. Steve Kascholk finally had that steady job he'd been looking for.[43]

The small town of Nanty Glo, Pennsylvania, later noted that two of its sons, Pat McDermott and Steve Kascholk, were associated with the murder of Mellett. On August 19 the local newspaper, *The Journal*, in an editorial titled "Canton a Typical Crime Center," commented, "It is high time that there was a cleanup all along the line. Officials who close their eyes and hold out their greedy paws for a share of the ill-gotten loot of bootleggers and gamblers anywhere are no better than the murderers of Don R. Mellett."

The Gang of Three

Ora Slater now had three suspects in a conspiracy to kill Don Mellett: Pat McDermott, Ben Rudner, and the mystery driver, Smitty. Since McDermott had initially come from Cleveland, Slater guessed that he might have returned there. He quietly asked Cleveland police to try to find McDermott. Detectives scoured Cleveland and learned that Pat had been seen hanging around the Hough–East 79th Street district just after the murder. A Cleveland poolroom operator recalled that Pat wanted him to help square an old bad check. The always-broke Pat had, the man estimated, around $60 or $70.[1]

Detectives managed to track Pat to Catherine "Kitty" Barnes's East 78th Street boardinghouse. They learned that around the third week of July, officers had stopped there to break up a noisy birthday party. A fellow identifying himself as Charles Collins opened the door for them. Collins, a new boarder, had arrived the evening of July 16 and paid for two weeks in advance. The police asked the proprietress if any liquor was present, and Kitty denied it. Unconvinced, the police searched the house anyway. On finding one inch of booze in the bottom of a glass, the officers threatened to arrest her. The gallant Pat McDermott, alias Charles Collins, apparently stepped up and offered, "Miss Barnes, if you have to go [to jail], let me go in your place." His noble gesture did not go unrewarded. A few days later, when Pat was broke once again, Barnes loaned him $3 and later $5 more. Boarder Thelma Harris told police that she noticed Pat grow increasingly nervous about the cops, and by the end of the month, Pat was gone. He didn't leave a forwarding address, but detectives did trace a long-distance telephone call from Barnes's phone to Ben Rudner on July 21.

Unfortunately, the story was too big to stay secret for very long, and Pat McDermott's name was leaked to the Cleveland press. With reporters hot on the story, Slater had no choice but to go public with the manhunt for McDermott on July 30. He concluded a briefing of the press by calling Pat the "key man" in the crime. When pictures of McDermott appeared on wanted posters and in the papers, *Daily News* circulation manager Charles Gaston told investigators that Pat, wearing only glasses as a disguise, had visited the paper the afternoon before the murder at about two or three o'clock. He asked for Mellett, "The big boss in the little front office." When Gaston pointed toward the business office, the stranger studied Don for a long minute before leaving without saying a word.

Cleveland police had failed to nab Pat McDermott in their dragnet, but they did snare another important, if reluctant, witness. Peggy Cavanaugh, later nicknamed "Pretty Peggy" by reporters, was a cute twentysomething waitress from the Hough district in Cleveland. Since this murder story lacked the requisite sex angle to really sell newspapers, reporters tried to mold Peggy into the role of murderer's girlfriend. But Peggy was reluctant to talk to detectives and steadfastly refused to accept the press-assigned role of McDermott's consort. She insisted that she was just a waitress who flirted with the dapper, talkative McDermott, a regular customer at the lunch counter where she worked. Peggy admitted to investigators that she had a chance meeting with Pat on the street in Cleveland on July 26, the date she recalled as the same day she quit her job as a waitress. Pat, who fancied himself a ladies' man, struck up a conversation. (When it came to women, Pat wasn't in Steve Kascholk's or Bill Bitzler's class—no wife, no ex-wife, no illegitimate children—not even a girlfriend.)

It is unclear what Pat wanted from Peggy, but he did convince her to go along with him on a car trip to Akron. Pat had succeeded in convincing Homer J. Connelly, an Ohio Bell Telephone lineman he had met the previous March, to drive him to Akron in Connelly's Ford coupe to "see a fellow." Pretty Peggy may have been invited because Pat was showing off, or she might have been an inducement to get Connelly to drive. The trio drove to a restaurant in Akron called Beck's Deli, where Homer and Peggy waited while Pat went next door to the smoke shop to see a man. Pat's contact was not there, so he returned to the deli, where they remained for an hour before Pat called his contact. After a brief conversation, Pat said they now needed to drive to Massillon. When the trio arrived in Massillon, they stopped in front of a store. Pat jumped out and instructed Homer to drive a couple of blocks to Sailors Hotel. Within ten minutes McDermott returned with $10, and the three headed back to Cleveland. On the trip back, Pat had Homer stop and he purchased three newspapers. Peggy said he read the sports sections, claiming he was playing the horses.[2]

Police brought Homer Connelly in for questioning, and he proved more cooperative than Peggy. He substantiated what Peggy had told them about the trip to Massillon, but he could not recall in front of what store Pat had left the car. Sketchy on details, it seems Homer and Peggy weren't paying much attention to McDermott. At this point, investigators believed the trip to Massillon was a "payoff drive" for McDermott to collect his blood money. Since Peggy Cavanaugh was such an uncooperative witness and had no real ties to prevent her from fleeing, after she told her story McClintock decided to place her in the workhouse under a $10,000 bond. Slater, writing in 1931, explained that the high bond would cast suspicion on anyone trying to bond her out.

Slater checked the telephone records for Beck's Deli on July 26. There was only one long-distance call to Massillon on that date between 5:30 and 7:00 P.M. The call was from a "Mister Jones" to Ben Rudner's hardware store. Under questioning, Mrs. Beck admitted that members of the Rudner family were regular customers. Slater's evidence against Rudner was growing.[3]

Suspecting that Louis Mazer might be involved, detectives decided to question Doll Carey, the local madam known to be Mazer's girlfriend (who reporters unflatteringly described as "fat, forty and not very pre-possessing"[4]). But Carey refused to talk, telling investigators when they asked about Mazer's whereabouts the night Mellett was killed, "That's for Louis to talk about."[5] One of Carey's girls was willing to talk, however. Mazer had sacrificed Thelma Harris in a police raid earlier in the year, and she was sore. She said that at about 6:00 P.M. on July 15, Floyd Streitenberger arrived and held a hasty conference with Mazer in the kitchen. The two men then left together. Mazer later returned alone to get his gun, a pearl-handled .38 Spanish revolver, the archetypical pimp's weapon. Mazer hadn't returned by 1:00 A.M.[6] She told investigators that she saw Streitenberger again on Walnut Avenue on Friday evening. This time he was pacing the street in front of Carey's place, nervously waiting for Mazer. Thelma also witnessed a July 19 meeting that took place when Detective Streitenberger stopped by briefly to pick up a revolver from Mazer.[7] The investigators decided it was time to lean on Louis Mazer.

"Limpy Louis" Mazer, age thirty-two, was a clever and elusive career criminal. He readily admitted that he came from the gutter and lived in a "resort." In 1918 he claimed to be a salesman when he registered for the draft. His perhaps only honorable act came when he joined the Pennsylvania National Guard field artillery in 1916; he was discharged for disability a year later. He joined the army in 1918 and was assigned quartermaster duty. To his credit, Mazer stayed clean while he was in the service. Detective Floyd Streitenberger said Mazer never did an honest day's work in his life. Mazer didn't deny it. He and Carl Studer were partners in a protection business for local brothels that was sanctioned by Jumbo Crowley. By 1926 Mazer had abandoned prostitution for bootlegging. Unlike some criminals of the day, Mazer shunned publicity; not a single picture of him could be located in July 1926.[8] Questioned by postal inspector Captain A. P. Owen, police captain Ben Clarke, Hexamer, and Slater, Mazer proved tougher than expected. All he would tell the inquisitors was what had happened to his Hudson car, which had mysteriously disappeared from the streets after the murder: he had to give it up to a finance company that had it stored in a Canton garage.

Investigators took Steve Kascholk out of the workhouse long enough for a trip to the garage where Mazer's reprocessed Hudson was gathering dust. Could he identify it as the car in which he rode from Massillon to Canton with "Smitty" behind the wheel and Pat McDermott riding shotgun? After a maddeningly slow trip around the garage examining the Hudson, Steve told investigators that it "might be the car." When acting chief Hexamer was at Doll Carey's place, he had noticed a large police dog. So, leaving no stone unturned, he had Kascholk visit the dog at the Walnut Avenue brothel. Was this dog his seat companion on the ride to Canton? Steve thought it was.

Attorney Norman Clark, thoroughly scared, told all he knew about the criminal operations of his clients Mazer and Carl Studer, Mazer's cousin and business partner. Studer was a Crowley lieutenant sometimes known as "the King of Canton's Vice Ring." His deceased parents, Joe and Caroline, owners of the famous Canton House brothel, had been fixtures in Canton's sex industry.[9] Carl, who was described by reporters as "debonair," was a bootlegger, bawdy house owner, and partner with Mazer in the Lyceum Pool Room, a Tuscarawas Street East clearinghouse for all types of criminal activity. Both men had reason to dislike Mellett, and were seen on more than one occasion outside the *Daily News* building observing who came and went. They also hung around police headquarters, where they had many friends.[10]

The Mellett family, understandably, had little faith that anyone in Canton was capable of bringing Don's killer(s) to justice. Their confidence in Governor Donahey was weakened by his lukewarm support for Prohibition and numerous pardons of its violators. The public face of the family's discontent was the *Daily News*'s new publisher, Charles E. Morris, who had served James Cox for years in a variety of troubleshooting capacities.[11] McClintock was perceived as a good man but was a lightweight as a prosecutor and distracted by his congressional race. (The primary election was August 12.) So the *Daily News*, even while providing Slater an office, acquired the services of Joseph R. Roach, a Chicago attorney and former law partner of Clarence Darrow with experience battling vice lords in Illinois and Indiana.[12] Roach had an abrasive style that almost immediately sparked resentment among investigators in Canton. Roach arrived August 4 and within a week was issuing scathing reports on crime conditions in the city.[13]

Roach's services were initially offered to McClintock, who icily rejected them, so Mayor Swarts reluctantly appointed Roach special counsel to acting police chief Earl Hexamer. The unrestrained Roach went to Cleveland on August 10 where he met with federal prosecutors who shared his view of conditions in Canton. This meeting produced a strategy that would circumvent the law that only state officials could prosecute murder cases. The feds gave Roach the authority to investigate liquor law violations that might relate to Mellett's death under agreement that he turn any evidence over to them for actual prosecution. The feeling was that at least the killer(s) would be tried for something.[14]

After being in Canton only a little more than a week, Roach was not bashful about telling reporters that he had enough evidence to convict several men of first-degree murder, irrespective of any Prohibition violations. Additionally, he alleged that members of the Canton police department were involved. This was the first time police were publicly implicated, and it confirmed what the Mellett family was charging. While Pat McDermott was important, Roach agreed, he was not key to solving the crime—an attack on Slater's key man theory. Roach further claimed that the murder probe in Canton, currently stalled awaiting McDermott's apprehension, was really stymied by vice lords who controlled public officials.[15]

But Slater and McClintock were not inactive. On August 16, using evidence of bribery and liquor violations, including attorney Norman Clark's testimony, they had federal authorities arrest Mazer and Studer.[16] Specifically, the pair was charged with moving illegal liquor from Canton to Detroit. Mazer's troubles didn't end there. Roach and Joseph Cleary, Governor Donahey's personal detective sent to Canton to keep the governor abreast of the investigation, pressured a justice of the peace into issuing a murder warrant for Mazer. Cleary had gotten wind of Steve Kascholk's story, slipped into the workhouse to interview him, and then announced that there was enough evidence to arrest Mazer and Ben Rudner for murder. Roach agreed and, continuing to grandstand, announced that Mazer owned a pearl-handled Spanish revolver that had fired the metal-jacketed bullet recovered at the crime scene. He also said that a Canton police officer had cleaned the gun for Mazer the day after the crime, though he never produced the weapon.[17] A frustrated McClintock appealed to the governor to restrain Cleary, and Donahey complied, recalling Cleary to Columbus.

When informed of the murder charge, Mazer reportedly sobbed and proclaimed that his pals knew he was innocent of murder. He declined, however, to identify his pals. Recognizing a bandwagon when he saw it, Ora Slater jumped on the Mazer murder charge, boasting to the press, "Louis Mazer is as good as in the electric chair," and then promising that Mazer would come in for some hard questioning from Canton authorities.[18]

New revelations appeared daily, both fact and rumor, and everyone in the county had a theory about the crime. As the *Plain Dealer* observed, "Stark County folk are a great people for reading newspapers. Everybody has read about the Mellett murder."[19] McDermott, Mazer, and Rudner were implicated, yet Cantonians seemed to be waiting for the other shoe to drop. The *Plain Dealer* summed up the prevailing mood in Canton, "Although no policemen are as yet charged directly with participation in the murder plot, there are those who feel sure that the Mellett case will prove a repetition [of other famous police corruption cases of the 1920s]."[20]

However, one of Mazer's pals in Canton came to his rescue and provided an alibi for the night of the July 15–16: Mazer claimed that he had been visiting the home of police detective Floyd Streitenberger at the time of the murder to examine a sick dog.

An alert editor on the staff of the *Buffalo (N.Y.) Courier Express* read Mazer's statement reported in the August 17 Associated Press dispatch and recognized Streitenberger's name on a list of delegates to the Fraternal Order of Police convention in Buffalo at the Statler Hotel. *Courier Express* reporter Clement V. Curry called the hotel and arranged to interview the Canton detective. Curry questioned Streitenberger closely regarding his movements the evening of the murder.[21] "Mazer is absolutely innocent, and I will do absolutely everything I can to clear him," Streitenberger declared, indignant that his friend had even been arrested. He told Curry that on the evening of the murder he left the police station at 5:00 P.M. At about 8:30 or 9:00, he and his wife drove over to see the fireworks at the fairgrounds, a short drive that, inexplicably, took an hour. Arriving at 10:00 P.M., the couple stayed until 10:45 P.M. Instead of going straight home, they took a leisurely drive around Canton to enjoy the night air, reaching Second and Walnut, in the heart of the red light district at 11:45, where they saw Louis Mazer. The police detective told the reporter that he was looking for Mazer because he had a German shepherd dog that was sick, possibly with distemper, and he knew from the dog's pedigree that Mazer owned a littermate. He wanted to have Mazer look at the dog. (Streitenberger said that he had arrested Mazer three years ago and described him as "a bootlegger of no account." He claimed that he had not spoken to Mazer—not even a "hello" on the street—since then.) They passed Mazer on the street and flagged his car down. Mazer agreed to look at the dog, at which point Kate Streitenberger told Mazer to follow them to their home twenty blocks away. They arrived there at about midnight. For the next forty five minutes, Streitenberger said, the two men talked only about dogs. Mazer said he didn't think the dog had distemper. Mazer left by 1:00 A.M. According to the detective, they retired for the evening, only to be aroused at 1:40 A.M. by Captain Clarke to investigate the murder.

Apparently, Streitenberger was aware of Mazer's arrest when he talked to Curry—significantly, the times the detective gave Curry matched what Mazer claimed. He told the reporter to "go ahead" and quote him. Streitenberger then talked off the record about the Mellett murder with Curry, who kept his word and refused to divulge what he had been told. Curry and Streitenberger were alone in the hotel room for forty minutes.[22] After he left the Statler, Curry called the *Plain Dealer* and, per an arrangement with the Cleveland paper to share news tips, gave over the details of Streitenberger's statement. Later that evening, learning of the interview, a fellow Canton police officer also in Buffalo for the FOP conference realized the danger Streitenberger had put himself in and suggested the detective head home immediately and try to revise his damaging comments.[23] It was too late. Two days later, on August 19, *Plain Dealer* reporter William Tugman delivered Curry's sworn deposition regarding the interview to Canton authorities.[24] Streitenberger's Buffalo statement was front-page news. And people were reading the papers. That July the *Daily News* hit an all-time circulation high of 34,000.[25]

On August 16 McClintock convened a grand jury to examine the evidence gathered thus far. In his methodical way, the county prosecutor was building his cases in what now appeared to be a murder conspiracy involving Mazer, McDermott, and Rudner. However, to the dismay of some, the grand jury adjourned without handing down any indictments.[26]

On August 17, Ora Slater checked Steve Kascholk out of the county workhouse and took him to Cleveland. He ushered the prime witness into federal distict attorney A. E. Bernstein's crowded office where Louis Mazer was being questioned in the presence of several men. Steve stared intensely at Mazer as agonizing moments passed for investigators until Steve nodded to Slater that Mazer was the man known as "Smitty." Studer and Mazer weren't telling much to investigators, except about their former attorney Norman Clark. Apparently they were convincing enough to get the federal district attorney to arrest Clark on charges of violating liquor laws. But unlike his former clients, Clark was out of jail on $15,000 bond in short order. According to Clark, Mazer said more than once that "if Mellett keeps things up, he will be bumped off." Clark also denied fixing cases for Mazer and being fired from his job at the law firm of Pomerene, Ambler and Pomerene. Clark recounted one angry exchange with Studer in jail before Clark's release on bond, during which Studer called Clark a "damned double crossing skunk." To which Clark promised, "I am going to tell all I know about you gang of whelps."[27] Studer managed to get himself finally freed on bond, but because of the murder charge, Mazer remained behind bars. And Ben Rudner, understanding that he would not be arrested on liquor charges, willingly went to Cleveland for questioning despite being generally viewed as having some connection to the murder.[28]

August 24, 1926, was a big news day in Canton. No doubt at the instigation of Joseph Roach, Florence Mellett's personal attorney, Frances Poulson, filed a civil suit for $100,000 on August 24 against Rudner, Mazer, and McDermott for the murder of Don Mellett. According to

Mrs. Mellett, this action was not for the money but rather to "secure vigorous prosecution of murderers." If she ever received any money from the suit, Florence said she would donate it to fatherless children.[29] This suit put the three conspirators in the public eye for the first time. For this, Roach received credit, especially among members of the press, who were always happy to reward investigators willing to go public.[30]

That same day McClintock recalled the grand jury to meet the next day, and he lashed out at Roach and all the criticism Roach had been heaping on him for failing to indict anyone thus far. He declared that he "will not be coerced or intimidated by anyone." He reassured his constituents that he would do his job until his term ended. (Whether he won or lost the congressional race, he would be leaving the prosecutor's office December 31.[31]) In addition, McClintock made it clear that all investigations of an official nature would originate from his office. To that end, Slater was moved out of the *Daily News* building and into the prosecutor's office.[32]

As the county grand jury reconvened on August 25, it received a special charge from common pleas court judge A. W. Angler. He reminded the jury members to demand to hear all the evidence, realize the important role in forming public opinion their results would have, and to base their opinions only on the evidence. Thus charged and forewarned, the grand jury settled in to hear almost thirty witnesses including Ora Slater and Joseph Roach, who gave documentary evidence.[33] Roach would soon bow out of the Mellett murder investigation having so thoroughly alienated all sides that forever after he would be referred to in Canton as the "Chicago Roach." On September 3, the grand jury issued indictments for Rudner, Mazer, and McDermott in the slaying of Don Mellett on July 16, 1926. Rudner knew what was coming. He had been hanging around police headquarters, talking to investigators and reporters and even inviting some of them to his home. He was enjoying his notoriety. When Sheriff Ed Gibson arrived at his Massillon store to arrest him, he said he was ready to go. When they arrived at the jail, Rudner bounded up the steps ahead of the lawmen waving to reporters and shouting, "I'm innocent. It's a frame up!"

Saranus Lengel's civil service hearing began September 8, with the dismissed police chief facing a much less sympathetic commission after Mayor Swarts's August 23 replacement of commissioners Jansen and Burris with George Melbourne and Charles Flory.[34] The three members heard a lot about Carl Studer, a known friend of Lengel. Prosecutor McClintock presented witnesses who testified that Studer both collected rent on the houses and took a portion of the receipts, some suggesting that Lengel shared in the take. Also testifying at the hearing was the police call box operator Laura Hardy, who told about the unusually slow response by police officers to Mellett's murder. Lengel never took the stand to defend himself, and his dismissal was upheld by the commission.

Mayor Swarts appointed Sergeant John "Jiggs" Wise the new chief of police. Wise moved quickly to consolidate his power in the department. He offered several officers the chance to resign, including Streitenberger; when they refused, he fired them. They all appealed, however, and won reinstatement. Undeterred, Wise almost immediately dismissed Streitenberger a second time and made it stick.[35]

. . .

When Ora Slater was in Cleveland with Steve Kascholk to identify Louis Mazer, *Plain Dealer* reporter William Tugman had pulled him aside and told him that there were relatives of McDermott in town who wanted to talk to Slater. Eager as Slater was to talk to Pat's kin, he felt he was duty bound to return Kascholk safely to the workhouse in Canton as soon as possible. He told Tugman to tell the family to come see him in Canton. Slater was taking a risk. What if this put the family off and they backed out of talking? Slater never explained why he didn't go immediately to see them and send Kascholk back to the workhouse with his assistant, C. B. Armstrong. However, one of Slater's best tactics as an interrogator was to seem disinterested in what someone had to say, hoping they would become even more eager to talk. Slater later admitted that all the while he was praying that the McDermott family would make the trip to Canton.

After returning Steve to the workhouse without incident, Slater went to his room at the McKinley Hotel, where he was joined by Armstrong. Together they spent the evening wondering if McDermott's relatives would show. Finally, at 10:30 P.M., there was a knock at the door. Slater answered it, and four men filed into the hotel room. Bernard and Tom McDermott were Pat's brothers in from Nanty Glo, and Jerry O'Rourke and Joe Piatica were brothers-in-law from Cleveland.[36] The four men, representing the family, had a simple request: convince us Pat was involved, promise us he'll get a "square deal," and we'll turn him in *if* we locate him.

The McDermott family was of some prominence in Nanty Glo. Pat's father, also Patrick, was a native of Dublin, Ireland, and had been a veteran of the British Army before arriving in America. The elder McDermott was deceased, but not his wife, Alice, a Scot, whose blindness literally kept her in the dark about her wayward son's activities. Bernard was the eldest son, and with his uncle, Martin, he currently owned the Shoemaker Hotel in Twin Rocks, Pennsylvania, not far from Nanty Glo. He also once owned a pool hall where Pat had worked. Martin McDermott was well-known in Cambria County, where he was a local political leader and small businessman. When a *Pittsburgh Post* article in September 1926 claimed that the family was hiding Pat in the Pennsylvania mountains, Martin filed a libel suit. He was not a man to be trifled with.[37]

Pat McDermott might have been regarded as the black sheep in the family, but his relatives still demanded proof of his involvement in the murder of Don Mellett. They appeared sincere to Slater and Armstrong, so Slater called McClintock and Hexamer. Why not bring in someone from Nanty Glo to convince the family? Steve Kascholk was brought over from the workhouse and told his story. Slater concluded the conference by pointing out the obvious advantages for Pat to voluntarily surrender or, at least, be peacefully apprehended. As they were leaving, Bernard told Slater that he was satisfied the detective had "played square with us." If the family located Pat, he said, they would be in touch. But Slater was destined to be disappointed if he expected a quick result from his meeting with the family. In the weeks ahead, repeated contacts with the McDermott clan always produced the same response: "still looking."

It wasn't until Saturday, October 23, that Slater heard from the McDermott family again. At home in Cincinnati for the weekend, Slater's phone rang at 1:30 A.M. It was Bernard McDermott calling from Twin

Rocks, Pennsylvania, urging Slater to come with the prosecutor and no one else. When he and McClintock arrived that evening, the family again sought assurances that Pat would receive fair treatment. Satisfied, they told them that Pat was in hiding near Twin Rocks.

Slater then learned that the family had known of Pat's whereabouts for about the last month or so. Both Jerry O'Rourke and Tom McDermott had visited Pat twice at his hideout, even while they were telling Slater otherwise. Pat's kin probably needed little more to convince them of Pat's involvement. The men told Slater that Pat suddenly had enough money in the days following the murder to repay a debt to Jerry O'Rourke. The family spirited the fugitive out of Cleveland and back home to Cambria County, Pennsylvania. They said Pat didn't know that they were turning him in, or "he would be on his way. He won't listen to reason, so we've had to take things in our own hands."

The three men had it all planned out. Slater and Bernard would go to the Shoemaker Hotel in Twin Rocks, which Bernard and Martin owned. Tom and McClintock would stay behind in Johnstown until Slater had charge of Pat. The family would deliver Pat the next morning. Promptly at 8:00 on Sunday morning, October 24, Bernard McDermott knocked on Ora Slater's door in the Shoemaker Hotel. He told Slater to have some breakfast, that he was going to church. Pat would be delivered to Slater's room by 9:30 A.M. At exactly 9:30, Slater heard someone bounding up the stairs. A moment later Pat McDermott burst through the door. He instantly knew he'd been betrayed. He recognized the famous detective from his picture in the newspapers. With Bernard blocking his escape and Slater facing him in the small hotel room, Pat McDermott was trapped. He went pale. Asked by the detective if he knew who he was, Pat answered, "Yes, I know you. You are Ora Slater." Pat turned on his older brother, who was clearly nervous in his role as Judas. "You double crossed me!" Pat snarled and cursed him. Bernard's shoulders sank, and his head dropped. "Pat, we thought it was best. . . . This way you'll get a square deal."

Slater asked Pat what he had to say, and the fugitive demanded a written promise from the county prosecutor to drop the murder indictment before he would talk. It wasn't long before McClintock and the rest of the McDermott clan arrived from Johnstown. Everyone urged Pat to talk, but he refused unless the murder charge was dropped. For his part McClintock refused to consider this compromise until he heard what Pat had to say. This was standard prosecutorial procedure. Pat remained obstinate. His family pleaded with him, "Don't protect Rudner and Mazer." But Pat continued to curse his kin. After much discussion, he agreed to return to Canton voluntarily with Slater and McClintock. The rift between Pat and his brothers would last for some weeks.

Pat was bundled into a car for the long drive back to Canton in a rainstorm. The trip took hours along mountain roads and through Pittsburgh. The two investigators no doubt worked on Pat during the trip back to Ohio, but they acquired little new information. The concept of a "square deal" meant different things to each of the participants. This would be an issue later, with the McDermotts believing Pat's surrender should count for something, and the prosecutor believing that Pat must talk before any deals could be made. It was late Sunday evening when the three travelers arrived at the Stark County Jail. The first glimpse waiting newsmen had of Pat was not that of the cocky, dapper, bigger-than-life murderer who gave away stolen clothing, but of a disheveled, carelessly dressed fugitive in an old pair of trousers, dirty shirt, torn sweater, and cap pulled down over his eyes. The elusive fugitive turned out to be much less impressive in custody.

McClintock and Slater took a big gamble in bringing McDermott in by themselves. Slater had gone with the McDermotts and stayed alone in the hotel with only his wits and the family's sense of right to protect him. There was no backup—no state police, county sheriff, or even local constable was present to assist if things went bad. Slater liked to claim he rarely carried a gun and never shot a man. But this time he had been armed and stated flatly that he would have shot Pat in self-defense if necessary. Slater also recognized that the only witnesses would have been the hostile McDermott family if he had used his gun, making self-defense hard to prove.[38] What would Slater and McClintock have done if Pat refused to surrender? McClintock had no jurisdiction in Pennsylvania, and Slater had no arrest powers. The two men took a huge risk that could have backfired and resulted in a serious, even deadly, outcome. The bloodless surrender of Patrick McDermott was the high point of Ora Slater's career, and the beginning of McClintock's incredible run of luck.

The defendants were housed in separate locations to reduce the opportunity for them to exchange information and alibis on the jailhouse grapevine. Pat was immediately moved to the county workhouse, where he joined Louis Mazer in solitary confinement. Unlike Steve Kascholk, McDermott and Mazer were working on nothing but their alibis in the workhouse. Despite the isolation, Pat kept abreast of all gossip via a hole in the wall of his cell through which he traded cigarettes for information from other prisoners. Mazer, for his part, was said to pass his time by doing sit ups, and reading novels about criminal court proceedings. The workhouse also held celebrity detainee Peggy Cavanaugh.

Rudner, Mazer, and eventually McDermott believed they should be free on bail while awaiting trial despite their first-degree murder charges. Common pleas court judge Edwin W. Diehl accommodated them by setting bails ranging from $60,000 to $100,000 for the three defendants. McClintock objected and, aided by former judge H. C. Pontius, appealed the issue all the way to the Ohio Supreme Court. The matter was finally settled in early December when the state's high court ruled against granting bond for first-degree murder, thereby setting an Ohio precedent. All three would remain behind bars until their trials.

Slater later learned that while on the run Pat had been indirectly helped by his old prison buddy Ben Rudner. For assistance in hiding Pat, Rudner had contacted another Atlanta federal prison alumnus and his cell mate, Morris "Ben" Nadel, who was a well-known Cleveland Packard mechanic turned bootlegger, who was described by the *Plain Dealer* as "a huge fellow with the physique of a heavy weight champion; a character out of one of Eugene O'Neill's plays." Toward the end of August, Nadel asked one of his lieutenants in the Cleveland suburb of Lakewood, Dan Pfaff, if he could hide a friend evading a liquor charge. Nadel knew who Pat was but deliberately remained vague. Pfaff begged off, saying he didn't have a place. About midday on September 1, Nadel took Pfaff to the Abigail Apartments on 105th

Street (which were owned by another Nadel associate, Stanley Slagle), and there, in a small ground-floor apartment, introduced Pfaff to Pat, now using the name "Wilson." Nadel instructed Pfaff to bring Pat food and reading material and to do any favors Pat asked. Nadel would pay all the expenses.[39] After a few days, Pat began complaining about his confinement in the small apartment. And sometime later in October, Pat contacted Pfaff wanting to talk to Nadel. Nadel was out, as he usually was for Pat's calls. Pat then told Pfaff that he was going away, was meeting someone at 7:30 that evening. Pfaff offered to drive Pat to his meeting. Pfaff drove McDermott to a bridge just five minutes north of the Abigail Apartments. No one was there, but Pat insisted upon being left. That was the last Pfaff saw of McDermott. Pat's secret meeting on the bridge was with his brother Tom and brother-in-law Jerry O'Rourke.

Cleveland police located Pat's hideout in the Abigail Apartments on October 27. In the first-floor apartment they found a shirt with a faint "mcd" laundry mark. Eventually the Cleveland detectives traced the apartment to Stanley Slagle and his wife, and they picked up Pfaff as well. The Slagles both subsequently testified against Nadel who now faced charges for harboring a fugitive for helping his buddy Rudner. Pfaff went one further and gave evidence against Nadel on liquor conspiracy charges.

In jail and facing a possible death penalty, Pat McDermott refused to talk, despite the best efforts of his interrogators. McClintock decided to move Mazer's trial back and try Pat first in December for first-degree murder. This drew howls of protest from the McDermott family and defense counsel who believed this was not the "square deal" Pat was promised for voluntarily surrendering. The trial of the *State of Ohio vs. Patrick Eugene McDermott* for the murder of Don Mellett promised to be front-page news across the country.

6

The Slugger Goes on Trial

The trial of Patrick Eugene McDermott for first-degree murder in the slaying of Don Mellett was set to begin December 6, 1927. This trial was more than a legal proceeding to determine McDermott's guilt or innocence. Canton was on trial. Would the rule of law prevail in Canton? The outcome would determine whether the "stench," as *Time* magazine had labeled it, could be removed from Canton. Bringing Don Mellett's killers to justice was the city's chance to redeem itself and rehabilitate its tarnished image.

The alleged co-conspirators were taken to the Canton Police Department on December 2 for photographing and fingerprinting by Captain Ben Clarke. No explanation was given regarding why this routine and vital piece of police business was delayed so long when all three had been in custody for weeks. Nevertheless, this occasion was a press opportunity not to be missed. Pat McDermott was described by the *Evening Repository* as "looking like a prosperous young businessman." Clean-shaven and wearing a brown business suit, white shirt, and black bow tie, Pat kept up a steady banter with Clarke, Chief Wise, his guards, and reporters. When a small vial of gasoline used to clean fingerprint ink was misplaced, newsmen suggested it was mistaken for moonshine. Not so, Pat quipped, "If that were the case, that bottle would've disappeared long before this." But when news photographers pressed Pat for a picture for the papers, he growled, "I don't need the help of the newspapers." Pat was the central character in this courtroom drama. For the next three and a half weeks, reporters would hang on his every word, gesture, expression, and change of clothes.[1] Pat didn't look like a murderer from central casting. He was just a short, average-looking guy with neatly trimmed hair and fashionable suits (this by design of his defense team). He did not look like the ruthless thug the public expected. He was just a petty thief and ex-convict who occasionally carried around a handful of pistol cartridges to demonstrate to acquaintances how tough he was.[2] The press endlessly speculated whether or not Pat would betray his guilt in some unexpected manner, or really prove his proclaimed innocence.[3]

Louis Mazer was also in a good mood for his fingerprinting. He joked with Chief Wise about their mutual military service on the Texas border in 1916, although they served in different units.[4] In contrast, Ben Rudner was ugly and defiant. He insisted that Clarke, not Wise, fingerprint him. "I'm going to settle an old score with Wise when I get out of this," he threatened. Authorities were careful to keep the three prisoners separated during their processing, lest they have a chance to work on their alibis.[5]

Interest in the trial of Pat McDermott was at a fever pitch and could have easily devolved into a media circus. The job of providing a fair trial and managing the press fell to common pleas court judge Edwin W. Diehl. The judge was of solid Dutch stock from the eastern Stark County city of Alliance, where his family had business and real estate interests. Diehl's education began with a teaching degree from Ohio Northern in 1895. While teaching he read for the law and was admitted to the bar in 1902. Appointed to the bench in 1923, Diehl, a Democrat, won a six-year term in 1924. In 1926, he was fifty years old.[6]

Judge Diehl was meticulous. He personally decided on the layout of the courtroom, the largest in the Stark County courthouse. It was a gloomy place, with arched windows and old-fashioned, heavy walnut-paneled walls and a skylight for added illumination. Except for a single portrait of William McKinley, once a county prosecutor, there was no adornment on the walls, and the only color in this austere room came from the American flag beside the judge's bench, which stood at the far end opposite the heavy doors. To its left was the jury box. Between the jury box and bench was the witness stand, a four-sided box. In front of the judge and the witness stand were the attorneys' tables. However, unlike the usual alignment of tables, end to end with the aisle between, these were arranged one in front of the other, with the prosecution in front and the defense in the rear. The judge knew his attorneys. He had cleverly devised this setup to slow down attorneys attempting to rush the bench with objections. Behind the lawyers was the rail, which separated two or three rows of seats for those spectators fortunate enough to be admitted. Last, but not least, to the judge's right stood three tables for the press. On one table was a muffled telegraph key, a first for an Ohio court, which would instantly transmit the proceedings around the country. Parked around the press tables were seats for a battery of press photographers, who were present only by the sufferance of the court and under strict guidelines only to take pictures when the judge permitted. Any violation would result in immediate removal. Judge Diehl also issued strict orders for ensuring security at the trial. No one could pass the rail without a written order signed by the judge. Outside the second-floor courtroom, potential spectators were to be halted at the top of the stairs to wait for a chance to be admitted. Suspicious-looking persons and those with packages were removed from the building. Rumors of gang attacks were rampant, and the sheriff placed machine guns at the courthouse doors. Once the seats were filled, a few standing-room spectators were admitted to line the back and side walls. When the courtroom was full, the doors were to be locked, and no one was allowed to leave until that session was complete. Armed guards manned the main entry doors. Inside, strict silence was to be observed at all times, and any violators would be ejected. A bailiff summed up the judge's orders and precautions: "Don't even whisper."

The defense and prosecution each had three attorneys of record. Leading the prosecution was outgoing prosecutor Charles B. McClintock, a man dismissed by many legal pundits as "a small town lawyer." Reporters described the forty-one-year-old "boy prosecutor" as "wiry," "solemn," "gayless," and physically unimpressive. A cartoon caricature presented him as a pinched-face fellow with heavy eyebrows. Distracted by the Mellett case, McClintock had only made six or seven campaign speeches, which may have been a blessing since he was a terrible stump speaker. He lost the election when the Canton Jungle voted Democratic for the first time in years. Perhaps he had been too honest a prosecutor. Recalling for readers that McClintock and Slater had brought in the fugitive Pat McDermott, something an army of lawmen failed to achieve, the *Plain Dealer* predicted that the prosecutor would be worth watching.

Assisting McClintock was prosecutor-elect Henry Harter, in his early thirties, the son of a prominent attorney who served fourteen years on the common pleas bench and was related to the Aultmans, for whom the hospital was named. Harter was a graduate of Williams College, where he had excelled at football in the days when players wore little padding and were occasionally killed pursuing the sport. He had a footballer's physique, an even temper, and an excellent legal mind. The *Plain Dealer* considered him an "excellent teammate" for McClintock. Rounding out the prosecution team was another assistant prosecutor, James M. "Jim" Aungst. Robust and athletic like Harter, Aungst was regarded as one of Canton's best young legal minds.

The prosecution team was not noted for its oratorical talents, but rather its methodical and logical presentation of the evidence. This strategy was dictated by the fact that the state's case against Pat McDermott was based on strong but entirely circumstantial evidence. No eyewitnesses had come forward despite the reward, and so far none of the defendants were talking. McClintock's courtroom style featured penetrating cross-examinations and quick retorts. Harter was more easygoing and could be counted on to admonish his more intense chief to relax and "laugh it off." Jim Aungst tended the reams of notes and reference volumes the prosecution brought to court. Behind the scenes providing valuable advice and courtroom experience to the prosecutors was former judge Hubert C. Pontius, who left the bench in 1924 after serving six years. He was Don Mellett's personal attorney and family friend.

Pat McDermott had rejected the attorney retained by his family in favor of Ben Rudner's old counsel, Everett L. Mills. This was a mistake on Pat's part and would play into Rudner's defense strategy when it became obvious that Mills was more interested in saving Rudner than McDermott. Pat may have been spiting his family for turning him in. The McDermott family feud was cooling, and they were said to be paying for Pat's defense and new wardrobe. Tom and Bernard McDermott were in Canton for the trial. They denounced the thought of receiving any of the reward for Pat's surrender, saying that instead it should go to Mrs. Mellett, and they categorically denied the newspaper rumor that they received $5,000 from Slater's agency for turning in Pat.

As the Canton bar went, no doubt Mills was one of Canton's top defense attorneys. Mills was a Republican partisan who was cocky, aggressive, pugnacious, and confident as a defender. He actually believed in the innocence of many of his clients and distrusted much of law enforcement. He believed that McDermott was being tried on flimsy evidence trumped up by a prosecutor who needed this case to further his political ambitions. It was no secret that Mills and McClintock disliked each other as only a prosecutor and defense attorney could. Speaking to reporters before the trial, Mills bragged, "Before you get through with this, you're going to know how to try a first degree murder case."

The man the reporters expected the most from during the trial was co-counsel C. Homer Durand, whose involvement had remained a secret until just before the start of the trial in order to shock the prosecution. Durand, from Coshocton, Ohio, was a former Republican candidate for governor on the "wet" ticket. He was an avowed antiprohibitionist who frequently defended bootleggers. He was expected to play the "heavy" on the defense side, as if Mills weren't heavy enough. A tall, physically large man with an admirable head of dark wavy hair worn in a pompadour style, the forty-four-year-old Durand offset the drabness of the local bar by wearing old-fashioned 1890s stiff collars with a black ascot and a Prince Albert coat. The members of the press were counting on Durand for oratorical fireworks, calling him the "legal firebrand from Coshocton." Clearly, since there wasn't much of a fee to be collected in this case, Durand was there for the publicity.

Easily overlooked was the third member of the defense team, James H. Ensley, a Canton city councilman. Relegated to taking notes and shuffling papers, young Ensley said little. His brief exposure to the press came in an affidavit he filed with the court in which he claimed McClintock asked him to try to talk McDermott into turning state's evidence. But when McClintock discovered that Ensley was secretly working with Mills on Pat's defense, the prosecutor questioned Ensley's ethics and dismissed him from the prosecutor's office.

Jury selection began promptly at 9:00 Monday morning, December 6, 1926. The question was whether a jury of thirteen men and women free of preconceived opinions about the greatest murder in Canton's history could be found in Stark County. The defense argued vigorously that this was an impossible task, and requested a change of venue several times before and during the selection process, producing a sheaf of dubious affidavits from local characters confirming that a bias existed in Canton. Judge Diehl denied the requests, citing the obvious fact that press coverage of the crime had been heavy all across Ohio. This argument was legitimate, but in reality no one in Stark County wanted the trial moved. It was time to show that Canton was a place where law and order could prevail.

Picking a jury was as much an art in 1926 as it is today. Each side had an idea of what they wanted in the perfect juror, an attempt that the *Plain Dealer* described as "something like bidding for a dummy in three handed bridge or drawing to a flush in poker."[7] Potential jurors could be rejected for peremptory, or arbitrary, reasons. The defense had a four to one advantage here, with sixteen peremptory challenges to the prosecution's four. Jurors could also be rejected for cause, obvious disqualifications for confirmed opinions or a relationship with either side.

Sixty-two Stark County voters were called in the first venue of possible jurors to be questioned by the attorneys and scrutinized by the press. Durand and Mills examined every potential juror carefully,

"like a surgeon studies a patient," according to one reporter. Pat Mc-
Dermott studied the list of prospective jurors but was rarely consulted. Instead, his lawyers talked around him while Pat assumed
"his professional pose as amateur lawyer."[8] The defense asked each
juror if they had any prejudices against Catholics (Pat was Irish
Catholic) or Jews (Rudner was Jewish) and if they had any association with the Ku Klux Klan, which was active in Ohio in the 1920s
and was known for its anti-Catholicism and anti-Semitism. Finally,
the defense wanted to know each person's reading habits, preferring
to have no readers of the *Daily News* on the jury. The prosecution's
primary issue was whether a potential juror was opposed to capital
punishment, since this was a first-degree murder trial. "Would you
flinch from a verdict which would send this young man to the electric
chair?" McClintock questioned. Opposition to the death penalty was
more widespread than expected and was grounds for dismissal from
the jury pool.

Mills and Durand insisted on asking every juror if they would accept the testimony of a bootlegger, meaning Ben Rudner. Each time,
McClintock objected, and finally the questioning of George Pierce, a
seventy-year-old blacksmith, touched off a debate among the lawyers involving case law citations. When finally allowed to answer,
Mr. Pierce laid the question to rest by replying, "If a man were in
the bootlegging business, I believe he would be in the lying business,
too." Judge Diehl rewarded Mr. Pierce's wisdom by seating him, but
the defense later dismissed him.

By Tuesday afternoon, all fifty-seven of the sixty-two potential jurors who responded to their summons had been examined, and only
eleven were tentatively seated after seven removals by the defense and
one by the prosecution. Prospective jurors came and went quickly.
Some were dismissed for illness or age, anyone over seventy getting
an automatic exemption. And some were excused for being too eager,
which raised red flags all around. With this venue exhausted, either
the defense or prosecution needed to request a second one, or jurors
could be selected from the bystanders in the courtroom. The sheriff
claimed it would take two days to draw and notify a second venue.
Mills invoked an Ohio law granting the defense three days to exam-

ine the new venue list. Not wanting any delay, Judge Diehl himself retired to his chambers to compile the list. Whether he got the forty names from the Canton city directory or from memory is unclear, but he directed the sheriff to go round up the people. Eventually, a third special venue of twenty was required. After six days, on Friday, December 10, twelve acceptable jurors were seated. All that remained was to find the one alternate, the thirteenth juror.

When Mrs. Ida Willingham of North Canton entered the courtroom, Pat instantly liked her. The defense previously had a definite preference for male jurors, fearing women might be too sympathetic to Mrs. Mellett. But Mrs. Willingham, middle-aged and motherly in a silver fox–trimmed gray cloth coat, was different. Pat indicated his approval to his attorneys. When asked by Durand if it was worse to kill an editor than anyone else, she replied, "A life is a life." She was seated. After a week, and the examination of 103 potential jurors, the jury was complete: three housewives, three tradesmen, four farmers, and three businessmen. Their names were published in the newspapers. Judge Diehl admonished the jury not to read any newspapers, which all agreed was a hardship. Furthermore, he sequestered them in the Northern Hotel just across the street from the courthouse and then, in turn, had a deputy sheriff escort each juror home to collect things needed for an extended hotel stay.

During jury selection, Judge Diehl disposed of "a number of legal skirmishes in which practically every legitimate remedy known to criminal law was taken advantage of."[9] The defense had three main technical issues. The first was a juror's ability to regard the defendant as innocent. Diehl ruled that it was acceptable for potential jurors to agree to lay aside previously held opinions and agree to be fair and impartial if seated. This ruling favored the state, but Judge Diehl did not hesitate to dismiss several prospective jurors who were either unclear about their opinions or how strong those opinions were. Second was the defense demand for three days to examine juror lists of the second and third venues. Diehl ruled that since he personally prepared the lists, they were exempt. Third was a list of complaints about the unavailability of prosecution witnesses for defense examination. This was dismissed out of hand. In case anyone in the courtroom missed it, the judge pointed out that all these defense motions were designed to build a case for an appeal of an unfavorable verdict. Commenting on the jury selection process to Durand, the colorful defendant offered the opinion, "By the time I get through this, I'll be able to hang out a shingle and start practicing myself."[10] ✦

Pat McDermott was the subject of the intense legal battle and an alleged hired killer, yet he was anything but intimidating. Seated between Mills and Durand at the second table, he looked more like a smallish clerk or bookkeeper. His hair slicked down and parted in the middle, he favored conservative suits, white shirts (a fresh one each day), and bow ties; his wardrobe was selected and paid for by his defense team. During jury selection, Pat chewed gum and nervously fiddled with a pencil that he parked behind his left ear when he needed to adjust his tie. He made notes, leaned forward on his arms to listen, and polished his fingernails. He sometimes stared down those attempting to make eye contact, and in unguarded moments his jaw drooped. Failing to present the picture of a hardened killer, he made a proper and almost debonair appearance. Looking at Patrick McDermott, it was easy to forget that he was a career criminal and that this was not his first criminal trial. If Pat didn't flinch when the prosecution mentioned the death penalty, it was because he was too much the experienced defendant and too young to believe it could happen to him.

With jury selection completed, Judge Diehl wasted no time and scheduled a session for Saturday morning, when the jury was taken to the murder scene. There, six months after Mellett's death, they saw little more than bullet holes in the garage door. A new house stood in the vacant lot. Florence Mellett and the children were gone, having moved back to Indianapolis a few weeks after the crime. The trial attorneys also made the trip, as did Pat McDermott, who was escorted by a workhouse guard twice his size. A large press contingent completed the tour group. The press described Pat as "serious" during the visit.

Courtroom proceedings were scheduled to begin Monday, December 13, after Judge Diehl disposed of further defense motions. By tradition, the prosecution would present its case first. Outside the courtroom, in the court of public opinion, the defense asserted that

Left: Patrick "Red" McDermott, smiling for the camera, viewing the murder scene on the opening day of his murder trial, December 11, 1926. Cleveland Public Library

Below: Defendant Pat McDermott (right) at opening of his murder trial. Cleveland Public Library

The prosecution and defense at McDermott's trial. In front of the table sit assistant prosecutor James Aungst (in the foreground in spectacles) and behind him prosecutor-elect Henry Harter and outgoing prosecutor Charles McClintock. On the other side of the table sit the defense (from left): James Ensley, Homer Durand (in spectacles), Everett L. Mills, and Pat McDermott (again, in a bow tie). Cleveland Public Library

McDermott was charged with murder because the prosecutor had wanted to squeeze a confession from Pat to enhance his failed run for Congress. Mills alleged that Pat was offered a deal to turn state's evidence but refused. In an effort to prove it, he produced an affidavit from the defendant swearing he was offered a 75–25 deal if he would turn against the two "Jews." If Pat refused, Mills claimed that McClintock said he would see to it that Pat didn't get a fair trial. "Pat was not able to give information," claimed Durand, adding in a racially tainted conclusion. "He was too white, and too decent to barter his own safety against other men's lives."[11] The defense insisted that it would call Ora Slater to testify about what offers were made to Pat. "We know that Slater knows that Pat is innocent," said Durand, and the "key man" theory was insincere. But Slater didn't rise to the bait and offered no comment on the accusation. Instead, Slater and McClintock produced their own affidavits denying McDermott's assertions. After the detective received a subpoena, all he would say about Pat was that if McDermott chose to, he could "tell plenty." An indignant prosecutor insisted that all Pat was offered was the "square deal." Both sides continued sparring in the press. The defense hinted at several aces up their sleeves, including the claim that it was Pat McDermott who telephoned those warnings to Don Mellett. Not to be outdone, the prosecution claimed to have a witness whose name had never been mentioned before.

Judge Diehl wanted a fast-paced and orderly trial. Christmas was just twelve days away. He set a grueling schedule by judicial standards: 8:45 to 11:45 A.M. and 1:00 to 4:30 P.M. The jury ate lunch across the street at their hotel, and Pat McDermott ate back at the workhouse. All recesses were limited to ten minutes.

In New Jersey, the Hall-Mills trial, a sensational sex-charged murder, conveniently ended just the week before, releasing hoards of crime reporters into Canton to cover the McDermott trial. Yet this trial lacked a key element to make it really sensational. As one cartoonist put it, "This won't be so good as the Hall-Mills case. T'aint got the love interest."[12] And Canton's civic conscience, Henry Timkin, said about the trial, "Were this an ordinary sex crime, the whole community would be maudlin for vengeance. A crime against society itself is an intellectual problem requiring thinking."[13] To their credit, some reporters did see the trial as an opportunity to reveal what ailed government in general during Prohibition—and not just in Canton.

Monday morning's session began with opening remarks by the prosecution and defense. McClintock promised that the state would show "that Mellett was killed by reason of a conspiracy because of the acts of his newspaper. McDermott was one of the conspirators who helped kill Mellett." Mills repeated his claim that the defense would prove that Pat was a victim of a conspiracy by the prosecutor to advance his congressional ambitions.[14]

The first witness on the stand was Dr. T. C. McQuate, the county coroner, whose official duty was to establish that a crime was actually committed. McQuate, who guessed he had been coroner "counting this year, off and on for ten years," was a large, jovial fellow who filled the witness chair. A bit of a showman (befitting his earlier career as a sideshow barker for Barnum and Bailey Circus), McQuate arrived on the witness stand complete with a black satchel. He was all business relating the pathological details of Mellett's murder. From the black bag, McQuate produced two skulls he used as props to illustrate the details. His conclusion was simple and exact: "The cause of death was due to a bullet passing through Don Mellett's brain."[15]

When asked how many bullets were fired at Mellett, McQuate replied that two went through the garage door, two left marks on the brick house, one went through the kitchen window, and one was the fatal bullet to the victim's head. Asked to produce the fatal slug, McQuate removed from his bag a large envelope. Three successively smaller envelopes and layers of tissue paper later, he handed the bullet to Mills for examination. After carefully doing so, the attorney disdainfully tossed it on the defense table. This sent bailiffs scrambling to retrieve it and place it in evidence. Mills meant to show his disdain for the prosecution, but his cavalier handling of the bullet that killed Mellett was seen as disrespect. He failed to appreciate the aura attached to the fatal slug. It was not a good beginning for an experienced defense lawyer.[16]

The highlight of the first day's testimony was the 1:00 appearance of Florence Mellett. Called by the prosecution as a witness, she was asked to relate her husband's movements the evening he was killed. She was also there to remind the jury that this trial was about Don Mellett's murder, not Pat McDermott's newfound celebrity. As Florence was sworn in, spectators half-rose in their seats to get a better look, and newsmen edged a bit closer. The press found her "a tiny creature" and "petite," and younger looking than expected. She was dressed entirely in black but wore no widow's veil. In a clever move by the prosecution, she sat in the witness box with her youngest daughter, four-year-old Mary Jane, on her lap. A well-mannered child, Mary Jane sat quietly smiling at the jury—and the defendant. News accounts noted that Pat did not smile back. The defense offered tepid objections to this arrangement but could not object too strenuously for risk of alienating the jury. No one in the courtroom was going to seriously challenge anything Florence Mellett did or said.[17]

Her voice a barely audible whisper (which prompted Mills to complain), Florence related the now-familiar events of the fateful evening. When she spent considerable time in describing the chocolate soda disagreement, Durand questioned the relevance of the story. He was met by an icy stare from Florence and was overruled by Judge Diehl. "I don't know why I let him go to the garage alone," was Florence's remorseful conclusion. The defense's cross-examination was brief and focused primarily on the interaction between the police and the Melletts that night. The same line of cross-examination was put to Carrie and Walter Vail, who followed Mrs. Mellett on the stand and told the same tale. The defense focused on demonstrating that animosity existed between the Mellett family and the Canton police.[18]

The first day concluded with a brief appearance by the prosecution's star witness, Steve Kascholk. Pat glared intensely at his former Nanty Glo buddy, but Steve seemed not to notice. His time in front of the jury was short, however. "Come on. I got a good job for you. Rudner wants us to go out and slug a guy tonight," was all Steve had to say, quoting Pat, before Mills and Durand were on their feet shouting protests. Judge Diehl dismissed the jury for the day, since it was almost 4:30, while the lawyers sorted it out. The defense wanted Kascholk branded a co-conspirator before his testimony was allowed in a move to diminish his credibility. The two sides exchanged heated words, and Durand, after being chastised by the judge, apologized to McClintock for questioning his integrity. The prosecutor assured Diehl that they would prove Steve was only a witness.[19]

Steve took the stand first thing Tuesday morning. Labeled a "boob," "dumb," and a "Polack," the slow-talking Kascholk was described by Fred Charles of the *Plain Dealer* as "the kind of colorless chap you'd take along on a camping trip because you'd know you could kid him into chopping all the wood and washing all the dishes." It would be pay enough to say, "Steve, you're all right." Kascholk was nervous, twisting his fingers as he testified about his visit to Canton in July with Pat McDermott. In eight hours on the stand, Steve failed to break under Mills's grueling cross-examination. Any attempt to confuse Steve merely made him back up in his response and start over in his maddeningly slow manner. Even Pat's full-bore stare failed.[20]

Mills and Durand wanted to show that Steve's main reason for coming forward was to claim the $27,000 reward. In an effort to demonstrate this to the jury, they had three letters that Steve had written while in the workhouse to his girlfriend, Mary Cherwinsky (who was the mother of his two illegitimate children). Homer Durand took on the task of reading Steve's missives to the jury. On August 12 he wrote to Mary, "There is a $27,000 reward in this case, and if this case is cleared up, it will be through my help, and the reward goes to the person who gives the best information and I happen to know the most about it. So if I make good, you will be the lucky one." In another letter Kascholk wrote, "Mary, if I get this money, I won't have to worry about getting along for I could give you enough to keep you. I expect at least $10–15,000 out of it, but, Mary please keep quiet about it. Don't even tell anybody that I wrote you this letter." How the defense came into possession of the letters was never explained, but Pat had plenty of sympathy in the workhouse, among both guards and inmates. Asked why he never wrote his legal wife, Steve said that she never contacted him.[21]

No one doubted that Steve was at least partially motivated by the reward money. After all, that was the purpose of the reward. A share of the cash would enable him to divorce his wife, a stern and unattractive woman, and marry Mary, who reporters described as "a pretty little thing, soft like a baby, with soft light hair, soft blue eyes, and soft translucent pink cheeks." The couple met in Nanty Glo, where Mary faced the disapproval of Steve's family, in part because his mother saw Mary with rouge on her cheeks. Mary and Steve's two children were staying in Canton during the trial and living on his dollar-a-day wages. Despite the hardship, she was said to be "devoted" to Steve. Steve's scandalous relationships notwithstanding, his straightforward acknowledgment of Mary and unshakable tale of a conspiracy to kill Don Mellett played well with the press and jury. His recall of the smallest details—like Ben Rudner's profanity and sore finger—amazed all observers and left Charles McClintock smiling. A *Plain Dealer* headline summed up Steve's eight hours on the witness stand with a four-word headline: "'Stupid' Steve Strong Witness."[22]

Wednesday afternoon brought ballistics engineer M. A. Robinson to the stand with all the hard evidence the prosecution had to work with. Robinson had reexamined the three bullets again just before the trial and created a stir by revising his original conclusion. The three bullets were fired from two, not three, .38 caliber revolvers, a very common weapon in the 1920s among criminals and lawmen alike. One revolver was in excellent condition, but with a rusty barrel; the other was well worn. The confusion was the result of his hasty first look at the slugs, Robinson claimed. Of the two bullets said to be from the better weapon, one was the fatal bullet and the other had been removed from the window frame. The third, picked up off the ground, was metal jacketed, of wartime manufacture, and had been fired from the worn pistol. Neither the press nor the defense raised the obvious question of whether the third, found bullet was even connected with the homicide. The Melletts rented the home and had only lived there a few weeks; what might have transpired there before they moved in was never considered. As for the prosecution, promoting the idea of a murder conspiracy involving multiple individuals was to their benefit.[23]

How many shots were really fired at Don Mellett that hot July evening? There was no clear agreement in the testimony the jury heard. The coroner counted six possible. Florence Mellett thought three. Walter Vail six or seven. Carrie Vail four. Joe Schumacher four or five. Schumacher and Bessie Zimmer both believed that they heard two men running away down the street. Based on these accounts and the physical evidence at the scene, four to six shots were probably fired, and two men were possibly involved.

The state's much-anticipated "mystery witness" also proved to be the trial's comic relief. The affable Bill Bitzler slowly told his story amid almost constant defense objections. He regaled the court with tales of his minor criminal record, his friendship with Pat, their perusal of Canton's bootleg joints, and their bragging and one-upping about fictitious past crimes. Bill's tale of purse snatching in search of liquor filled the courtroom with laughter. While most witnesses were nervous and tight-lipped on the stand, Bitzler was willing to tell more than most wanted to hear. After all, he was not a suspect, and he stood to profit from the reward. His amiable manner soon had everyone, even the defense attorneys, calling him "Bill." Even Pat managed a smile. Bill admitted he was the recipient of the stolen clothes that Pat and Steve had found under the bed in the hotel room but said he had eventually turned the clothes over to the police. Bill also denied defense allegations that he was after the reward but conceded that he was now working in Akron under the name "Blair" to avoid creditors.[24] Mrs. Bitzler followed her loquacious husband on the stand, substantiated his testimony, and identified Pat. The Bitzlers' testimony was not as damning as Steve Kascholk's, but it did place Pat in Canton the five days before the murder.[25]

Thursday morning was reserved for the appearance of the girl the press called "Pretty Peggy." Red-headed and fiery Peggy Cavanaugh strongly denied press allegations about having a romantic relationship with McDermott: "Pat and I lovers? Absolutely not!" Peggy was decked out in a brown fur-trimmed coat, green scarf, and a stylish close-fitting black hat. For Peggy's turn in the box, Pat ditched his gray suit for a navy blue one complete with handkerchief in the pocket. The male reporters and jurors gave Peggy their full attention. But three months in the workhouse had left her lifeless and unsmiling. Speaking in a monotone and biting her lip, Peggy gave automatic answers to questions about her relationship with Pat, the famous car ride to Massillon, and her lack of knowledge about the crime.[26] Everything Peggy said was substantiated by Homer Connelly, who was a much more cooperative and helpful witness.

The appearance of the prosecution's primary witnesses was interspersed by a parade of less exciting, but necessary, boardinghouse operators, hotel clerks, Cleveland police officers, telephone and telegraph operators, and neighbors of the Melletts, each of whom added a small piece to the case McClintock was methodically building against Pat McDermott. Even a traveling salesman, Mr. William Angus McDonald, whose clothes were stolen, put in an appearance to identify them.[27] The last witness for the prosecution was William Brumme, a German-born hardware salesman who frequented the

Rudner hardware and auto parts emporium in Massillon. Brumme testified that he had twice seen Chief Lengel in Rudner's Massillon store. This proved nothing but did succeed in casting suspicion on the former police chief.

The state rested at 9:23 A.M. on Saturday morning after presenting a parade of fifty-two witnesses whose testimony was meant not only to convict Pat McDermott but to lay the groundwork for the upcoming conspiracy trials of Mazer and Rudner. But would it be enough, since in reality their case was entirely circumstantial? There were no witnesses who saw McDermott shoot Don Mellett, none who could even place him at the scene of the crime. Perhaps that was why a smiling Pat answered a reporter's question about how he would account for his activities on July 16 by saying: "I won't have to tell that. By that time it won't be necessary."[28]

The prosecution's case completed, the defense wasted no time. The strategy was simple: provide an alibi for anyone the state said was even remotely connected to McDermott. In a short Saturday session, Everett Mills and Homer Durand presented a parade of nine witnesses, all meant to provide an alibi for Ben Rudner. Although he may not have realized it, Pat McDermott was a stand-in for Mills's primary client, Rudner. If Pat was acquitted, the state's entire conspiracy theory was doomed; if he was convicted, Mills had already laid the foundation for Rudner's defense. Everyone could see the defense strategy—except perhaps Pat.

The star witness that Saturday morning was Mrs. Sarah Rudner, Ben's wife of ten years. Seen by the press as pretty, quiet, and of obvious refinement, Sarah Rudner, her deep auburn hair hidden under a stylish tight blue turban, had a clear devotion to her husband. Camera shy, she had earlier fled the courtroom pursued by photographers wanting a picture of the bootlegger's wife. "Ben would never have permitted anybody to annoy me so," Sarah complained. Nervously jerking her head as she took the oath, Mills asked if the popping flashbulbs bothered her. Yes, she said they did, and Judge Diehl was happy to put a stop to it. Mrs. Rudner's story was that of a young couple who lost two children in infancy, suffered through Ben's imprisonment in Atlanta, and now lived modestly as legitimate businessmen within the family hardware empire (even Sarah worked in the hardware store). Led by Mills, she gave a detailed account of Ben's activities on July 8, 9, and 26, days the state asserted he met with Pat McDermott. Sarah Rudner stood by her man, even recounting Ben's travails with an infected finger on the 8th and 9th.[29]

Cross-examination fell to Harter, who needed to show it was all a ruse. He did this carefully, questioning Sarah's excellent, but selective, memory. How could she be so certain about specific days and times yet so unsure about others? No satisfactory answer to these rhetorical questions was really expected from the witness. Harter's questioning was for the benefit of the jury.[30]

Rudner's alibi parade continued with a steady stream of friends, relatives, and hardware store employees. Ben's brother, Eddie, once arrested for bootlegging but now running a store in Dover, Ohio, was presented as a verbal and visual alibi for his brother. Bearing a modest resemblance to Pat, Eddie claimed it was he with Ben when earlier witnesses said it could have been Pat. This line of defense was continued to the point of having Eddie dress like Pat and asking witnesses to identify him. It worked and succeeded in defusing prosecution attempts to place Rudner and McDermott together.[31]

There was more of the same when the trial continued on Monday morning. Nearly every hour of Ben Rudner's life on July 8 and 9 was accounted for by one witness or another. By now the jury was certainly wondering who was being defended, Pat McDermott or Ben Rudner. Some interesting testimony did come from Harry L. Van Gutten, a Canton city bus driver, who claimed that Steve Kascholk rode his bus alone out to Mellett's neighborhood on July 10. However, cross-examination by the prosecution revealed that in May Van Gutten had sold Louis Mazer a .38 caliber Smith and Wesson revolver designed to fire metal-jacketed bullets along with a handful of cartridges, all for $20.[32]

In an attempt to break the chain of circumstantial evidence linking Pat to Ben, the defense placed Ben's brother-in-law, Jack Greenburg, on the stand. Telephone company records for July 26, when Pat made his trip to Massillon with Cavanaugh and Connelly, were introduced as evidence that showed a "Mr. Jones" placed a collect call from Beck's Deli to Ben Rudner that evening. Greenburg claimed that it was he who called Ben and denied using the name "Jones." On cross-examination, McClintock confronted Greenburg with the telephone record of the call from the deli at 7:00 that evening.

"Is that your call?" the prosecutor demanded.

"No!" Greenburg emphatically denied.

McClintock had him. "Did you ever look up the records, and notice there was only one call from Beck's to Massillon on July 26?"

It was not just Greenburg caught in this trap, but also Mills and Durand for not doing their homework and checking Greenburg's story before putting him on the stand. Harter later told reporters that Greenburg had "perjured himself to save the lowest type of man."[33]

Spectators and reporters were surprised—and disappointed—by the appearance of ousted police chief S. A. "Ed" Lengel as a witness for the defense. Lengel acknowledged being acquainted with Rudner since the bootlegger's youth. The former chief admitted that the two talked before and after the murder and that during his suspension in March he had visited Rudner in Massillon—just once, to pass the time.[34]

The star witness, and one who could actually speak to defendant Pat McDermott, was boardinghouse proprietor Hattie Gearhart. A very large woman, she was so infirm that she couldn't climb into the witness box; instead, she was allowed to sit in a chair facing the jury. Hattie claimed that McDermott returned to her Cleveland Avenue house at 10:30 the night of the murder and couldn't possibly have left again without her knowledge. According to her, someone returned to the rooming house at 10:30 P.M. Gearhart said she asked, "Is that you, Johnny?" "No," was the only response. She assumed it was McDermott, who she knew as Charles Thompson. She heard two shoes hit the floor and concluded that the boarder had gone to bed. Pressed by McClintock on cross-examination, she conceded that she hadn't actually seen Thompson's face that night. Nevertheless, she was unshakable, mumbling under cross-examination, "I swear to God I'm telling you the truth!" Hattie Gearhart's testimony was headline news.

December 21 was the shortest day of that year but the trial's longest, as Judge Diehl pressed for a verdict by Christmas. The defense put both Tom McDermott and J. J. O'Rourke on the stand in an attempt to get into the record allegations that Pat was offered immunity if he would turn state's evidence. Suggesting that the prosecution double-crossed Pat, Mills challenged, "If McClintock was honorable and above board, he shouldn't be ashamed of what this witness will testify to," referring to brother Tom. Judge Diehl refused to admit testimony regarding any alleged deals. The defense lost the fight. About all the two McDermott family witnesses could say was that they recalled Steve Kascholk's story as being less polished and that Steve said Pat had a .45 caliber pistol, not a .38. McClintock drew admissions from both that they had visited Pat while he was hiding in Cleveland and that Pat purchased clothing on his sister Alice O'Rourke's account. Both men were fortunate not to be charged with aiding a fugitive.[35]

Ben Rudner wasn't the only one in need of an alibi. Louis Mazer got help from two former business partners, Louis Heller and Jack Dixon. Both men claimed that Mazer was hanging around the poolroom playing cards and helping out on July 9, when he was accused of driving Pat and Steve around, and again on July 15, the evening of the murder.[36] But Mazer's primary alibi witnesses were no surprise. Dismissed Canton police detective Floyd Streitenberger and his wife, Kate, now residing in Dayton, were entertaining neighbors at home the evening of the crime. Both stated that Mazer was sitting in his car in front of their home until 12:45 A.M. Streitenberger said he went out and talked to Mazer but did not invite him inside. Later, two of the guests, W. D. Craft and W. H. Young, confirmed the presence of Mazer's car.[37] In cross-examination, McClintock attacked Streitenberger's credibility. When asked why he was dismissed from the police force, Streitenberger responded, "They asked me to resign, and I refused, and they preferred charges." Next the prosecutor questioned that odd interview the former detective gave to a reporter in Buffalo, especially the claim that he barely knew Mazer. Streitenberger said he was misquoted.[38]

Mrs. Steve Kascholk also appeared as a defense witness. She claimed to have been married to Steve for almost three years. She said that Steve left her after three months, but she stayed on in Nanty Glo and bore him a son, Theo. She had Steve arrested for nonsupport and the Mary Cherwinsky affair, and he was jailed from November 1925 to

May 1926. She claimed that Steve wanted her to come to Cleveland in mid-June when he had a job washing dishes, but she refused. From a defense standpoint, Mrs. Kascholk's job was to paint as unflattering a picture of the state's star witness as possible. So far, Steve seemed to be a sympathetic character to the press, and his plain, humorless, vindictive wife failed to tarnish his image.[39]

On Wednesday, December 22, Ben Rudner and Louis Mazer took the witness stand. There to help Pat's defense on the surface—but really to defend themselves—their appearance alone was enough to cause the defendant to lose his half-mocking nonchalance. Pat listened intently to every word of testimony, his face flushed and veins in his forehead prominent.[40]

Louis Mazer was first. Speaking in an even, barely audible monotone, the thirty-two-year-old Canton native was a strong, unshakable witness. He flatly denied the accusation by the prostitute, Thelma Harris, that he had a gun the evening before the murder. (When the defense tried to recall Harris, she could not be found.) Asked if he knew Pat McDermott, Mazer replied, "I never saw him in my life." Asked the same question about Steve Kascholk, Mazer was emphatic that he first saw the star witness in the Cleveland federal building in August. As for the revolver he bought from Van Gutten, Louis Mazer said it had been stolen from under the seat of his Hudson.[41] He was at the poolroom on July 8 and 15 instructing the new owners about the business. At midnight he went to Streitenbergers'. Although Mazer admitted visiting Mellett at the *Daily News* per Chief Lengel's advice, he denied threatening the Melletts. He readily admitted to bootlegging and living in a brothel, but he hotly denied having any part in the murder. He also claimed that Kascholk identified him in Cleveland only because investigators had pointed him out.[42]

Then came Ben Rudner's turn. Neatly dressed, his hair slicked back, a faint smile on his lips, Rudner told in great detail the same story of his July activities already provided by his wife and associates. This included his trouble with an infected finger. Only rare flashes of temper marred his performance of doing nothing more than working in his family business. When asked, "Do you know this man McDermott?"

he replied, "No, Sir, I do not." The press felt that in the main Rudner gave a clear and perfectly definitive account of himself.[43]

When the prosecution's turn came at questioning Ben Rudner, McClintock scrutinized the inventory sheets placed in evidence by the defense purporting to support Ben's alibi that part of his time in question was spent doing store inventories. When asked about the famous R. L. Strang telegram, Rudner denied authorship. McClintock handed Ben a blank Western Union form and had him write the message verbatim. A confident Mills offered to make the copy a defense exhibit. (Later the prosecutor had Ben brought back to court to spell "Thompson" correctly.) The stage was set for the battle of the handwriting experts.

The press credited the prosecutor with scoring a shot in the dark when he asked Ben if he knew Cleveland bootlegger Ben Nadel, who had been indicted for hiding Pat. With little effort, McClintock made Ben admit that Nadel was his cell mate in Atlanta. Rudner denied having any contact with Nadel since. (Nadel was refusing to talk to investigators.) He also denied knowing McDermott in Atlanta. In an effort to damage Rudner's credibility, the prosecutor reviewed Rudner's criminal record of assault, robbery, and bootlegging. Rudner's excellent memory deserted him when McClintock wondered if Rudner, who insisted that friends join him in a long, rambling drive around Stark County that evening, had noticed all the activity in Mellett's neighborhood after midnight July 16. After all, Tuscarawas was a major thoroughfare, and Rudner's father only lived a few blocks away. "I didn't notice them, no," was his response.[44]

December 23 marked the long-awaited appearance of Pat McDermott on the witness stand. Upon entering the witness box at 9:42 A.M., and at Durand's urging, Pat turned and grinned at the assembled photographers as the flashbulbs popped. Mills wasted no time in getting to the point: "Do you know Steve Kascholk?" Suffering from a bad cough, Pat replied in a husky voice, "I know him." And off the defense went, leading McDermott through his version of events in July while maintaining the overall defense theme that the defendant was framed by McClintock and Slater. The courtroom was packed, including Florence Mellett, who attended, as she had every day, only this time she brought her four children—a not-too-subtle reminder of what this trial was about.

For an hour the defense walked Pat through his story, which began with meeting Steve in Cleveland and then going to Massillon to look for work and then moving on to Canton. Pat claimed that it was Kascholk's proposition that they beat up Mellett for a mysterious fellow called "Smitty," to which Pat purportedly exclaimed, "Are you crazy?" He said that the last time he saw Steve was July 10 in the company of two other unknown men. Between July 10 and 15 he said he loafed around Canton waiting for something to turn up. On the night of the murder, he went to a movie and then to bed at 10:30 P.M. When he got the Strang telegram the next morning, he told the court that he immediately thought it was from Steve and went to Cleveland. Pat said that he went to Massillon on July 26 with Peggy and Homer to try to find Steve. When he learned that he was wanted, he went into hiding. He refused to say where he was or who helped him until late August, when Nadal and Pfaff hid him. Pat not only denied telephoning Rudner July 21 and 26, he claimed not to know Rudner at all. He said that it was he who called Mellett to warn him, that he spoke to a lady between 8:00 and 9:00 the Saturday evening preceding the murder. Pat claimed to have called Don Mellett to "tell him there is something coming off tonight." Pat's motivation for making warning calls to the publisher was never adequately explained, even in the light of subsequent events.[45]

The remainder of Pat's time in the dock was spent under relentless cross-examination by McClintock. Getting right up in McDermott's face and thumping the witness box for emphasis, the prosecutor made his questions personal, despite Harter imploring him, theatrically, to move back for his own safety. McClintock quickly got under the defendant's skin, reducing Pat to half-whispered, savage retorts to his inquisitor's questions. The press likened Pat to a sullen schoolboy. Pat's replies drew reprimands from the judge, followed by protests from the defense. Denying all prosecution allegations and contradicting their witnesses, McDermott complained, "They're framing me!" Of onetime pal Bill Bitzler's testimony, Pat shouted, "It's a lie!"[46]

Reverting to a monotone, McClintock methodically drew from Pat the story of his conviction by army court martial for stealing from a warehouse and his subsequent escape from the guard house. The defendant claimed he was only under unguarded arrest and that his escape was a misunderstanding. He claimed a general court martial only convicted him on one of thirty-six counts and did not deny his twenty-seven months spent in Atlanta's federal prison beginning February 1, 1922. After his release, Pat said he worked as a sign painter in Boston and as a barber in Toledo, Atlanta, and Nanty Glo. He denied knowing Ben Nagel in Atlanta. He said he arrived in Cleveland only a week before first meeting Kascholk.[47]

The prosecution's constant verbal hammering took its toll; Pat became more confused in his answers. Asked about the telephone call he made from Beck's Deli outside of Akron, he first refused to admit making a call, then claimed it was to a girl and then to Steve in a Massillon poolroom. How did he get the phone number in Massillon? McClintock demanded. From the phone directory, Pat replied. The clever prosecutor was quick to point out that Massillon numbers were not in the Akron directory. McDermott's worst moment on the stand came when the prosecution asked him whether he had ever been in jail for robbery in York, Pennsylvania. The defendant denied it emphatically. Slowly and methodically, McClintock returned to the question time and again during his cross-examination. Each time McDermott denied being jailed. Finally, the prosecution produced a letter from jailers in York describing Pat and his family in detail.[48] Checkmated, McDermott concluded his testimony for the day.

For a professional defendant like McDermott, it was a terrible performance that courtroom observers agreed left an unfavorable impression on the jury. His legal team had just watched their client scuttle their well-planned defense. They had no more witnesses and scarcely a thing to add. Outmaneuvered by a prosecution with only a circumstantial case, Pat McDermott's defense rested. Ora Slater never took the stand, for either side. "He has hung himself," McClintock said of McDermott's testimony as the day concluded.[49]

Rebuttal arguments lasted a full day and featured dull and lengthy presentations by dueling handwriting experts over who actually wrote the original Strang telegram received by the defendant. The state presented Dr. Harry Jenkins of Cleveland, a self-proclaimed expert in nervous disorders and handwriting. Dr. Jenkins presented a mind-numbing lecture on his credentials, the evidence, and how handwriting traits relate to personality. His long-anticipated conclusion was that Ben Rudner wrote the telegram. At this point, Mills prompted a series of feisty exchanges concerning Jenkins's compensation, motives, and possibility of error. These verbal battles tried Judge Diehl's patience, and he threatened an evening session if the trial continued to drag on.[50]

Not to be outdone, the defense had its own handwriting expert, George W. Pengalley. To no one's surprise, Pengalley concluded that Rudner was not the telegram's author. On cross-examination, Harter asked if this might not be the result of an attempt to disguise the handwriting by Rudner. "Yes, it frequently happens," Pengalley replied. In the end, handwriting analysis proved of no use to either side.[51]

Finally, at 10:15 A.M., Friday, December 24, closing arguments began, with each side allotted two hours to summarize its case for the jury. Prosecutor-elect Harter led off for the state. In rhetorical hyperbole, he said the fusillade of shots fired at Don Mellett were "aimed at the freedom of our press, and without which our institutions cannot stand," and declared, "It is a matter of war. It must stop or America is not safe." He depicted Mellett as a "young, virile editor whose only faults were courage and honesty." When he described the murdered publisher lying in a pool of blood, three men in the jury brushed tears away. (The three women, press reports noted, stayed dry-eyed.) Mrs. Mellett and her four children listened intently. Harter's most quotable statement came when he said Ben Rudner was a "smart aleck wolf, he is the big fellow"; Louis Mazer, the man who supposedly wouldn't hurt anybody, was "a slinking fox"; and Pat McDermott was "the jackal who has done their dirty work for them." With this, Harter provided the papers with a ready-made headline. He summarized the state's case against the defendant asserting that both McDermott and Mazer were triggermen. Admitting that the state's case was circumstantial, Harter asserted that these are often the strongest sort of cases because of the volume of solid evidence required. Harter closed by telling the jury, "If this man [McDermott] is guilty, he is guilty of the most dastardly, cowardly crime in the Decalogue. He is the hired assassin who takes life for money." He ended his remarks just before the noon recess.[52]

Homer Durand was first for the defense, finally displaying his oratorical talents in the closing arguments. But no matter how great his skill, Durand had the difficult task of making the co-conspirators look like upstanding citizens. He charged that the state's case was constructed by the five "ferrets," as he called them: Ora Slater, his assistant C. B. Armstrong, postal inspector Captain Owen, Columbus detective H. B. Burton, and Governor Donahey's man Joseph D. Cleary. Attacking the sincerity of the prosecution, Durand pointed to Mrs. Mellett and said, "That little widow doesn't want a sacrificial goat offered up for the murder. She wants justice." As for Steve Kascholk, he predicted that "within six months Kascholk will be charged with the murder of Mellett." There was, he suggested, very little connection between Mellett's newspaper crusade and his slaying—something no one in Canton believed. As for Pat McDermott, Durand told the jury that he shook Pat's hand every morning and was convinced that it was not a red hand dripping with blood. He ridiculed the idea that Pat would kill for a mere $200. "Think of it, an Irishman" standing 200 feet away to start a fight. Continuing to play on ethnic stereotypes, Durand called Mazer a "soft-spoken, inoffensive type of Jew who lived with a Magdalene" (a biblical reference to his prostitute girlfriend). Concluding with an allusion to the death penalty, Durand reminded the jury of what execution was like: "A life, perhaps an innocent life, is sent hurtling into eternity with an accompaniment of burning hair and flesh." He then told the packed courtroom, "I'd want more evidence . . . to send a man to that little white room in the big gray building to be electrocuted."[53]

Everett Mills was next, and he proclaimed that the defense had "met every issue of this case." For Mills, Bill Bitzler was the biggest liar he'd seen in twenty-one years of practice. This case, he told the jury, was not about silencing the press, which could be both constructive and devilish at times. Florence Mellett wept as Mills told the jury that nothing could excuse the dastardly murder of Don Mellett: "I am as sorry for Mrs. Mellett and her fatherless children as anyone can be, but that must not sway me or you in sending this man to the chair on the day when the spirit of love is abroad in the world—on Christmas Day."[54]

The honor of the last remarks to the jury went to Charles Mc-Clintock. Striding back and forth in front of the jury, the prosecutor stopped suddenly and turned to McDermott and shook his finger, shouting, "This man lied to you! Don Mellett would have given his family a happy Christmas, but you murdered him!"[55] Pat stared back, his face flushed, his cheek propped against a clenched fist. McClintock told the jury that not all the murderers had been found yet. As far as this case was concerned, he said, the Canton Police Department had "a bad odor." "When you murder an editor, you are murdering civilization and society," he lectured the jury. McDermott had no mercy in killing Mellett and deserved none from the jury. The final verdict, he said, should "serve notice to law violators that murder in Canton will be punished." It was a powerful performance, and when McClintock was finished, eight jurors were left weeping or wiping away tears.[56]

All that remained was for Judge Diehl's charge to the jury. Spectators were offered the chance to depart, but most chose to stay. The judge began with an abbreviated law lesson on reasonable doubt and circumstantial evidence. "Circumstances taken here and there must fit to make a proof or a deduction that is reasonably certain and beyond reasonable doubt." Last he listed the possible verdicts: first-degree murder as charged, which carried the death penalty; first-degree murder with mercy, which carried a life sentence; second-degree murder, which carried a life sentence with possibility of parole; manslaughter, which carried a sentence of up to twenty years in prison; and, of course, not guilty. At 4:29 P.M. on Christmas Eve, he handed the case over to the jury. Now it was up to those twelve residents of Stark County who had listened patiently to the evidence.

Considering the hour, most of the players, including Pat McDermott, went to dinner. But just fifty minutes later, at 5:43, the jury was back with a verdict. A surprised defendant blurted out, "Gee, they were fast." With the faint tinkle of Salvation Army kettle bells audible in the background, foreman Bert H. Sweitzer rose to read the jury's decision to a nearly empty courtroom. "We have found the defendant,

Patrick Eugene McDermott, guilty." A pause. "And we do recommend mercy." Many of the jurors with children Pat's age wept. Pat, his face cupped in his hands, reddened but showed some sign of slight relief.[57]

Florence Mellett and her children were at dinner in their hotel dining room when the jury came in. Tracked down by reporters, she commented, "I feel that justice has been served. I have never had a desire for vengeance as such. But to permit the escape of those who slew my husband would have been to fail him in the work he as an editor had attempted."[58]

Most observers felt that Pat's testimony sealed his fate. Prosecutor McClintock said afterward, "He was his most damaging witness." Mc-Dermott's conduct as an unruly adolescent alienated the jury, none of whom made any significant post-trial statements. A few days later, Pat himself admitted the obvious: "I made a fool of myself on the witness stand. But, gee, everybody was telling lies on the stand, and I thought I'd tell my share. I guess I didn't do it very well either." Pressed by reporters about whether he would tell all he knew now, Pat was vague. Maybe he'd wait, or maybe once he got to the penitentiary he'd change his mind.[59]

"That's that," was Louis Mazer's comment when told of the verdict back in the workhouse. His friends urged him to do whatever he could to save himself, whether it hurt Rudner's case or not. The prosecution made it clear that they intended to continue to pressure Mazer. Meanwhile, Ben Rudner, when told of the verdict, commented, "The hell they did. That's tough, ain't it."[60]

On Christmas Day, Pat McDermott, once the center of nationwide attention, had only one visitor, Everett Mills, who dropped off a basket with turkey and all the fixings. Mills promised to launch every appeal of Pat's conviction he could, something he never did. Tom Mc-Dermott left Canton to tell his mother Pat's fate. He never spoke to his younger brother again. In the days following the end of the trial, before his transfer to the Ohio Penitentiary in Columbus, McDermott resumed his self-satisfied demeanor. According to workhouse superintendent John Boyer, "this chap takes his place as one of the coolest and cleverest criminals in the country."[61]

The verdict was national news the day after Christmas. The *New*

York Times, which had been carrying daily reports of the trial's progress, gave the verdict a bold, front-page headline: "McDermott Guilty; Jurors Urge Mercy." There was no editorial comment, however. *Editor and Publisher* on January 1 said of McDermott's conviction, "The first chapter in the prosecution of Mellett's slayers has been concluded." The press trade journal went on to remind its readers, "The murder of Don R. Mellett was intended to serve notice on newspaper editors to keep silent against obvious misconduct. Instead, the murder has aroused newspapers to further vigilance."

Charles McClintock received hundreds of congratulatory telegrams from around the country. Previously dismissed as "a small town lawyer," McClintock had gambled big on a trial based on circumstantial evidence provided by sketchy characters and won. Using a baseball analogy, *Plain Dealer* reporter Fred Charles wrote that the prosecutor had "batted out of the crime bushes." Charles went on to sing McClintock's praises in a front-page article on Sunday, December 26, pointing out that he had bested the more famous "Chicago Roach." The article concluded that "the ex-boy prosecutor will be worth watching."[62]

Not all the letters McClintock received were congratulatory. Two anonymous letters containing death threats arrived bearing Canton postmarks. Judge Diehl received one from Cleveland warning him "not to punish Pat." The prosecutor's home was placed under twenty-four-hour guard. And threats to break McDermott out of jail or kill him were also received, requiring extra guards.[63]

Peggy Cavanaugh was released from the workhouse by McClintock on a personal recognizance bond on December 30. She picked up a county check for $120 and hurried to Cleveland. Of her four-month stay in the workhouse she said, "I hope I never see Canton again." Steve Kascholk remained in the workhouse; more trials were to follow.[64]

An editorial in the *Plain Dealer* on Christmas Day offered that "the detection and trial were to test the question whether in a civilized state the publisher of a newspaper could ever hope for immunity from murderous attack if he had the courage to uncover vice and corruption." It called the verdict the "first fruit of Canton's effort to redeem herself."[65]

The Rich Man Faces a Jury

With Pat McDermott destined to spend the rest of his life in the Ohio Penitentiary,[1] the state turned its attention to the man Henry Harter called the "smart aleck wolf" of the evil threesome, Ben Rudner. The decision to try Rudner next delayed Louis Mazer's trial once again. This may have been a strategic error. Mazer could see the direction Stark County justice was taking and might now have been induced to talk if his trial for first-degree murder was imminent. Unlike hardened ex-convicts Rudner and McDermott, who would never talk, Mazer was seen as less resolute; a little more serious pressure and he might break. However, Harter was prosecutor now; it was his decision who to try next, and he chose Rudner.

Ben Rudner's trial was scheduled to begin in early February 1927. Once again, Everett Mills was lead defense counsel, and this time he also tried to get a venue change based on extensive press coverage in Canton. This idea failed to gain any traction with the judge this time around too. Mills was partially successful when Judge Kirtchbaum was replaced as presiding judge, his objection being that Kirtchbaum, who had been appointed by Governor James Cox, was close to Don Mellett's friend and attorney, former judge H. C. Pontius.[2] The new judge for

Rudner's trial would be Abram W. Agler, a Republican appointed to the bench in 1923. A native of Wilmot, Ohio, and alumnus of Mount Union College and Ohio State University's law school, Agler was elected Stark County Clerk of Courts in 1908 and served until 1912. He was known as a tireless worker, busy lawyer, and award-winning orchardist. For this trial, Agler was given temporary use of Judge Diehl's large courtroom. Perhaps at Diehl's urging, one of Agler's first acts was to ban photographers from the courtroom.[3]

Ben Rudner's day in court was scheduled to begin Monday, February 7, at 9:15 A.M. The week before, fifty-six summonses went out to potential jurors. Ben Rudner liked being in the center of things, and the role of defendant in a murder trial certainly offered that opportunity. So Ben must have been a bit disappointed when only a small crowd of spectators and reporters was present when court opened that Monday morning for jury selection. It was the same drab courtroom with only two large windows to the east and two to the west to admit February's limited color and light. A row of spectator chairs remained empty all morning, and the only female in the small crowd was Mrs. Anna Rudner Rubin, Ben's sister. By noon, however, things were looking up as the crowd in the corridor had grown to McDermott proportions, and a hundred or so press and onlookers were admitted for the afternoon session before deputies closed and locked the doors.

Lead defender Mills had help in the form of out-of-town hired gun George Gordon Battle, whose role on the defense team was, like Durand's, kept a secret until just a week before the trial. The prosecution was the same, only now Henry Harter was county prosecutor and Charles McClintock was his special assistant. Never mind the reversal of titles, this was clearly McClintock's case.

Ben Rudner looked younger than his thirty years. He had gained weight during his incarceration and was described as "opulent" by the press and nicknamed "Big Ben." He appeared unworried, laughing, joking, and paying particular attention to the answers of the defense's primary question of prospective jurors: "Do you belong to any associations whose attitude is unfavorable toward members of the Hebrew race?"[4] Family patriarch Max Rudner sat at the defense table with his son. Max Rudner had begun as a junk dealer, but through hard work had risen to prominence in Canton as a hardware merchant. In 1912 he had testified against police corruption in the firing of police chief Billy Smith. He was essentially an honest man.[5] Unfortunately, his son had chosen another path in life. When Ben showed an early propensity for trouble, Max shipped him off to military school for a brief stint. When his son was in trouble with the law, Max hired the best lawyers, and when Ben was released from federal prison, his father gave him a position in the hardware business.

This time around the prosecution did not ask candidates about their feelings on the death penalty, perhaps in recognition that this case was weaker than the one against Pat McDermott. The state's case was based solely on Steve Kascholk's testimony and telephone records. No wonder Ben Rudner was laughing and claiming this was all a frame-up by the *Daily News* and its private investigator, H. B. Burton.

Both sides spent less time on legal skirmishes during jury selection than in December, and by 1:30 P.M. Wednesday, the full jury was seated. Not all the challenges were used, the state leaving one and the defense five. Ben's jury of his peers was composed of seven men and five women and one female alternate. This time around the defense wanted women on the jury. Again, these thirteen Stark residents would be the guests of the county at the Northern Hotel.[6]

The press anticipated that the workings of the Cleveland-Canton bootlegging ring would be exposed. Of the state's list of forty-nine potential witnesses, half were Clevelanders. This interested the Cleveland reporters as much as who killed Don Mellett. Included on the list were McDermott acquaintances Peggy Cavanaugh, Thelma Harris, and Kitty Barnes from the Hough neighborhood of Cleveland. So were the Stanley Slagles and Dan Pfaff, who had testified against Ben Nadel and the Cleveland bootlegging ring. Not called was Nadel himself, who had been convicted of hiding Pat but was free pending appeal.[7] Without delay, Judge Agler sent the jury out to visit the murder scene that afternoon and then had them go on to Massillon. Ben declined to make the trip, raising the question of whether he ever visited the site of the murder.

Mills's opening remarks on Thursday morning, February 10, the first day of testimony, revealed the defense strategy as being similar to that used in McDermott's trial. "Mellett's death resulted from his conduct as editor" because "he made a great many enemies by publishing his better articles," while he "never published a word against Ben Rudner." If that failed, the defense was prepared to fall back on a claim of anti-Semitism.[8]

Coroner McQuate was the first witness for the state. He was followed in rapid succession by Dr. Guy Maxwell, Leo Schumacher, and Patrolman Clarence Pollack. Florence Mellett was the fifth prosecution witness. At her appearance, the spectators quieted, the judge stopped rustling papers, telegraphers rested their keys, no one coughed, and two gum-chewing jurors ceased. Alone in the witness box, seated on the edge of the chair and staring at the floor, Florence spoke in a low but clear voice. Ben was attentive as she repeated the story of her husband's slaying. Neither Florence nor any of the first four witnesses were cross-examined by the defense. The lack of legal wrangling and fighting had reporters commenting on the air of urbane gentility that had been a hallmark of the trial thus far.[9]

But late Thursday afternoon, Steve Kascholk took the stand, and that air of civility evaporated. Steve was showing the strain of his months-long confinement. Very thin, almost emaciated, with prominent cheekbones and a wan complexion, he was battling a rasping cough.[10] His answers to the prosecution's questions were even slower and more plodding than they had been in December. When asked to identify Ben Rudner, whom he hadn't seen since July 9, Steve took a suspense-filled minute before pointing him out in the courtroom. Steve's story was the same as in December, but this time he concentrated more on the Rudner connection. Led by prosecutors, Kascholk recalled being introduced to Ben by Pat as "another jailbird." Ben lauded Pat, Steve recalled, calling him the "whitest man ever walked" and saying that Pat "had more guts than any." And, importantly, Steve also remembered that Ben Rudner had a bandaged finger.[11]

Now was the time for the man from Manhattan, George Gordon Battle, to earn his fee. The kind of high-priced, high-profile attorney only a rich man could afford, Battle had a deeply lined face, white eyebrows, and an obviously refined nature, at least by Canton's standards. The press corps immediately pegged him as a gentleman and accorded him a rare respect not afforded members of the local bar association. Battle was in Canton primarily to break Steve Kascholk's story, something Mills had failed to do during McDermott's trial. Battle's strategy was to ask his questions in no logical order, addressing them to the jury and not Steve, and to present his queries as fact—all to confuse the presumably slow-witted witness. Steve admitted to two arrests for abandoning his wife, to fathering illegitimate children, and to his need for the reward money. Battle's aggressive questioning left Kascholk "befuddled" but his testimony unshaken.[12] Steve's reward for his solid performance on the witness stand was a little more freedom in the county workhouse; he would be moved to the larger chapel where he was able to talk to the guards.

Following Steve was Bill Bitzler, who repeated his tale of hanging out with Pat McDermott in July. Both Mills and Battle attempted to discredit Bitzler by bring out his arrest record and questioning his motives for testifying. But Bill stuck to his story and his motivation of placing personal protection above the reward money. Mills failed to shake Bitzler. The trial was moving along at a good speed. At 3:00 the trial adjourned until Monday. It was now clear that Pat McDermott would not be called to testify.

The next witness for the prosecution took the stand on Monday morning, February 14. German-born hardware salesman William Brumme told the court that he saw former police chief S. A. Lengel in Ben Rudner's hardware store in Massillon twice during 1926. More interesting, Brumme said that he was introduced to Pat McDermott by Rudner in early July as "another unfortunate fellow who served with me in Atlanta." Brumme testified that he and Rudner weren't linked strictly by the hardware business. They were partners in a dog-breeding scheme that began when Rudner got Brumme to purchase a German shepherd bitch and puppies from a breeder in Mansfield, Ohio. Rudner then told Brumme he couldn't pay for them, and the German kept the dogs. Instead, Ben offered to try to sell the dogs and take a commission. Unfortunately, by this time, Ben was under suspicion in the Mellett murder, and no one would even buy a dog from him. Brumme said that when Detective Floyd Streitenberger told Mazer he wanted a German shepherd, the bootlegger bought one of Brumme's for him—the animal that became part of Streitenberger and Mazer's sick dog alibi.

Not unexpectedly, Brumme came in for fierce cross-examination by a "vehement" Mills and a calmer Battle, who preferred rapid-fire questions delivered in a gentle voice.[13] When asked why he hadn't mentioned meeting Pat in Rudner's during the trial in December, Brumme asserted that he tried but the judge told him to just answer the questions he was asked. Pressed by the defense, Brumme conceded that he had been arrested for assaulting both his brother and mother-in-law. In the end, the former German sailor proved a tough nut and withstood the attacks of the defense. He had proven that someone other than Steve Kascholk saw Pat and Ben together before the murder.

Attesting to Ben's reputation as a tough guy was Massillon druggist Stanley A. Baltzly. Ben had a habit of hanging out in Baltzly's drugstore, where, in early July, the druggist complained to him that he'd not been paid for a camera he sold to someone. The ever-helpful Ben offered the services of two "friends" who were coming to town, who he said could beat up the recalcitrant customer. Baltzly wisely declined the offer. The druggist also claimed that in casual conversation just before Mellett's slaying, Ben had told him there would be "big doings in Canton."[14]

Dr. Harry Jenkins made a return appearance on Tuesday afternoon and testified for four long hours on handwriting analysis. According to the *Plain Dealer*, "Jurors looked on vaguely; one or two appeared interested."[15] The state then offered a second expert, George Woods of Pittsburgh, who, not surprisingly, concurred with Jenkins's determination that Ben was the author of the R. L. Strang telegram.

On Wednesday, February 16, the trial was delayed in the morning when Clevelanders Dan Pfaff and Stanley Slagle were late in appearing. Both were arrested the evening before on bootlegging charges. Released on bail, Pfaff told the court with a smile, "We were arrested for possession of a still in Euclid village. But of course, we did not own it." Pfaff told the jury he met Pat McDermott through Ben Nadel, who paid the bills for Pat's lodging first at Catherine Barnes's boardinghouse and then at Stanley Slagle's apartment. Pfaff also said Pat McDermott told him that "Mazer may have squawked, but Ben Rudner never would."[16] He reported that Pat also said that if he could get a .45 pistol to Massillon, he would have an alibi for the murder. Slagle's testimony confirmed what Pfaff had said. The defense team did not cross-examine the witnesses, saying that they were not interested in evidence or testimony given concerning events after the murder, claiming it was inadmissible, which later proved a significant error. With Slagle the last witness, the state rested its case at 1:42 P.M. amid rumors that the defense had no plan of action or any subpoenaed witnesses.

The defense, it turned out, had plenty of witnesses eager to testify without subpoenas. The first that afternoon were their two handwriting experts, William Pengalley of Columbus and John Friendly of St. Louis. Both told the jury that while there were similarities between the script on the telegram and Ben's writing, it was not a match. (Pengelly did inject some unintentional humor into this dry subject when he informed the jury, in explaining the room for variation, that there were twenty-six capital and twenty-six lower-case letters in the alphabet.)

The defense strategy for saving Ben Rudner that would emerge in the days ahead was a simple one: deny everything and provide alibis for everyone. Mrs. Sarah Rudner was first to take the stand. In a soft voice, and following Battle's lead, she gave the most complete account of Ben Rudner's movements on July 8 and 9 presented in either trial. When she finished, there were tears in her eyes. As Harter began his cross-examination, she broke down for a minute, weeping. She composed herself, straightened, and answered each of Harter's gentle and polite questions willingly. After Sarah Rudner left the stand, a line of ten other witnesses corroborated parts of her account.

Former chief of police S. A. Lengel appeared as a defense witness, much as he did in December for McDermott. Lengel told the jury that he had known Rudner since he was a boy but had only been to Rudner's in Massillon once. Lengel claimed it was he who arrested Ben in 1921 when he was wanted on federal charges. (Lengel's assertion was later challenged by other police officers but resolved when it was discovered that Rudner was arrested twice in 1921.) He said that Rudner called him at about 4:00 A.M. the morning of the crime to ask about it and then made the drive to Canton to see Lengel personally, arriving about 5:00 or 6:00 A.M. Lengel did not find it unusual that an ex-con and local bootlegger would be so interested in the murder of Don Mellett.

The last witness on Friday, February 18, was Ben Rudner himself. The *Daily News* described him as "sleek and confident with a perfect memory."[17] The *Plain Dealer* commented on his shifting from polite to defiant to cocky and back to polite.[18] Gently guided by Everett Mills, Rudner's testimony was one of denial. He claimed that prior to the murder he didn't even know who Don Mellett was. He said that his visits with Chief Lengel concerned vandalism at Rudner's Canton hardware store. The defense was done with him at 4:10 P.M. McClintock took the remaining twenty minutes of the day. After getting Ben to admit that he was arrested for hitting a man over the head with a pipe during a robbery, for assaulting a police officer, and for bootlegging, the former prosecutor launched at Ben with nonstop, rapid-fire questions. Ben parried McClintock's questions, smiling when he thought he scored a point. Although he denied nearly everything, he did admit meeting Mazer the morning after the murder to discuss police dogs. At this, Sarah Rudner wept, and Max Rudner sat coiled on his chair ready to spring to Ben's defense.

The weekend was quiet. Judge Agler did not go to his farm as was his habit. The newspapers reported seeing Henry Harter, Judge Agler, and George Gordon Battle together at a luncheon meeting of lawyers that Saturday at the Courtland Hotel. Also in a newspaper sidebar was a mention that Massillon hardware salesman William Brumme had requested police protection for unstated reasons.[19]

Back in court on Monday morning, February 21, Ben Rudner's cross-examination wrapped up by 10:30. He generally acquitted himself better in court than Pat McDermott did, who had been his own worst enemy. Rudner had not seemed to do himself any real harm while on the stand.

George Gordon Battle then re-called William Brumme to the stand. He asked Brumme if he wanted to recant his previous testimony. "No," Brumme said. A surprised Battle sat down, opening the way for Harter to ask Brumme why Battle should think he would want to change his testimony now. This was the moment Brumme was waiting for. Last Friday night, he told the court, he had met Herman Rubin, Ben's brother-in-law, on the street in Canton near Rubin's clothing store. Rubin, accompanied by two burly "clerks," had offered to settle the long-standing dog purchase debt while suggesting that Brumme might want to change his story. They went to Rubin's establishment, and there an argument broke out, with Brumme claiming he was threatened before escaping the store. When reexamined by the defense, Brumme admitted he was only in the store about five minutes.[20]

The defense then called Herman Rubin, who denied threatening Brumme. The good brother-in-law also stated that neither he nor Ben arranged the murder-night party that gave Rudner an important alibi. On cross-examination, McClintock decided to take a shot from left field, asking Rubin, "Didn't you tell him [Pat McDermott] he wasn't entitled to any money because it wasn't a bullet from his gun that killed Mellett?"[21] The defense objections were immediate and sustained. The prosecutor was trying to shock the jury. Court didn't adjourn until 6:00 P.M. so that final arguments could begin first thing in the morning. The strain of the long trial had frayed everyone's nerves. The judge, jurors, and attorneys breathed a collective sigh of relief as the last rebuttal witness was dismissed.[22]

The *Daily News, Evening Repository,* and *Plain Dealer* ran front-page stories on the 22nd describing the palpable tension in Canton awaiting the conclusion of Rudner's trial. An underworld rumor transmitted to Mayor Swarts indicated that a gang from Toledo was heading to Canton to either free or kill Rudner if he was convicted. The reports likened the excitement to that following Mellett's murder the previous July. The sheriff had his machine guns oiled and redeployed at the jail and courthouse.

The next morning, February 22, Judge Agler allowed closing arguments to begin in front of a packed courtroom but cleared the corridors outside. Prosecutor Harter asked for the death penalty. At this suggestion, Ben, his wife at his side, yawned in response, but the press duly noted that his face drained of color.[23] Harter told the jury, "Ben Rudner is a gangster with a rich man's means behind him." Don

Mellett's only fault, Harter told the jury, was his honesty, his courage in using the power of his newspaper to attack what he believed was corruption, vice, and crime of all sorts.

Hired gun George Gordon Battle lectured the jury for a full two hours and ten minutes, basically arguing that poor Ben was a scapegoat. The witnesses for the state, he said, were "a sewer of jail birds, wife beaters, wife deserters, reward seekers, men and women at the mercy of police." Closing in a soft voice, Battle pled for Ben's life. Sarah Rudner burst into tears, Max Rudner cried, Anna Rubin wept, and tears welled in Ben's eyes.

One man not weeping was Charles McClintock. According to the former prosecutor, who made the final case to the jury, the state had only begun to smash the "unholy alliance between police and crime" in Canton. "If civilization is to endure, ladies and gentlemen of the jury, someone must go. Either respectable law abiding people like you and I, or people like Rudner!" McClintock told the jury how "Rudner conspired to have Mellett shot down just like Booth was hired to shoot down Lincoln. . . . If you do recommend mercy in your verdict, why? Was Ben Rudner merciful?" He closed his remarks by quoting John A. Bingham, the prosecutor of the Lincoln conspirators, "You must see that wrong must be redressed, crime must be avenged and the majesty of the law must be vindicated."[24]

When the closing statements were over, Judge Agler read a 12,000-word charge in which he went out of his way to tell the jury that the state must prove that a motive existed for Ben Rudner to want Don Mellett dead in order for there to have been a conspiracy. The possible verdicts open to the jury were the same as at Pat's trial—except Judge Agler, whether by accident or intent, omitted second-degree murder as a choice. At 10:10 A.M., Wednesday, February 23, the jury took the case and filed out of court to the fourth-floor deliberation room. All through the afternoon as the jury deliberated, in drugstores, poolrooms, hotel lobbies, homes, and on street corners the question was, "Has the jury reported?"[25]

At 8:10 that evening, the jury returned. Tight-lipped and unsmiling, forewoman Margaret Snyder handed the verdict to clerk Milo Cathon.

The clerk, known for his flair of the dramatic, made the most of his moment in the spotlight. "Not guilty of first-degree murder," he read. Then, after a long pause, "Guilty of second-degree murder." Rudner smiled. Second-degree murder indicated no premeditation and carried a life term with the possibility of parole or pardon. Agler asked the jury not to discuss their deliberations. They did not.[26]

The *Daily News* said of Rudner's conviction, "Justice is being done as verdicts are being found based on facts." The *Cleveland Plain Dealer*, in an editorial titled "The Second Step" in Canton's regeneration, wrote, "A difficult task confronted the state. So far it has been well performed." Ben's longtime attorney Everett Mills asked for a new trial based on the verdict. He lashed out at the jury to reporters: "It is one of those well known 'compromise' verdicts which American juries are so fond of. Ben Rudner should have been given the whole penalty or none at all. A child would know that, but a jury wouldn't."[27]

On February 28, 1927, the *Daily News* reported that Ben Rudner was hustled out of town to Columbus in the dead of night. Ben's parting comment to a reporter was, "I am an innocent man. . . . I have been the victim of newspaper publicity and perjury."[28] Incarcerated by the State of Ohio, Ben became prisoner number 56,796 in cell 13. For Ben Rudner, the unlucky cell assignment would be a sign of what he could expect for the rest of his life.

8

Mazer Confesses

Prosecutor Henry Harter reconvened the county grand jury at the end of February to hear new evidence concerning the Mellett murder conspiracy that had come to light during the Rudner trial.[1] Louis Mazer, whose trial was next on the docket, remained in jail in solitary confinement, where he was silent and unwilling to discuss the case with investigators. His defense counsel of record, George W. Spooner of Cleveland, had not visited him in months. His only regular visitor was his brother-in-law, who came two or three times a week with fruit and other luxuries approved by his jailers. The workhouse warden denied rumors that Mazer was cracking up.[2]

During this time, prosecutors tried again to get Louis Mazer to talk. The prosecutors were surprised and frustrated that the supposed weak link had held out this long. These overtures included visits by attorney Oscar Abt representing Judge Agler, who would have to approve any deal prosecutors made with the defendant. What investigators said to Mazer is unknown, but the first man arrested in the murder conspiracy could see which way the tide was flowing. He knew it was likely that if he came to trial, he would be convicted as well and face life in prison. Around the first of March, Mazer finally began talking to authorities, telling his story in bits and pieces. He appeared to be talking off the cuff, though this was an act, since in reality Louis Mazer had months to work on his tale and sort through jailhouse rumors about what had occurred in the earlier trials. Finally, on Saturday, March 5, he gave a sworn statement of his version of events to prosecutors. Even his new defense counsel, D. E. Kramer, who was present, didn't know for certain what his client would say.[3]

According to Mazer, the plot was hatched when Detective Floyd Streitenberger approached him during Chief Lengel's first civil service hearing in early 1926. More than once Streitenberger suggested to Mazer that "Mellett ought to have a beating so he would quit running down people."[4] On July 8 in Canton, Ben Rudner introduced "Red" to Louis Mazer. Mazer and Rudner were boyhood friends. Ben said Red was from Boston and real tough. During this meeting outside a South Market Avenue poolroom, Rudner told Mazer, "Lou, here's a man that just came in from the east, and he's all right—he's a good fellow and he's broke and willing to do most anything." Rudner further identified Red as a "lambaster," a slang term for someone who has skipped on an arrest warrant.[5]

Mazer contacted Streitenberger at police headquarters. "There's somebody here, you know, that's supposed to be from the east, and I guess he would give a fellow a beating for money." The detective responded, "Bring them on by all means."[6] Mazer drove to Massillon on July 9 and picked up Pat at Rudner's store. Together, they went back to Canton, and McDermott was registered at the New Barnett Hotel. Mazer introduced Pat to Max Kane (or Cain or King), an associate of Mazer's, and then borrowed Kane's Hudson to take Pat out to what he thought was Mellett's residence on Broad Avenue.[7] Mazer apparently didn't want his car seen around Mellett's neighborhood (this despite the fact that both Kane and Mazer drove similar cars). The address was supplied by Streitenberger, Mazer said, who got it from Canton police headquarters. After ascertaining the lay of the land, Pat wanted to return to Massillon. Mazer suggested that Pat take the interurban train, but Pat begged off, claiming he had too much luggage to bring back to Canton. (His luggage was Steve Kascholk.) So Mazer, again using his own car, drove to Massillon. On this return trip, he said, Pat wanted $200 to give Mellett a beating. Once again at Rudner's hardware, they picked up a second man called "Smitty," later identified as Steve Kascholk.

According to Mazer's story, during the return trip to Canton, Pat asked Mazer for a gun, "just for protection."[8] Mazer eventually gave Pat the new, unfired .38 Special revolver with a black barrel that he bought in the spring of 1924 from bus driver Van Gutten.[9] Sometime later, McDermott came around and told Mazer that Smitty wanted to leave. But Pat assured him, "I will stick around and see you through myself." In the following days, Mazer claimed that he rarely saw Pat, despite the fact that Pat was staying in Canton and had almost no acquaintances in town.

The day before the murder, Streitenberger, Mazer said, realized that the Melletts had moved. "Louis, this Mellett don't live out there anymore." He then told Mazer he would get the correct address to him after supper. When the two met again later at Doll Carey's Walnut Avenue home, Streitenberger handed Mazer a typed slip of paper with the correct address and an important description: "two trees in front of the house." The police detective told Mazer that tonight was the night for McDermott to do his job. With the sham battle and fireworks at the fairgrounds less than two blocks away, it would "be a good time to pull this," since there would be lots of people around and plenty of noise. According to Mazer, Streitenberger instructed him to drop Pat off in the neighborhood later that evening. When Pat had finished the job, he was to go to the nearest fairground gate where Streitenberger and his wife would be waiting to pick him up in a Willys-Knight sedan. Streitenberger told Mazer to tell Pat to "croak him," meaning Mellett.[10]

At this point in his deposition, Mazer told his inquisitors that he "just didn't have the spirit to be in it," that he was "led in a little at a time." Ignoring his conscience, however, Mazer said he got his own revolver, picked Pat up at the boardinghouse, and drove him out to Mellett's. Mazer then retreated to his only real home, the poolroom he used to own. Between 10:30 and 11:00 P.M., Pat called Mazer at the poolroom and wanted to be picked up. But before doing so, Mazer went to see Streitenberger. When prosecutors asked how he knew where Streitenberger lived, Mazer said he'd been to the detective's current and previous homes to deliver liquor several times. "Streity" now took charge of the operation, according to Mazer. The two of them drove out to Mellett's in Streitenberger's car to pick up Pat. McDermott, known to them only as "Red," said no one was home. Their car was gone, he said, and their hired muscle was tired of waiting. Streitenberger ordered Pat to "just stick around, he's [Mellett] got to come home." Mazer told prosecutors that Pat returned to his post in the weeds of the vacant lot next to Mellett's house, where he had found some boards to sit on. This time Streitenberger instructed Pat to "cripple Mellett if possible, but don't be too particular."[11]

Mazer and Streitenberger then cruised the area. While cruising around, Streity told Mazer that a plot was in the works to frame fellow officer Jiggs Wise by taking him a load of corn liquor. The city would be better off with "that fellow out," Streitenberger said. About the time Mazer said he wanted to call it a night, the two men heard police sirens. Assuming that McDermott had done something, they began a search for him, first by driving out to the streetcar junction. No McDermott. So they drove east several blocks on Tuscarawas until, by chance, they overtook their man rapidly walking along the street. Pat jumped into the car and announced that "the angels sure must be singing to him [Mellett] now."

According to Mazer, when they asked what he did, Pat bragged that he aimed and shot Mellett, and then fired a few more rounds just to excite the neighborhood. Neither man questioned McDermott's marksmanship. Mazer asked Pat for his gun back, but Pat said that he left it in the street when he ran away, covered with a newspaper, not an illogical move for a gunman fleeing the scene. But Streitenberger didn't want that gun left lying in the street, so they hastily returned to the scene of the crime. Mazer noted, ironically, that most of the way they were followed by a police motorcycle. Mazer said that Streitenberger ordered him to pick up the revolver, but he refused. "No, I'm not going to get out of this car." McDermott retrieved the gun from the street and shoved it at Mazer, who again said he refused to touch it. Mazer said that's when Streitenberger, clearly disgusted, assumed command and said, "I'll take charge of it."

Mazer and Streitenberger dropped off McDermott on Cleveland Avenue so he could walk to his boardinghouse. They returned to Streitenberger's house, where Mazer retrieved his car and drove home to Walnut Avenue.[12] The next day Kate Streitenberger brought the gun to him, cleaned and oiled—like a good neighbor returning a borrowed lawnmower. But only a day later, Mazer said, he saw Streitenberger and gave the revolver back to the policeman. "I can't look at it," he told the prosecutors he said to Streitenberger.[13]

Louis Mazer, trying to sound believable, told his interrogators that although he knew the pistol had been fired, he didn't know Mellett was dead until he read it in the paper the next morning. He said that when Ben Rudner appeared at Doll Carey's house a little later, he asked about the murder, "Did Red do that?" Mazer replied, "No one else— he's the one, I guess." According to Mazer, at the moment Rudner was proud of his man: "Pat's a pretty tough guy." The two then went to the D&E Sandwich Shop. As they were leaving, they met and talked with two Canton police officers, one of whom was Malcolm Cline. After they parted, Mazer went for a haircut. As he was leaving the barbershop, Mazer ran into Streitenberger and Detective Fats Metzger who were out checking cars. "Don't worry," Mazer claimed Metzger told him, "everything is all right."[14] Asked by Harter about the evidence supporting a two-gun theory, Mazer appeared baffled, because, according to him, McDermott—"just that one man"—was there.[15]

Continuing his deposition, Mazer said that early Friday afternoon, July 16, Rudner took Mazer out of the poolroom and told him "you have to get that fellow out of town." Mazer then told Rudner, "Jesus, I don't want to see him again." This time Rudner made it an order: "you will have to get rid of him." (Rumors that police would be picking up strangers on the street for questioning probably motivated Rudner.) Together, the duo went out to search for Pat, each in his own car. Mazer found him standing on the corner of 7th and Cleveland SE. Mazer said that when they told McDermott he had to leave town, he said he needed a suitcase. They then took him to a secondhand store near the New Barnett Hotel, where he bought a cheap cardboard suitcase for a dollar. They drove McDermott back to his boardinghouse and arranged to pick him up again in an hour on the corner of 7th and Cleveland SE. Then, according to Mazer, he and Rudner returned to the poolroom, where Ben told Louis to pay off Pat "so he won't be sore." Again, Mazer claimed he balked, saying, "My God, why should I pay him?" Apparently Rudner could be persuasive, because Mazer went to the Canton Bank and Trust Company, where he had $240 on deposit, to make a withdrawal, but he had arrived at 2:15 P.M., fifteen minutes after closing. Nevertheless, he managed to talk a teller into cashing a check for $200 postdated to the next business day.[16]

With $200 in his pocket, Pat left town for Massillon, Mazer driving him there. He reported that McDermott had said Boston was his ultimate destination, but something changed his mind and he now wanted to go to Cleveland. So Mazer drove Pat to an Italian roadhouse near Akron and left him. Mazer's associate Max Kane was nearby, and he drove McDermott to Cleveland. Max Kane (or Cain or King) was, according to Mazer, an acquaintance whose wife was one of Doll Carey's girls. Kane, a small-time gambler who had no real occupation, proved to be elusive; investigators across northern Ohio never found him. (In fact, they never even discovered the correct spelling of his name.)

Mazer said that at this point he decided it might be a good time to leave town, so he went to a lakeside cottage to stay with Doll Carey. He wasn't out of touch, however. He said that he and Streitenberger would call each other using the code name "Bill" to signal the need to meet, usually on an unpaved street near the Pennsylvania Railroad tracks. The pair talked or met daily to discuss the case and their alibi. One evening after the murder, Streitenberger wanted some beer, so he and Mazer drove out to North Industry to get some. On the way back to town, Streity asked Mazer to look at his German shepherd puppy, which was sick. From this, he said, the two created the famous sick dog alibi.[17] Streitenberger's advice to Mazer was "don't worry" and "keep quiet." Mazer said that Streitenberger never implicated Chief Lengel in the murder plot. When Pat was finally apprehended, and Rudner and Mazer already jailed, Rudner told Mazer that McDermott "will never say anything—don't worry about him." After his indictment, Mazer said that he told attorney Everett Mills the true story but was told to "keep quiet."[18]

As the deposition concluded, Harter asked Mazer to explain his involvement. Mazer said he didn't pay attention to what was in the newspapers and had no ill feelings toward Mellett. "They [Streitenberger and McDermott] just seemed to lead me into it. I ask myself that question a thousand times." The career criminal tried to ingratiate himself by telling Harter, "I would like to have you talk to me often. I know it will all come to me."[19] When asked about the testimony he previously gave under oath, Mazer readily admitted that he lied: "The story that I told at the McDermott trial was all fake." Once more he placed the blame on Everett Mills.[20]

The picture Louis Mazer painted of himself as an unwilling accomplice was obviously self-serving. Certainly Ora Slater and Charles McClintock knew this, although they were not present at Mazer's "official" confession. Yet Mazer's willingness to talk without conditions or a deal was a major break in the case. Former police detective Floyd Streitenberger had been secretly indicted just the day before, Friday March 4, on charges of conspiring to murder Don Mellett, an indictment based on the detective's relationship with Mazer, inquiries about Mellett's address, and the lawman's whereabouts the night of the crime. Mazer's testimony would greatly enhance the state's case against the officer. But Mazer's involvement in the whole plot was no doubt greater than he was admitting. The investigators knew it, but they were willing to let him off the first-degree murder hook if they could use him to secure convictions of others they believed were involved. Mazer's reward for talking, as all the parties understood, would be reduced charges for his role in the murder. How much a reduction would depend on how persuasive a witness in future trials the former perjurer would become. To be safe, the deposition of Mazer was not made public at that time. In fact, for some weeks to come the press would have to be satisfied with rumors that Mazer was talking. The prosecution had decided to play its cards close to the vest.

9

The Detective's Day in Court

D on Mellett's "classic martyrdom"[1] was recognized on May 2, 1927, when the *Canton Daily News* was awarded the Pulitzer Prize "for the most distinguished and meritorious public service rendered by any American newspaper during the year (1926)." The $500 gold medal was posthumous recognition of Mellett's sacrifice as well as the paper's "brave, patriotic and effective fight for purification of municipal politics, and for the ending of a vicious state of affairs brought about by collusion between criminal authorities and the criminal element, a fight which had a tragic result in the assassination of the editor of the paper."[2] Mellett's successor as publisher, Charles E. Morris, said of the award in a press release:

There is humility, because only in humility can there be real service such as that for which the life of Don Mellett was sacrificed: there is pride because a civic fight has been won against great odds, successfully only because of awakening of public consciousness without which society cannot last; and there is gratitude because of the recognition that the work for Canton is a work of the best traditions of journalism, which include, above all, honesty, independence, fearlessness and persistence, unselfishly or at personal loss, to render public service. . . . Canton now stands proudly before the world as a city which will not tolerate the evils which are eating at the heart of popular government everywhere.[3]

Floyd Streitenberger, who had been under suspicion of being part of the Mellett murder conspiracy ever since his hasty and enthusiastic pronouncement of Louis Mazer's innocence back in August 1926, was indicted on Friday, March 4. Mazer's assertion that Streitenberger was an active participant in the conspiracy as well as a conduit between local vice lords and the police was going to be tested in court.

Shortly after Streitenberger had been dismissed by Chief Wise in September, he had left Canton for Akron, where he stayed with a stepdaughter until he got a job as a carpenter in a power plant in Springfield, Ohio. It was there authorities arrested him in March, transporting him back to Canton still in his work clothes. The once-cocky police detective was a sorry sight, depressed and disheveled. He had anticipated his arrest and probably reasoned that any attempt to flee the state would hurt his chances in court.[4]

Streitenberger's bare-bones defense team featured no famous orators or out-of-town legal minds. In fact, the ex-cop, who was almost broke, was defended by court-appointed counsel. Leading the defense was sixty-five-year-old James H. Robertson of Canton; his assistant was Frank T. Bow, a newly minted attorney whose bright future would include twenty years in Congress representing Stark County.

Streitenberger's trial was set for May 9, 1927. A visiting judge would preside, since all of the local judges were assumed to be too familiar with the police. The Ohio Supreme Court picked Frank M. Clevenger, a common pleas court judge in Clinton County in southwest Ohio.[5] In his long judicial career, Judge Clevenger presided over trials across the state, reminiscent of the circuit judges of an earlier time, and his resume included presiding over a 1919 trial challenging Ohio's ratification of the Eighteenth Amendment—Prohibition. Clevenger was widely respected and was very active in the state and national bar associations, yet this distinguished jurist was virtually unknown in Canton in the spring of 1927.[6] All concerned agreed that

Streitenberger's trial would be short. His court-appointed defense was not going to waste time debating legal technicalities and planned to call only eighteen witnesses, including the defendant.

Even before the trial was formally called into session, on Saturday, May 7, Captain Ben Clarke gave sworn testimony. Clarke, who was accidentally wounded with his own sidearm on New Year's Eve, was partially paralyzed and bedridden. Mellett supporters saw something sinister in this gun accident, but in actuality it really was just a freak accident.[7] Unable to testify in person, his deposition was taken at his bedside. Present were Prosecutor Harter, defense attorneys Robertson and Bow, and Streitenberger. Once the defendant's superior, Clarke was a defense witness and was expected to bolster the detective's alibi. But he turned out to be a disappointment to the defense. He could only account for Streitenberger at around 10:00 P.M. and 2:00 A.M. on the night of the crime, not the four hours in between, during which Mellett was shot. He also claimed not to know of a plot against Mellett. (At that time the Canton police force was divided between supporters of current chief Wise and those who backed former chief Lengel. Clarke appeared to be a fence sitter, trying to lean whichever direction the political wind was blowing.) Yet the fact that he gave the victim's address to the conspirators twice placed him in the sights of those who believed in a broad conspiracy within the police to harm Don Mellett. Were it not for his medical condition and the sympathy it engendered, Clarke might have been indicted as well.

By the conclusion of the first day of jury selection, Monday, May 9, a tentative jury was seated.[8] Observers considered this remarkable, since by now everyone in Stark County had either heard about the murder or previous trials—and it was planting season. The defendant passed his first day in court with a coolness that impressed reporters. He grinned at the mention of the death penalty, winked at people in the courtroom, and laughed audibly as he perused the newspaper comics. It was a brave front not destined to last.[9]

By noon on Tuesday, a jury of nine men and three women was seated. Once more they would be guests at the Northern Hotel for the duration. The prosecution's case rested primarily on weak circumstantial evidence and the testimony of Louis Mazer. The defense was going to attack Mazer, press the multiple gunmen theory, and say that Streitenberger, although mentioned negatively in Mellett's editorials, held no grudge toward the editor. Five witnesses, and none of them a surprise, appeared that afternoon for the prosecution, concluding with the reliable Steve Kascholk, who did not link the defendant to the crime but did link Mazer to the crime. Florence Mellett was unable to travel from Indianapolis to Canton in time to see the trial open.

Louis Mazer, who replaced Steve Kascholk as the prosecution's key witness, took the stand first thing Wednesday morning, May 11. According to reporters, Mazer gave his testimony with evident relief, sitting up straight and telling the jury he wanted to clear his conscience. He looked healthier, his face unwrinkled and an extra eighteen pounds on his frame. He held his right hand almost in a salute when the clerk swore him in. He kept his hands folded in his lap and didn't twitch or portray any sign of nervousness. Mazer told the court that he was at various times a salesman, poolroom operator, and store owner, and he readily admitted that his "home" was a Walnut Avenue "resort." On the stand, he acknowledged that prosecutors had offered him a deal to come clean but said that he declined it: "I decided it would be best for everybody concerned if I threw myself on the Court's mercy and took my medicine." Louis Mazer as reformed man had them laughing in the Jungle, but it was well-presented in court so as to seem plausible.[10]

Under oath and Streitenberger's steady glare, Mazer quietly and, according to reporters, with "apparent sincerity," related his account of the conspiracy and the murder. "Detective Hears Betrayer's Story" announced the *Plain Dealer*. He told the jury, as he'd told Harter, that in the past two months spent in solitary confinement, the events of July 1926 had "come to" him. His testimony was letter perfect; he never lapsed. Reports noted that only the newspaper boys outside the courthouse shouting "Mazer takes the stand!" caused him to take a moment's pause. He readily confessed that his previous trial testimony was all false—"Oh, it's all perjury. Lies which Streitenberger and I planned to tell as our alibis."

By 1:30 that afternoon, Mazer was finished. At the close of his testimony, attorney Oscar Abt confirmed Mazer's assertion that he rejected immunity, explaining, "Mazer said that he felt he didn't deserve complete immunity." Appearances by Bill Bitzler and Florence Mellett in the witness chair rounded out the day. Yet despite his sensational testimony, Mazer had to share the day's headlines when the story broke that ex-chief Lengel had made a habit of giving special police badges to his cronies. Among them were Ben Rudner's brother Louis, Norman Clark, and several other sketchy characters.

Doll Carey and Thelma Harris testified for the prosecution on Thursday, May 12. Before Mazer confessed, their testimony was regarded as critical to the state. Now their stories bolstered Mazer's. The defense, attempting to impugn their integrity, made them concede to prostitution-related arrests. The state rested at 2:00 P.M.

Kate Streitenberger was first to come to her husband's defense. The defendant's second wife was unflatteringly described by the press as a "swarthy brunette," but was a good witness for her husband. She knew the evening activities of July 15 "like a railroad timetable," according to the *Daily News*.[11] After visiting the fairgrounds, Kate said the couple went for a drive to cool off at about 10:30 P.M. They came across Louis Mazer during the drive and asked him to come look at their sick police dog. Mazer said he would stop by later that evening. When the Streitenbergers arrived home, they decided to hold an impromptu gathering and invited their neighbors, according to Kate. When the party broke up, Louis Mazer, who had been waiting by the curb in his Hudson, came in and examined the sick puppy. After staying an hour, when the detective and the bootlegger talked of nothing but dogs, she claimed, Mazer left, and the Streitenbergers went to bed at 12:45 A.M.

McClintock's cross-examination failed to substantially shake Kate's testimony, although he did rattle her when he questioned the Streitenbergers' relationship with drug lord Teddy Abbey, described by Judge Pontius as "one of the shrewdest, cleverest, most dangerous criminals" in northeast Ohio.[12] Questioned about correspondence Kate sent from Springfield to Abbey's cook in Canton, the detective's homesick wife replied, "Well, I would have been tickled to hear from anybody in Canton."[13] When she was finished, Kate flashed her husband a smug smile as she exited the witness box.

Floyd Streitenberger was his own best witness. He denied absolutely Mazer's story, referring to the state's star witness as "a liar, just a no good and a no account bootlegger." Floyd was known for his country-boy "Kaintucky" accent, but this southern Ohio boy was no rube. He possessed a policeman's experience in the witness chair. Still, when forced under cross-examination to depart from his well-rehearsed alibi, he fell back on "I don't remember" a little too often.[14] When McClintock asked about trips he made to Canton after his dismissal from the force, Streitenberger said he and Kate visited once a month to see friends and make payments into his retirement fund. Pressed on why he, a lawman, rented a house from well-known underworld figure Teddy Abbey, he answered, "I just as soon rent from him as you as long as the house is good, and in the best part of the city." As for Louis Mazer, the defendant claimed he was not a friend or associate, just a stool pigeon. In fact, he said he had not even seen Mazer in three years, until the night of the murder when he asked him to look at his sick dog. As for that Buffalo reporter he talked with, the former cop explained, he was misquoted.

Reporters were astounded at Streitenberger's ease in the courtroom, his coolness, "as unconcerned as a tomato."[15] He joked and laughed at McClintock's questions, knowing the prosecutor's style from the days when he testified *for* the prosecution as a police officer. And he probably knew what the state's witnesses would say. Ora Slater's theory about men on trial for vicious crimes was evident in Streitenberger: "An innocent man will be utterly unnerved when he faces trial for murder. A guilty man knows what is coming. If he weren't hard enough already, not to be bothered, he would have time to prepare himself, to steel his nerves."[16] Streitenberger had had eight months.

After Streitenberger stepped down, the defense made a small attempt to discredit Mazer by having Leo Schumacher and Bessie Zimmer tell the jury that they heard several shots and more than one man running away from the murder scene, raising the question of how many shooters there might have been. With that, the defense rested.

The state called the Gussett family in rebuttal. Most impressive was ten-year-old Carl, who, despite his obvious nervousness, testified that a man came to the Streitenbergers' door during the July 15 party and that their host left with the man wearing a blue suit and straw hat. His sincerity and courage impressed the courtroom crowd. His story was confirmed by his parents, Emil and Elsie.

In closing statements, the best the defense could do was tell the jury that Streitenberger, an Army veteran, was being framed by a mere bootlegger. They were more convincing in their feeble attempt to discredit the state's one gunman theory. In his closing statement, McClintock addressed the jury: "The people of Ohio have provided that anyone who unlawfully kills a policeman who is performing his duty shall be guilty of first degree murder and sentenced to death. Will the people of Ohio provide the same penalty for a policeman who, using his position as a cover, conceives and carries out the murder of an editor who was exercising his constitutional right to free speech?" At this, Streitenberger buried his face in his hands and his wife left the courtroom. Lengel was never called to testify.

Judge Clevenger's charge to the jury was remarkable for its brevity. He instructed the jury that there was no law keeping them from giving full credence to Mazer's confession, even if he previously lied. But, he said, they should consider that Mazer might be lying to get off easier. At 1:20 P.M., Tuesday, May 17, the jury received the case. At 10:15 P.M., after deliberating for eight hours, the jury had reached a decision: guilty of first-degree murder with a recommendation of mercy. It was a life sentence with no parole, and for good measure, Judge Clevenger sentenced Streitenberger to spend each anniversary of Don Mellett's murder in solitary confinement. The defendant had been sober, even despondent, all day; after the verdict was announced, he appeared stunned and broken. The *Daily News* called him a "miserable spectacle."[17]

The trial faded fast from the front pages. Since McDermott's conviction, interest in the Mellett murder had declined significantly, not just nationally but in Ohio as well. The *New York Times* continued to cover the trials but rarely accorded the stories space on the front page.[18] Even Ohio's largest newspaper, *The Plain Dealer*, and one deeply involved in the investigation, buried most coverage of Streitenberger's trial deep in the paper. The same cast of characters kept making repeat appearances, and from a news standpoint they were becoming bor-

THE DETECTIVE'S DAY IN COURT · 149

ing. Even Mellett's Pulitzer wasn't front-page news outside of Canton. Lastly, Strietenberger's trial coincided with one of the twentieth century's landmark events: Lindbergh's solo flight across the Atlantic.

The day after his conviction, a revived Streitenberger told reporters, "Sure, I'm innocent. I never thought that a jury would believe a guy like him [Mazer]." But any hopes he entertained of the verdict being overturned on appeal were desperate as long as Mazer was available to testify. Yet, despite his conviction, Streitenberger had friends in Canton, while Mazer was seen as a weakling, even by his underworld cronies, who considered him a squealer. Although he was now seen as the mainspring of the plot to silence Don Mellett, Streitenberger was a sympathetic figure to many.

It leaked from the prosecutor's office that Judge Agler and Prosecutor Harter offered Mazer immunity on the murder charge in exchange for his testimony. Ora Slater and Charles McClintock had not been consulted on this offer and might have disagreed with it, feeling Mazer should face a jury. Perhaps because of a guilty conscience, or perhaps knowing that if he served time for the murder he would be immune to further prosecution, Mazer declined the offer. Had he accepted, Harter and federal district attorney A. E. Bernstein had arranged for Mazer to be turned over to the feds for prosecution on liquor charges. In the end, Judge Agler sentenced Louis Mazer to five to twenty years for manslaughter. Many people in Canton were outraged at what was perceived as a light sentence for cold-blooded murder. Nevertheless, a majority of Canton's citizenry, and those directly involved in the murder investigation, quietly accepted Mazer's lighter sentence as the price of his cooperation, without which the connection to Canton's police could not have been made.

The effort to clean up Canton after Mellett's slaying had begun with the police department. Lengel's successor as chief, Jiggs Wise, banned the loitering of bail bondsmen and criminals from police headquarters, which ran rampant under Lengel. Lieutenants replaced sergeants in command of the night shift. And he began methodically purging inept or corrupt officers like Streitenberger and Van Gunten from the ranks, all moves applauded by the *Daily News*. Unfortunately, because of civil service rules, these moves were stymied for months as the officers appealed their decisions. Eventually Wise succeeded in removing many of the worst offenders. Pressure was applied to the vice lords, and even Jumbo Crowley decamped in early 1927 for the small city of Wooster twenty-five miles west of Canton.[19]

That week, in a little-noticed but related move, Governor Vic Donahey pardoned Canton bootleggers turned state's witnesses Harry Turner and Harry Bouklias. Apparently no longer concerned about the *Daily News*'s reaction, he claimed that their testimony in the Curtis brothers scandal was a service to Canton and justified their pardon after serving the minimum eighteen-month sentence. The *Daily News* was unimpressed, calling the governor "weak" and suggesting that the pardons were "used to pay political debts."

Three days after his conviction, Streitenberger decided to talk. That Friday afternoon, May 20, he sat down with prosecutors Harter and McClintock along with Ora Slater. The convicted conspirator was clearly upset. Some of his answers were contradictory, and parts of his confession were of little value. The Kitzig murder, for example, he said was carried out by Mazer and Rudner—or maybe it was Rudner and McDermott. Mazer removed liquor from the locked evidence cabinet in the police department after getting the key from another unnamed police officer. When Streitenberger objected to McDermott—who was supposed to only beat up Mellett—having a gun for fear he might get scared and shoot somebody, Mazer reassured him, "He's an old hand, don't worry about him." And finally, McDermott shot Mellett but just maybe some other unknown person was present. When asked about the murder weapon, Streitenberger said he returned it to Mazer after cleaning it. Streitenberger speculated that Mazer later tossed the gun into Meyer's Lake. However, the police detective did admit that he buried the spent shell casings behind his garage. Five empty .38 caliber casings were later recovered by Ora Slater from the exact spot Streitenberger said he hid them. This was as close as investigators would ever come to recovering the murder weapon, or weapons. When the prosecutors asked about Ben Rudner, Streitenberger said that Rudner's first comment to him about the murder the morning after outside police headquarters was "Well, the SOB is dead," followed by advice to "stick to one story, regardless of what happens."[20]

The investigators wanted most of all to hear about Lengel. Streitenberger said that Lengel promised to take care of him and his family should anything like this happen, but Lengel had not, so Streitenberger decided to talk. He reported that Lengel had said about Mellett, "All the SOB wants to do is get rid of the whole bunch of us." The morning after the murder, Lengel told Streitenberger, "There's liable to be a lot of hell, so you want to watch yourself." And later the chief expressed his frustration over the killing by telling him that "the dirty SOBs [Mazer, Rudner, and McDermott] had intended to kill Mellett all along, not just beat him up or cripple him."[21]

Streitenberger also discussed another officer he said knew about the plot to "get" Mellett: Captain Ben Clarke. He spent about as much time implicating Clarke as Lengel but denied any bad feeling toward Clarke, who had sent him some cigars and chewing gum in jail. He said that Clarke told him to watch himself around Mellett. In a bizarre statement that should have raised some red flags about Floyd's sanity, Streitenberger said Clarke told him he had peeked in Mellett's window one evening and seen the publisher wearing a .45 automatic pistol and a bullet-proof vest. Clarke's motives and actions remained murky in Streitenberger's tale. Those in Mellett's circle— his family, friends, and the prosecutors—considered Clarke as guilty as any of the others. Regarding the police captain, Judge Pontius noted in his files that "a guilty conscience needs no accuser." Yet much of what those in the Mellett camp considered incriminating was open to interpretation. Was Clarke just genuinely confused when he mistook Lloyd Mellett for his brother at the fairgrounds the night of the murder? Was he destroying evidence at the crime scene when he was suspected of erasing footprints or merely shifting the dirt looking for spent bullets? And lastly, was Mazer, a confessed perjurer, telling the truth when he claimed Clarke told him the investigation was off track and "we have them guessing?"[22]

During Streitenberger's confession, prosecutors brought in Louis Mazer, presumably to see if the two agreed on anything. After calling each other liars, their discourse further deteriorated. "I wish to God McDermott would confess because he has nothing to lose and nothing to gain," Mazer said to Streitenberger. "So do I. It would sure make a fool out of you if he ever confesses." In a move that didn't help his credibility, Streitenberger said that while in jail, a mysterious voice whispered to him twice in his cell an offer of $800 if he would back up Mazer's version of events. Mazer's assertion that he was an unwilling messenger for police higher-ups was very questionable, as was Streitenberger's claim that he was just a "handy man" in the plot. Little of value came of the confrontation. For the most part, Streitenberger simply unwittingly confirmed Mazer's confession.[23]

Eager prosecutors summoned a grand jury for 9:00 Monday morning, May 23, to hear Streitenberger's revelations. Everyone present was sworn to secrecy, but leaks to reporters were inevitable. A rumor circulated that Streitenberger told the grand jury that two high-ranking former police officials planned to kill the editor of the *Canton Daily News* for his editorials. These same men met in Massillon with Rudner and Mazer after the slaying to arrange alibis and make plans to kill McDermott. Mazer and Rudner went to Cleveland to kill McDermott, Streitenberger said, but were unable to find him.[24] Who, reporters wondered, were the two cops Streitenberger fingered? Meanwhile, defense attorney Robertson suggested to reporters that the elusive Max Kane could have been the mystery gunman.

The Monday meeting of the grand jury failed to result in any indictments. They adjourned until June 6, and Harter claimed this was in order to allow time to investigate new angles. The jury was not sufficiently moved by what it had heard from the two witnesses, Floyd and Kate Streitenberger. Part of the doubt may have come from Kate. Unaware of what Floyd had told investigators, she repeated her courtroom testimony that Floyd was at home at the time of the murder, risking perjury. Further doubt may have arisen because of Streitenberger's condition. Reportedly he was quite nervous and also in a bad mental and physical state. After three hours with the grand jury, he was said to be "very bedraggled."[25] Clearly the prosecutors had been overeager, and the grand jury had not heard enough evidence to convince twelve of fifteen jurors to indict anyone.

That week the *Cleveland Plain Dealer* offered its take on Streitenberger's confession. The editors wrote that the state's main theory had been that the plot had its origins in high police circles, and the idea that Streitenberger was the brains had many weaknesses. If Streitenberger's story was true, the editors said, it would not help him but could crimp Mazer's hope for a better outcome. Nevertheless, no matter how questionable these confessions were, "In any case, it works for justice."[26]

10

The Dutch Baker Defends Himself

B y the conclusion of the next session of the Stark County grand jury, June 9, former Canton police chief Saranus A. Lengel was indicted for the murder of Don Mellett. In an ironic twist, that day also marked the twentieth anniversary of Lengel joining the police force; if he hadn't been fired, if he had worked until June 23, he would have been eligible for a pension of $137.50 a month.[1] Instead he faced a murder charge, with his trial set to begin July 11.

Jury selection for Lengel's trial began Monday, July 11, 1927, in the same large courtroom in the county courthouse. Judge Clevenger presided again as visiting judge. However, unlike some of the previous trials, "the spirit of brevity was apparent in the proceedings," according to the *Daily News*.[2] Lengel's senior defense counsel was Frank Rollin Hahn of Youngstown. The forty-seven-year-old Hahn was a defense attorney with years of experience, and the first of several from the Mahoning Valley who would aid Lengel's defense. Hahn's primary assistant was W. Bernard Rogers, who represented Lengel in his first civil service hearing. Seated beside the defendant and volunteering to assist in the defense was old Lengel friend W. K. Powell, a newly licensed attorney who, until a few months ago, had been chief of police in Youngstown.

Lengel, despite all the allegations of being on the take, had almost no money in the bank. He requested public assistance to pay for his defense. This was denied when it was discovered that his house was in his wife's name and that he had $1,500 in cash value in a life insurance policy. He had to mortgage his $7,000 home to pay his attorneys. Expecting acquittal, Lengel made it known that he intended to press for reinstatement to the police force and refile his $50,000 libel suit against the *Daily News* as soon as the criminal trial concluded. This Dutch baker, as the sharp-tongued Jansen had derisively called him, would be more of a test for prosecutors than the previous four defendants had been.[3]

Lengel's defense strategy was straightforward: attack the weakness of Streitenberger's accusations; rely on the strength of Lengel's reputation and denial of what the state's star witness had to say; let Lengel's standing in the community contrast with the words of a convicted murderer and perjurer who admitted that all he knew of the ex-chief's involvement he got secondhand from Louis Mazer.[4]

Jury selection proceeded with lightning speed on Monday, July 11, with forty-six potential jurors examined and some seated. For Tuesday, a new group was ordered up. The courtroom was hot, and everyone had to talk over the incessant whine of electric fans.[5] Judge Clevenger, in a rare break in decorum, invited the gentlemen to remove their coats because of the oppressive heat, but only the spectators did so.

By Tuesday afternoon, a jury of five men and seven women was seated to determine Lengel's fate. As with the other trials, the jury was taken to the murder scene immediately after being sworn in and before being sequestered. The press reported that Lengel was quiet and drawn. The gravity of a murder charge was sinking in, and the confidence he'd expressed days before—"Streitenberger knows I'm not guilty"—had faded.[6] He frequently turned to his wife, Carrie, and daughter, Daisy, but otherwise he shrank from the stares of reporters and spectators. The experience he'd gained in the courtroom in twenty years as a police officer deserted him.

After dispensing with the usual parade of prosecution witnesses testifying to establish a crime for the legal record, the state commenced by putting Steve Kascholk on the stand. His now-familiar

Former Canton chief of police Saranus A. Lengel confers with his daughter, Daisy, and wife, Carrie, during his first murder trial in July 1927. Cleveland Public Library

story received no cross-examination. Select *Daily News* editorials and articles were read into the court record since the state contended that the January 2, 1926, editorial and the March 1, 1926, article under Mellett's byline were inciting factors in the murder. Then Florence Mellett took the stand. Teary-eyed and sitting on the edge of the witness chair with her daughter in her lap again, she said of hearing the *Daily News* read aloud in court: "It sounds just like Don talking. They said then that he wasn't telling the truth."[7] Florence had nothing of substance to add to the prosecution's case except to keep the memory of her slain husband alive. The defense objected to the child in the lap ploy but could ill afford to attack her openly. Instead, Hahn silently left the courtroom during her testimony to protest this obvious and unusual attempt by the state to influence the jury.[8]

Mayor Swarts testified about his decision to fire Lengel for his incompetent investigation of the murder. Safety director Earl Hexamer testified that when he told Lengel he was fired, the defendant left his office and took an envelope, contents unknown, from the office safe before leaving the premises.

During the prosecution's case, defense attorney Hahn's tactics included jumping up and shouting to no one in particular, "That's all?" just when the prosecution finished with a witness. During cross-examinations he paced while looking at the floor as if disinterested in the answers to his questions. When the state objected to this behavior, Judge Clevenger was compelled to "sit on" and admonish Hahn for his actions.[9]

On Wednesday, two days into the trial, the state put Floyd Streitenberger on the stand. The man the press referred to as a "living dead man" because of his life sentence went straight to the point. "Chief Lengel knew they were going to get Mellett, and said the blankety-blank ought to be gotten. Louis Mazer told me the Chief wanted it done."[10] Testifying in prison denims, Streitenberger asked to stand rather than sit because his side hurt. (The first week of July, while working in the prison woodshop, he had been tripped by another inmate and nearly fell into a large saw.[11]) His voice was "so hopeless and emotionless that it cast an uncanny sort of chill" in the courtroom.[12] According to him, Lengel said of the alibi Mazer and the detective concocted, "Stick by it, keep to your story right straight through."[13] He said he learned of the plot against Mellett when he took McClintock's letter about Doll Carey's place to Mazer. The bootlegger told him that Lengel wanted the editor beaten up and that Rudner was supplying muscle in the form of "Boston Red" and another thug. Streitenberger painted himself as an unwilling participant who went along because Mazer said Chief Lengel wanted the detective to. As for the missing murder weapon, the ex-cop admitted only to cleaning it and burying the empty shell casings under his garage, which were recovered by investigators. Mazer, he said, got rid of the gun. On the stand Streitenberger stated that sometime after the murder, he and Mazer went to see Lengel, who said he was sorry the affair resulted in murder and that the conspirators should stick to their alibis. He said he visited Lengel at his home once after being fired and moving to Springfield. Once convicted, Streitenberger claimed, Lengel directed him to go to prison and keep his mouth shut; and Lengel promised he would do whatever he could for his protégé. Throughout his testimony, the obviously tired Streitenberger stared at the floor and talked slowly, giving a generally moribund performance.

Defense attorney Frank Rollin Hahn pounced on Streitenberger, who repeatedly answered "I don't remember" to Hahn's questions.[14] The witness did recall telling the former chief of a rumored plot to harm Mellett in early 1926. The defense suggested that there were multiple threats, in addition to the real plot, against Mellett. As for Lengel's advice to stick with the alibi, Streitenberger admitted that Lengel didn't really know that the dog alibi was false.

Lengel's defense succeeded in getting Ohio Penitentiary warden P. E. Thomas to agree to place a hidden Dictaphone device in Floyd Streitenberger's cell. In late June a recorded conversation between Rudner, who knew of the bug, and Streitenberger, who did not, reportedly had the former cop saying that the "Old Man" (Lengel) knew nothing of the actual murder and that Streitenberger only knew what Mazer told him. For his part, Rudner was interested in securing his own release, and he thought a Lengel acquittal could hasten that.

Hahn produced a transcript of the prison Dictaphone conversation, and Streitenberger agreed that he did not know he was being recorded. Dictaphone technology at the time was not totally reliable when used for electronic eavesdropping; gaps in the conversation occurred when speakers spoke too softly or background noise was too loud. Judge Clevenger, an old-school jurist, did not allow the Dictaphone transcripts with their gaps and incomplete sentences to be admitted into evidence. So the defense was forced to waive the transcripts, quote from them, and rely on Streitenberger's recollection of the conversation with Rudner and his willingness to tell the truth. No doubt the jury was somewhat confused by this scenario. Hahn confronted Streitenberger with Rudner's allegation: "You know you lied, why don't you go back and tell the truth?" Streitenberger denied this was said. Instead, the witness claimed that Rudner said in a very low tone, possibly not picked up by the machine, "You can save the Chief or break him." Hahn pointed out, and Streitenberger did not deny, that he said to Rudner, "The Chief didn't have anything to do with the murder, and other than what Mazer told me, I don't know anything against Lengel. I can't prove a thing against the Chief."[15] Streitenberger didn't disagree when the defense quoted Rudner from the transcript regarding Lengel: "He's a square fellow."[16]

Judge Clevenger adjourned court for the day in the middle of Streitenberger's cross-examination. This interruption in the momentum of the defense's assault on the witness's credibility did not make counsel happy. Further distraction arrived later that evening when Streitenberger's attorney, Frank Bow, told reporters that his client had dropped his appeal. The former police detective was coming to terms with the reality of life behind bars. Returning to the stand the next morning, it was evident that the rhythm of yesterday's cross-examination was broken. Streitenberger reverted to answering most questions with, "I don't know whether that was said or not." After less than an hour of this, the witness was dismissed.[17]

Comic relief, which this trial desperately needed, was again provided by Bill Bitzler the next day. An experienced witness by now, Bitzler told his story so fast that he had to be asked to slow down. Warming to his tale, Bill filled the record with "Pat says to me" and "I says to Pat says I" until even a now-somber Lengel was seen smiling faintly. After Bitzler, the prosecution rested.

On Friday, July 15, the defense began its brief case, which primarily consisted of the former chief rebutting everything Streitenberger said. In general, observers felt that he carried himself well, although he was occasionally tripped up by details thrown at him by an aggressive McClintock.[18] The former police chief admitted that he took no action when a Canton attorney told him that a local Black Hand leader had threatened to kill Mellett. This threat, McClintock pointed out, later became the basis of Lengel's flawed theory on the murder. With this, the defense rested, seemingly confident that the jury would not take the word of a former-policeman-turned-convict-and-perjurer, who turned in a terrible performance on the stand, over that of a longtime respected Canton resident and chief of police.

Harter took the lead in closing arguments, telling the jury and crowd in a sweltering courtroom, "[The state] prosecutes this defendant in self-protection, for he violated its most sacred right, the right of life which alone our Constitution puts ahead of liberty." Lengel showed no emotion while Harter spoke, but his wife and daughter, sitting just behind him, covered their faces with handkerchiefs.[19] Across the room sat Mrs. Mellett, her four children, and two of Don's brothers. Their turn to weep came when Harter described for the jury tiny Florence struggling to carry the lifeless body of her slain husband into their home just one year ago. (This didn't really happen.) "I doubt that Don R. Mellett knew how right he was," Harter told the jurors in conclusion. "I think no man did. By the use of his newspaper, he set out to stop this unholy alliance, and without the press, the great mass of people would always remain unheard. . . . Free government cannot exist if its press is subservient to vice or any other malign influence."[20]

Defense counsel Bernard Rogers took the floor. Pounding the jury box and shouting in a high-pitched voice, he told the jurors that Don Mellett's murder was an atrocity of historical proportions. But, he cautioned the jury, "There has been a hue and cry for blood, and we hope you will hear the evidence and the law, and not the hue and cry." The state, Rogers asserted, failed to prove its case beyond Lengel's incompetent investigation of the crime. Mellett was courageous, he said, but before he came to Canton, Saranus Lengel had a blemish-free record as a police officer and chief. "The press is a powerful instrument, but it can also be a most dangerous instrument," he warned the jury. Lengel, he said, was being tried for knowing Ben Rudner and being accused by Streitenberger, a confessed murderer and perjurer. "We do not want your sympathy, we do not want your pity, all we ask is a just verdict."[21]

Frank Rollin Hahn's final argument was more brief. After reviewing Lengel's career and thirty-plus years as a Canton resident, he simply addressed the jury: "Would you convict a man on no evidence, for the State has produced no proof."[22]

Charles McClintock again closed the prosecution's case, and his supporters said he delivered the best closing statement of his career. He started by asking the jury rhetorically, "Who is the defendant?" Then he pointed out Lengel's readiness to testify for each of the conspirators. What about his attempted jailhouse visit to the convicted Streitenberger? If Lengel was innocent, why didn't Mazer or Rudner testify for him? As for Streitenberger's allegations, he said, all had been corroborated by other witnesses. And as a threat, he said that if Lengel was not convicted, Rudner's chances of being released from prison were better. He told the jury, "I do not believe that Lengel ever planned to murder Don Mellett." But, he asked, "why didn't Lengel work with Don Mellett to drive vice out of Canton? The state, McClintock reminded the jury, was not asking for the death penalty, only a guilty verdict.[23]

One critical point in Judge Clevenger's characteristically brief instructions to the jury would later prove important. He told the jury that they should consider Lengel an equally guilty member of the conspiracy even if he had no knowledge of the actual murder plot. The jury was sent to deliberate at 1:20 P.M. At 5:20 the jury passed the judge a note, and most of the remaining spectators present assumed that the jury was going to supper. But, after deliberating for only four hours, jury foreman Perry Doll of Massillon announced that they had a verdict. Returning to the courtroom, a confident defendant, who never doubted acquittal, removed his cigar and patted his worried wife on the shoulder. A clerk read the verdict: "guilty of murder in the first degree. And we do recommend mercy."[24] Saranus A. Lengel froze, and his wife and daughter recoiled. Judge Clevenger looked up sternly, drew a long breath, and thanked the jurors for their service. The five men and seven women quickly hastened from the courtroom, never looking at the defendant.

The courtroom was stunned. Lengel moaned, tottered on his feet, and exclaimed, "My God! My God!" Carrie Lengel screamed and flung herself on her husband. Their daughter wailed, "Daddy, Daddy, you didn't do it!" The tension in the room broke, and disbelieving spectators asked each other, "Did they find him guilty?" Did the jury actually believe Floyd Streitenberger? Above the buzz of confusion, the Lengels could be heard sobbing. A bailiff shouted for order. Lengel, his wife and daughter clinging to him, rose, squared his shoulders, raised his right hand and protested to all who could hear: "Before God I didn't do it. I am innocent. There is no justice."[25] For ten minutes the Lengels remained rooted there before being led toward the back door of the courtroom. As the defendant approached the door, he proclaimed, "As God is my judge, I had nothing to do with it!"[26]

None of the prosecutors were present when the verdict was read. Harter rushed in after it was all over. He told reporters, "I'm not sorry they didn't give him the death penalty, but I think the other conspirators should have had it. . . . The jury's verdict, it seems to me, was exactly what Lengel deserved. We are grateful." He later admitted that the prosecutors expected no more than a manslaughter conviction. When asked for her reaction, Florence Mellett said she believed the verdict justified her husband's burning editorials attacking the former police chief and his lax enforcement of the law.[27] The Lengel verdict story ran on the front page of the *New York Times* under the heading, "Canton's Ex-Chief of Police Is Convicted in Killing of Mellett and Gets Life Term."[28]

Lengel's overconfident team, their bare-bones defense a failure, immediately asked Judge Clevenger for a new trial, a formality he was certain to deny. The real legal action would shift to the appellate court, and all the lawyers knew it. "Lengel was convicted by public sentiment, not by the evidence," Hahn declared. "We wanted to try the case in another county, but the old fellow insisted that he be judged by his fellow townsmen."[29] Again jailed, Lengel sat in his cell under a suicide watch after telling a fellow inmate, "I don't want to live now." Many in Canton felt the verdict was too harsh. Not Charles McClintock. He told the press, "Lengel, of all men, should have known better than to sit back and encourage the use of violence when he might have known murder could result."[30]

One year to the day after the murder of Don R. Mellett, the State of Ohio completed its work. Five men were imprisoned for the crime, four with life sentences based on guilty verdicts that rested primarily on circumstantial evidence and the testimony of admitted perjurers. It was a stunning success for the prosecution team, primarily Charles McClintock and Ora Slater, which began with nothing but managed to assemble five compelling cases.

Lengel's conviction was the most sweeping application of the conspiracy rule in Ohio legal history, a fact that troubled some legal experts. Higher courts would decide the fairness of this interpretation. The *Daily News* ran an editorial on the verdict in the July 17 edition that depicted the former chief as a victim of the vice machine, a man to be pitied. Yet, the editorial concluded, "The work of Don R. Mellett has been vindicated."

Long-suffering Steve Kascholk walked out of the Stark County Workhouse a free man on July 18, leaving his dollar-a-day job behind. With a handshake and best wishes from Florence Mellett, Steve left on the train for Nanty Glo. The county common pleas court, which oversaw the reward money, wisely decided to delay any distribution until Rudner's and Lengel's appeals were decided. Steve would have to wait a little longer for his big payday.

Of the five conspirators, only Lengel and Rudner pressed their appeals vigorously. Rudner was able to do so because his family had money, and Lengel, who never doubted his own innocence, did so out of sheer stubbornness. After Judge Clevenger denied a new trial for a guilty defendant, which was virtually automatic, the next appeal in Ohio was to the District Court of Appeals. The task of this elected multijudge panel was to review the trial record for errors. In general, appeals courts were reluctant to overturn unanimous verdicts by juries unless serious errors occurred during the trial that could have prejudiced the outcome.

Lengel's defense team and supporters weren't about to give up. With the former chief locked away in the Ohio Penitentiary, Lengel's attorneys went to the Seventh District Court of Appeals in Youngstown, home to Lengel's lead counsel, Frank Rollin Hahn. In mid-October, Hahn presented his argument to the court that Lengel's conviction was based on incensed public opinion, not evidence. That same day an appeals court in Toledo upheld Rudner's second-degree murder conviction.

On November 3, 1927, the appeals court ruled that improper evidence was admitted during Lengel's trial and that Judge Clevenger erred in instructing the jury.[31] Specifically, the appeals court said that Clevenger committed four errors: failure to admit the actual Dictaphone recordings as evidence; improperly admitting testimony of a conversation between Streitenberger and Rudner when Lengel was not present; admitting testimony by Streitenberger that some of Lengel's defense in his first civil service hearing was paid with money collected from vice lords; and instructing the jury to consider Lengel as guilty as any conspirator although not even the state claimed that he had prior knowledge that murder would result from the plot.[32] A new trial was ordered, much to the surprise of Mellett's supporters in Canton. In early December, Lengel was transferred back to the Stark County Jail. On the 13th, his friends posted a $25,000 bond, and Lengel went home, to be reunited with his wife and daughter.

The prosecution objected to the appeals court's decision and took their case to the Ohio Supreme Court, which, on December 20, heard the argument against a new trial as well as Ben Rudner's final appeal. Lengel traveled to Columbus to observe the proceedings, the first time a defendant had been granted that privilege in Ohio legal history. A week later, on December 28, the Ohio Supreme Court declined to overturn Rudner's conviction, leaving him to sit in prison; his only hope now was an eventual parole or governor's pardon. The court also let stand the appeals court ruling ordering a new trial for Lengel.[33]

Given the circumstances, the defense's request for a change of venue could hardly be denied. It was determined that the second proceeding would be held in Lisbon, the county seat of rural Columbiana County, almost due east of Canton on the Lincoln Highway. The trial was set to begin on Monday, February 13, 1928. Columbiana County, intent on putting its best foot forward in this high-profile case, undertook an extensive cleaning of the courtroom, which included replacing spectator benches with chairs.[34] The local hotels, rooming houses, and lunch counters prepared for additional business, and the county jail allotted space for potential inmates/witnesses from the Ohio Penitentiary. Yet despite the nationwide publicity the case brought to the village, the local papers reported widespread apathy among county residents regarding the Lengel trial.[35] Sixty-eight people were summoned to appear as potential jurors. The presiding judge assigned to the trial was W. Frank Lones, a Columbiana County native.

In addition to Hahn, Rogers, and Powell from the first trial, three local attorneys were added to the defense team, including George E. Davidson, who was once Judge Lones's law partner. The prosecution relied on Harter and McClintock, who were assisted by Columbiana

County prosecutor R. M. Brookes. Spectators and potential witnesses included Florence Mellett, who, with one of her daughters and one of Don's brothers, was seated in a conspicuous spot near the bailiff's desk, as well as Ora Slater, Steve Kascholk, Bill Bitzler, and Coroner T. C. McQuate. Waiting to be summoned from the penitentiary were Ben Rudner, Carl Studer, and, of course, Floyd Streitenberger.[36]

By Tuesday, a jury of ten men and two women was seated. An additional twenty-five potential jurors who had been called were not needed. This jury was not sequestered, only warned by Judge Lones not to read about or discuss the case. With that admonition, they were taken to Canton to visit the murder scene. When court resumed the next day, there were "lively" legal battles initiated by a defense once stung by complacency. A wary defense also employed a Dictaphone to record the proceedings lest anything be missed, a first in Columbiana County. Reporters commented that a new legal battle seemingly erupted every time Lengel's name was mentioned. In this round, the defense even challenged the idea of Kascholk testifying. As for the prosecution, it stuck with the first-degree murder charge. Harter told the jury, "A plot to beat up Don Mellett resulted in murder," and, the appellate court notwithstanding, "The defendant is equally guilty of murder as if he had fired the fatal shot." As the trial heated up, the courtroom filled with spectators, most from Lisbon.[37]

On Wednesday the jury heard from Coroner McQuate, Steve Kascholk, Florence Mellett, and Bill Bitzler. On Thursday Floyd Streitenberger took the stand. The prosecutors had heard rumors that the former detective might refuse to testify, so when he arrived in Lisbon, they asked him if he planned on giving evidence. He said he would. However, once on the stand, he declined to answer McClintock's questions. After a half-dozen refusals, Judge Lones pointed his finger at Streitenberger and threatened him with contempt of court. The recalcitrant witness shot back: "So what, I am doing life right now."[38] With this setback, the prosecutors argued that his previous statements, given under oath, should be admissible as evidence. They even summoned Florence Travis, court stenographer in Lengel's first trial, to read the transcripts. McClintock complained, "Streitenberger comes here refusing to testify, and the State is taken by surprise. He proved to be a hostile witness. . . . It seems a travesty of justice if we should be deprived of that evidence."[39]

The defense saw things differently, and so did Ohio law. Hahn pointed out that Streitenberger's refusal to testify could not be subverted by reading previous statements into the record. This was because a transcript could not be cross-examined, thus giving the prosecution an unfair advantage. Streitenberger, they said, was alive, present, and sane; he refused to testify for "private reasons" and no one could do anything about it.[40] Columbiana County prosecutor Brookes observed to reporters, "Someone, I do not know who, has coached this witness."[41]

The next day, Friday, February 17, Judge Lones ruled against admitting Streitenberger's previous testimony: "[Given] the decision of the Supreme Court in an exact similar case, I must rule that the previous testimony may not be used in this trial. . . . It is not for me, a common pleas judge, to say the Supreme Court is wrong." McClintock called the ruling "a mortal blow" to the prosecution's case. There simply was no other evidence linking Lengel directly to the Mellett murder. The state rested its case at 11:25 A.M. on Monday, asking for a verdict of guilt for first-degree murder. Immediately, the defense rose and demanded a "directed verdict of acquittal" on the grounds that the state had not presented sufficient evidence to prove its case.[42]

Judge Lones agreed. In his charge to the jury to issue a directed verdict of acquittal, the judge explained: "It takes more than mere gossip, suspicion or guessing to convict a person charged with a crime. Had it not been for [Streitenberger's] testimony, Lengel would not have been indicted." The judge further declared, "All the cowardly assassins who, on July 16, 1926, took or aided in taking the young life of Don R. Mellett, should receive the most severe punishment provided by law, but only the guilty should be punished."[43] He pointed out that Streitenberger's testimony was admitted under the conspiracy theory because the state promised to prove him a conspirator. "When [Streitenberger] took the witness chair, he refused to give any testimony. As he is already in prison for life, there is no way to force him to testify, and there is no law permitting his former testimony to be received." Lones pointed out that the appeals court read the trial record with Streitenberger's testimony and concluded it "was not sufficient to sustain the verdict of guilty." What would the appeals court say of a guilty verdict without Streitenberger's testimony? Thus, "as there is no evidence proving Lengel's connection with the conspiracy, the jury is directed to return a verdict for the defendant."[44]

There was absolutely no reaction in the courtroom filled largely with local spectators. Lengel, however, was jubilant. Quietly, both jurors and spectators came up to the ex-chief at the defense table and expressed support as they shook his hand. The general feeling in the courtroom, removed from Canton by thirty miles, was that Lengel's acquittal was justified. Outside, on the courthouse steps, Lengel told reporters, "This is the end of what has been a terrible ordeal for me. You will never know what it is to be unjustly accused of having taken a human life. . . . The result of this trial restored my faith in the impartiality of courts and the justice of the law." The former chief vowed to press his libel suit against the *Canton Daily News* and to seek $5,000 in back pay, his reinstatement, and a reduced $85 a month pension.[45] If Lengel's conviction was front-page news for the *New York Times*, then his acquittal was in the classic style of yesterday's news. Under the heading, "Lengel Acquitted by Court Direction," the story was buried deep in the paper's second section.[46]

On February 22 the *Daily News* published an editorial on Lengel's acquittal that reversed the position it had taken since the days when the Mellett brothers wrote the editorials: "So far as the real concern of Canton goes, Lengel's guilt or innocence is secondary. . . . Lengel's failings and faults as a guardian of the peace and safety of our citizens stand as a warning for eternal vigilance."[47] Florence Mellett chose to view the acquittal in more general terms: "Change in Canton after my husband's death helped make Canton a good place to live."[48]

McDermott Has the Last Word

Just two weeks after Saranus A. Lengel's acquittal in Lisbon, and in a surprising turn of events, Pat McDermott decided to break his public silence. For months rumors had reached Canton that Pat was telling his fellow inmates at the Ohio Penitentiary his version of the slaying of Don Mellett.[1] Now he was willing to go on the record. However, Pat didn't want to talk to anyone from Canton. Instead, he granted an interview to a pretty young newswoman from the *Youngstown Vindicator*, Ella Kerber Resch.

Pat's choice of Resch was no accident, nor was the reporter a disinterested journalist. Resch, whom Pat had met a year before, was a friend of Ben Rudner's family through his sister. Some in Ben's circle thought that he had a better chance of getting out of jail courtesy of the appeals court in Youngstown, which had been so helpful to Lengel. The notion that Lengel's acquittal would help Rudner was long odds, but the family was willing to try anything. For that reason, Rudner wanted Pat's confession to break in a Youngstown paper, not an unsympathetic Canton one. For her trouble, Resch would have the best story of her young career when she went to Columbus.[2] The interview was published in its entirety on Saturday, March 10, 1928, beginning on page one of the *Vindicator*, which didn't fail to take advantage of its promotional value. The paper claimed that it was reporter Resch who had gained McDermott's confidence, which led to the exclusive interview.[3]

Like any good Irish storyteller, Pat embellished his rambling and self-serving tale. Nevertheless, there was the ring of truth to much of it. He said he decided to talk because some of his fellow conspirators had done so. His silence thus far had been a matter of principle; he was keeping his word. He explained to Resch that sometimes he was known by the nickname "Boston Red." However, in the Atlanta federal lockup, where he had been a barber for the "aristocratic" prisoners, including the well-heeled Rudner, he was known by the generic "Butch."[4] Loafing around Cleveland's "Little Hollywood" neighborhood in the early summer of 1926, he heard rumors of a fellow in Canton looking for a couple of tough guys to beat up someone. McDermott needed a partner for the job and by chance ran into hometown acquaintance Steve Kascholk, also out of work, and suggested they check out the Canton scene. But a wary and streetwise Pat knew of no one in Canton he could trust to ask. However, he said, he did recall that former fellow Atlanta prisoner Ben Rudner lived in nearby Massillon where Rudner's father had a business. So Steve and Pat went to Massillon, where a helpful cabby directed them to Rudner's store. At first Ben failed to recognize Pat, who had only been a prison barber after all; but when prompted, Ben remembered him as Butch.

Once Pat's bona fides as an ex-con were established, the ever-helpful Rudner drove Pat to a pool hall in Canton, where he introduced Pat to Louis Mazer, Carl Studer, and Max Kane. McDermott said he took an instant dislike to Kane, whom he disdainfully described as a "doper." Next, according to Pat, Mazer drove him out to Don Mellett's old address on Broad Avenue and offered him $300 to beat up the editor. Offer made and accepted, the two men returned to Massillon to retrieve Steve and their luggage. The trip to Massillon and back was made in a black Hudson automobile, Pat remembered.

Pat said he wasn't in Canton very long before Mazer introduced him to Detective Streitenberger. Mazer also suggested McDermott get rid of Kascholk, whom Mazer correctly sensed was weak and unreliable. It was Mazer's advice to Pat that he tell Steve he was going to Chicago as a hint for Steve to leave Canton. Pat said that this ruse figured in Kascholk's decision to leave town as much as any moral qualms about employing violence. McDermott admitted that they found the trunk of clothes in the hotel room before Steve left and stole them to sell later. Pat added what the trunk's owner neglected to mention in court: the trunk contained a half-pint of whiskey that Pat and Steve finished. The clothing went to Pat's old pal Bill Bitzler, he said, who, in Pat's opinion, was rather shabbily dressed and would benefit from a less-threadbare wardrobe.

Pat told Resch that he met with Mazer every day he was in Canton, usually in the afternoon or evening. He said he twice remembered telephoning the Mellett home to warn him of impending danger. Once, on the Sunday before the murder, when he identified himself as "the enemy of your enemies," he warned Don about three men hanging around the garage. He said he called again later in the week, this time speaking to a woman who said Don was at his office. But he never explained to Resch why he called his intended victim, and the reporter apparently failed to inquire. According to Pat, Mazer told him there was no reason to hurry the job. Still, they made nightly visits to the Broad Avenue address. Pat said he was told that Mellett was single and lived with his brother and sister-in-law. Yet the people he saw on Broad Avenue didn't fit that description. Pat questioned this, and that prompted Streitenberger to get Mellett's correct address from the police department. McDermott also thought that the Mellett car was a Reo, having been told that one of Mellett's friends sold them. Pat admitted to drinking every night that week.

Pat said that on the night of the murder Mazer dropped him off in the correct neighborhood to scout around. Mazer told him to report to Streitenberger, who, with his wife, would be parked in a Chevy or Willys-Knight sedan at the fairgrounds gate closest to the Mellett home. But when Pat saw Kate Streitenberger in the car, he decided against approaching it. He called Mazer at the poolroom instead. Streitenberger and Mazer returned to pick him up some time later. He had grown impatient skulking around Mellett's neighborhood with the editor nowhere in sight. But Streitenberger wasn't giving up, however, saying that Mellett had to come home eventually. The three men drove a circle around the Mellett home several times. Finally, they saw that their victim had returned. When they pulled up to the curb near the house, Pat said, Streitenberger told them he heard voices from the front porch. This, the detective said, wouldn't do, so they parked farther down the street and walked back to the vacant lot across from the garage where Pat had found there was a good hiding place behind tall weeds.

In perhaps the most interesting part of the story, Pat denied being armed. When Mazer tried to press his gun on Pat, he told the *Vindicator* reporter, Streitenberger ordered Mazer to keep it. Pat was emphatic that he was not armed. He never mentioned the revolver Mazer had given him earlier; his co-conspirators each had .38 caliber revolvers, and the detective had a second smaller pistol in his pocket. According to Pat, they had to wait just five minutes before someone came out of the house to put the car in the garage. When that man exited the garage, Mazer and Streitenberger opened fire. At that same moment, he said, the car driven by Leo Schumacher pulled into a driveway only feet away. On hearing the car, the three men scattered, with Streitenberger and Mazer running west down Glenn Place past Schumacher's garage, separating, and then meeting up at Streitenberger's car. Pat ran south to Tuscarawas, crossed the street, and ran east, passing in front of the Mellett house, where he had a clear view of the commotion after the shooting stopped. He said he was two blocks down Tuscarawas when he was picked up by his accomplices.

Once all three were in the car, Streitenberger asked Mazer where his gun was. Back in the street, Mazer told him. Pat said that this caused Streitenberger to hastily turn the car around and return to the crime scene to recover it. They made this trip carefully, especially after a police motorcycle passed them. Streitenberger, appearing nervous, assured them that it was probably all right for a police detective to be out there that night. He then took charge of Mazer's gun.

The next morning, Pat said, he read in the newspaper about the murder and went to see Rudner. Ben asked Pat if he was involved. Pat said he was and wanted to know what to do. At that point in the interview McDermott stretched his credibility by claiming that he sent the R. L. Strang telegram from Massillon to himself to cover his hasty exit from the boardinghouse. Pat said that Hattie Gearhart had the wrong night in mind when she testified that he was in early Thursday evening.

Pat said he went to see Mazer and informed him he wanted to leave town. Pat told Resch that if he in fact had known Mellett was dead, he would have left town earlier. Leaving Canton made good sense, since, according to what Streitenberger had told him, the police would be hauling in strangers for questioning. Mazer drove Pat to the Akron roadhouse, and there Max Kane picked him up and drove him to Cleveland. In Pat's version of events, Kane said to call him if he wanted to talk to Rudner. The July 26 trip Pat, Homer, and Peggy took to Akron was, according to Pat, to meet the elusive Max Kane, who failed to show. The threesome then drove to Massillon, where Pat found Ben with his pal Fessler. The tightfisted Rudner had Fessler give Pat $10 to get rid of him.

According to McDermott, Lengel and Rudner knew nothing of the crime beforehand or about Pat's Cleveland hideouts. Later, when he and Mazer were arrested, Pat said he offered to take the blame. Resch never asked him to explain why, especially since the death penalty was a real possibility. In prison in Columbus, Streitenberger told Pat that if he, Streitenberger, was going down for the crime, someone was going with him, and it might as well be Lengel. Pat didn't deny that he didn't want to see Mazer—whom Pat said was also a drug addict—get off easy for being a stool pigeon.[5] As for Kascholk, in line for a large reward, McDermott said he thought Steve's story was "about right."[6] In a surprising revelation, Pat told Ella Resch that in February or March of 1926, Mazer had paid two men to beat up Mellett or blow up his home, but the thugs had skipped town with the money instead. This confirmed rumors of threats against Mellett in the spring of 1926. Pat said he was paid $40 dollars before the crime and $200 after. As for Ben Clarke, currently bedridden and fighting dismissal from the force for giving Mellett's address to the conspirators *twice*, he was not involved, Pat said. Recently an unsubstantiated story by an ex-con named Arthur Heinman had implicated Clarke.[7]

Because the interview was copyrighted by the *Vindicator*, the Canton papers could not print it verbatim. The Canton press downplayed this confession, giving it little credence. Prosecutor Harter labeled it a "smoke screen" designed to help Ben Rudner get a governor's pardon or parole, although little in Pat's tale actually helped Ben.[8] And it was in no one's interest in Canton to reexamine the case now, even if Pat was being completely honest. Still, to Harter's credit, he went to Columbus to see Warden Thomas, where he learned that no transcript of the interview was made. This lack of an official record of Pat's story further diminished the value of what he had said in regard to any further criminal charges being sought against any of the conspirators. Nor did it help anyone's appeal. In the warden's opinion, McDermott's confession didn't clear Rudner; rather, it implicated him. Pat's motivation was seen as loyalty to his old friend Rudner and as an attempt to make Mazer appear more involved than Mazer's confession had indicated. As if to confirm this, Pat threatened Mazer's life in prison just days following the interview, and for good measure Pat accused Mazer of killing the Kitzig boy. Mazer's only recorded comment to Pat was honest and to the point: "You're a fool." Not to be left out, Streitenberger, close-mouthed only a month ago in Lisbon, declared that Rudner gave him first chance to talk to the Youngstown reporter. This, he said, was at the instigation of attorney Powell, who had a reporter waiting in the prison should Streitenberger agree.[9] Rudner was grasping at straws to escape life in prison, as he would until his death. At last the once-tight-lipped conspirators, who had well-rehearsed alibis, were now turning on each other as they contemplated life behind bars and out of the spotlight.

Unanswered Questions .

W ho really was Don Mellett? Was he a pure-of-heart crusading journalist, or was he a ruthless business manager striving for profit? Who really shot Don Mellett? And, more interesting, why?

More than eighty years later, the answers still elude us. Mellett never had a chance to explain his motivation or his strategy. The myth that grew up around the martyred editor has clouded the real truth. Who really initiated the plot to assault Mellett? Which of the conspirators actually fired at Mellett that July night? Three self-serving confessions raised more questions than they answered. All of the principle players in one of the most important crimes of the Prohibition era are dead, and these questions will forever remain unanswered. The crime has never been completely solved.

Bullets from two different guns were found at the murder scene. Forensic science was in its infancy, but no great expertise was required to determine that the bullets were fired from two weapons whose rifling rotated in opposite directions. Also, Florence Mellett, Leo Schumacher, and Bessie Zimmer all thought there was more than one gunman. Yet no weapons were found, and it seems likely that Pat's revolver ended up in Meyer's Lake.

Three men gave self-serving confessions. As far as the shooting goes, McDermott's story comes the closest to being credible. It seems likely that all three men were in the vacant lot when the shots were fired. This was necessary to bolster McDermott, a reluctant hit man who was more talk and bravado than substance. Mazer's assertion that he was only going along is plausible. Streitenberger's claim to only be following Mazer was out of character.

When the *Cleveland Plain Dealer*'s editors questioned the idea of the police detective being the leader, they were blinded by stereotypes. A southern Ohio farm boy in speech and manner, Streitenberger was no rube. He had been an army top sergeant and Canton police night sergeant. He was used to giving orders to the likes of Mazer and Mc-Dermott. He would have been the one to keep going until the job was done, when Mazer and McDermott had given up. Moreover, the limited forensic evidence pointed to two bullets, including the fatal one, coming from a new but carelessly maintained revolver. This was probably the one Mazer loaned Pat. The third bullet, steel jacketed and of military manufacture, came from a well-used revolver—the type of weapon and ammunition a police officer might be expected to carry.

A plausible case could be made that McDermott shot *at* Don Mellett (shooting at and hitting a man from a range of 100 feet with an unfamiliar and unfired handgun was luck, not skill) and that Streitenberger, said by some to be a crack shot whose revolver was worn from practice, intentionally aimed to miss. Mazer, who had no history of assault with a weapon, only watched in stunned silence.

What of Ben Rudner and Saranus A. Lengel, neither of whom was involved in the actual murder? Rudner was drawn into the conspiracy by the unexpected appearance of Patrick "Red" McDermott. Playing his favorite role of big man in town, Rudner simply introduced McDermott to Mazer. After that, he worked primarily to limit his liability in the crime. His visits with Lengel, rides with McQuate and Slater, and schmoozing with police and reporters were done in order to find out how much complicity he was suspected of. Rudner was guilty of arranging to hide Pat, a wanted fugitive, after the crime. Evidence implicating Ben as a full-fledged conspirator is thin at best, and the verdict in his trial indicates that the jury agreed. Lengel was even further removed from the conspiracy. The police chief had no doubt heard rumors of a planned assault on Mellett in 1926, but which rumors were true? Lengel probably thought the editor deserved a beating, considering the editorial condemnation he and his department had endured. Lengel's failure was in placing his personal feelings above his professional duty. As chief of police, it was his responsibility to protect all law-abiding citizens of Canton, and he should have initiated some type of investigation into the threats Mellett received. Such an action by Lengel might have caused Streitenberger to back off. Instead, the detective mistook Lengel's indifference for approval. This failure to do his duty was, by itself, sufficient enough to warrant Lengel's removal. But his prosecutors, riding a wave of incredible luck, let their success go to their heads, and their conviction of Lengel for first-degree murder, on the flimsiest of evidence, was vengeance, not justice.

Was Don Mellett's investigation of the Kitzig murder the true motive for the attack on him? Ella Resch was a novice reporter on the trail of an exclusive for her paper. She was too inexperienced and awed by Pat to press him on the issue of motive. The Mellett family and Walter Vail always maintained that Don's death was because of his investigation of the Kitzig murder. So did Ora Slater, who said, "I could not help thinking that [the Kitzig murder] was the one thing which would have been most likely to precipitate Mellett's murder."[1] No evidence was found to substantiate Don's claim that he had solved the crime. But perhaps his poking around was dangerous enough. Yet it could be argued that murder was not the plan at all. Perhaps the perpetrators should be taken at their word, that only a beating was planned. They wanted to show Mellett just enough intimidation to get him to back off. Mellett's incessant editorial attacks on the police and crime bosses had a dampening effect on vice in Canton. Pat McDermott said that he didn't like the *Daily News* running his new Canton friends down, but he was too new to Canton to have arrived at this opinion independently. The crime could have escalated to murder only after Mellett proved difficult to corner for an assault, and the few shots meant to scare him went awry. This does not excuse his murderers, but it does put the crime in a slightly different light: conspiracy to assault the editor gone wrong rather than conspiracy to commit murder from the outset; a bunch of amateurs fumbling around instead of a group of hardened professional criminals. If that was the case, this would make Don Mellett's death even more tragic.

Don Mellett was a complicated personality. He was determined to succeed in his chosen profession as a journalist. Yet he understood as well as anyone in the newspaper industry in the 1920s the importance of making a profit. John Barlow Martin wondered, "Would it be unreasonable to conclude that Don Mellett came to Canton an intelligent, ambitious, right-thinking newspaperman who had made no conspicuous success, who was not getting any younger, and who found himself arrayed with the forces of righteousness—because that way lay fame and success also?" Helen Bloom, after extensively researching the slain editor, concluded that Don Mellett was "a six foot tall question mark." Jerry Updegraff concluded that Mellett "must have been a hard, cold, calculating businessman" who nevertheless "deserves to be called a martyr to American journalism," and Glenn Himebaugh called Mellett "a martyr with a smaller than deserved niche in the history of American journalism."[2]

The *Canton Repository*, fifty years after Mellett's death, said about its old rival: "He (Mellett) was accused of being opportunistic, of using his crusade against crime as a circulation builder to improve his own chances of advancement in Cox Newspapers and, in his crusade, of employing questionable methods—both in print and behind the scenes." Yet, the paper concluded, Mellett was "a full fledged American journalistic hero, and that is how it should be."[3]

No one in Canton was a closer friend to Don Mellett than Walter Vail. In an interview with the *Repository* in 1976, he recalled that his old friend "Don was a courageous and aggressive newsman. He also wanted to boost the *Daily News* circulation, but he did not try to do this through sensational stories." Evan Mellett summarized how the family felt about his father in a 1963 letter: "I simply see him as a young aspiring editor, trying to make a name for himself, and losing . . . [had he lived he] would never have been heard of . . . other than being a good, sound newspaperman."[4]

Perhaps all Donald Ring Mellett wanted to be was a good, sound newspaperman. It was fate that thrust him into a larger role.

The Aftermath

O ne last detail remained to be resolved before Canton could put the two-year saga of the murder of Don Mellett to rest: distribution of the reward money. Of the nearly $28,000 pledged, $24,113 was actually collected and held by the common pleas court. Wisely, the overseers chose to withhold the final distribution until all the trials and appeals were completed. By March 1928, all the appeals were over, and the time had come. Ultimately, thirty people filed with the court for a portion of the reward worth about $250,000 in 2009.[1]

Finally on March 26, 1928, the lucky recipients were announced. Twenty-four people were deemed to be entitled to some of the money for their assistance in bringing the conspirators to justice. Former prosecutor Charles McClintock had lobbied hard for Steve Kascholk and the Bitzlers as the most deserving, and the court agreed. Steve Kascholk received the largest share, $10,000.[2] The Bitzlers, who had a history of frequently moving and changing their name to avoid creditors, received a combined $6,000. Next on the list, despite previously denying interest in any reward, was the McDermott clan. Tom, Bernard, and Pat's two sisters received a total of $2,500.[3] The two reluctant female witnesses, Peggy Cavanaugh and Thelma Harris, each received $500. Homer Connelly was awarded $250 for testifying about driving Pat to Massillon. The hot-tempered German salesman, William Brumme, received $500, but it was held in escrow pending the settlement of an old debt. For being honest about the events at the Streitenbergers' murder-night party, Clare Welshimer received $500, C. O. Groner, $250, and the elder Gussetts, a combined $200. Brave young Carl Gussett so impressed prosecutors that he was awarded $300. W. A. McDonald, whose clothes Pat and Steve appropriated, was given $100, the half-pint of whiskey notwithstanding. Norman Clark, Mazer's former attorney and police prosecutor once held for liquor law violations, also got $100 for his trouble. Authorities may have had more help in apprehending Pat in Pennsylvania than they admitted, since two Nanty Glo residents, Dr. H. A. Collins and C. R. Dinninger, each received $100 for their aid in capturing McDermott.

Lastly, and somewhat surprisingly, three paid investigators received rewards over and above their salaries. The court said this was for the extraordinary time they put into the investigation. Ora Slater, who said he drove more than 1,000 miles in chasing down leads, was given $1,000. Although he didn't admit it, he had lobbied hard for it. In a letter dated July 16, 1927, Slater suggested to the common pleas court that he was as entitled as Bitzler and Kascholk because "without my apprehension of Pat McDermott I am satisfied that the murder of Don R. Mellett would now remain an unsolved mystery as other murders are in Starke [sic] County." And in a handwritten note dated March 16, 1928, he claimed to have "cleaned up the case." His assistant C. B. Armstrong received $250, as did the current chief of Canton police, Earl Hexamer.[4]

Ora Slater emerged from the Don Mellett murder case as the detective of last resort for unsolvable crimes in Ohio, Indiana, and Kentucky. He eventually rose to direct the Cal Crim Detective Agency in Cincinnati. On October 3, 1941, Slater chanced on a robbery in downtown Cincinnati while on his way to lunch. He grabbed the thief as the man ran down the street, and in the ensuing struggle Slater was shot point blank in the face. He held the man until police arrived, at which time the seriousness of the wound was discovered. Slater recovered, however, saved by his upper denture, which had stopped the bullet and limited its destructiveness. Slater died quietly at his home on February 1, 1945, after a two-year illness. He was buried in his hometown of Lawrenceburg, Indiana, in a ceremony for which the Cincinnati chief of police chose the pallbearers and the Indiana state police served as escorts. There's no question that Ora Slater was a premier private detective in the heyday of gumshoes.[5]

Although prosecutors Henry Harter and Charles McClintock did not receive monetary rewards, they were able to parlay their successful prosecutions into something far more impressive. McClintock was elected to Congress in 1928, where he served until the Democratic landslide of 1932, led by Jim Cox's old running mate Franklin Roosevelt, swept him from office. In 1946 he was elected to a seat on the Ohio Fifth District Court of Appeals, where he served until resigning in 1963 due to failing health. When McClintock died in 1965 in a Canton nursing home at the age of eighty, his longtime secretary, Mildred Haag, was the legal guardian of the widowed and childless judge. Miss Haag discovered that the former prosecutor had saved every scrap of evidence dealing with the Mellett murder. Unfortunately, she had it all destroyed.[6]

Henry W. Harter Jr. followed in his father's footsteps and was appointed a common pleas judge in 1929 on the death of Judge A. W. Agler. In 1934 he was defeated in a bid for reelection and returned to the practice of law. He died in 1949 at the age of sixty-three.[7]

Florence Mellett and her children stayed in Indianapolis, where she lived as a single parent surrounded by Don's family. She managed on Don's life insurance and workmen's compensation awards and the help of relatives. (In 1930 she and her children were living with Lloyd's family in Indianapolis.) She attended every trial and worked tirelessly to keep her husband's memory alive. Florence Mellett died in September 1971 at the age of eighty. Her brother-in-law Lloyd Mellett left journalism and in 1930 was managing an advertising company in Indianapolis. During the Depression he became a publicist for the U.S. Housing Administration in Texas. He died in Dallas in February 1953.[8]

Saranus A. Lengel, acquitted of murder, proceeded with his battle for reinstatement and back pay. He lacked the service needed to collect a twenty-year pension, however, and his libel suit against the

Daily News was never refiled. In November 1928, the police pension board ordered him reinstated with the understanding that he would resign immediately and collect a $91-a-month pension based on fifteen years of service. But it was discovered that the fifteen-year pension law was passed *after* he left office and was not retroactive. Lengel was therefore not eligible, and the deal collapsed.[9] In 1937 a state board of claims rejected his request for $15,000 in damages for his wrongful imprisonment. Instead, a $4,000 award was granted, about equal to his back pay. But the Ohio Legislature never approved the funds. Failing to get a police pension or award, Lengel returned to baking and "other employment." He died at age seventy-two of a stroke in January 1941 and was buried in Canton. There was no official police presence at his funeral.[10]

Pat's nemesis, Steve Kascholk, was true to his word and married Mary. In 1930 the couple and their two children were living in Cleveland where Steve was earning $2,700 a year working as a mechanic in the auto industry. Steve was going by his middle name, Frank, and the children's ages were adjusted to avoid the stain of illegitimacy.[11] He died in Cleveland in 1944. The Bitzlers, always on the run from their creditors, successfully disappeared from the historical record.

Ben Rudner never gave up in his quest to get out of prison. His attorneys argued in vain for years that his conviction for second-degree murder was invalid because he had been charged with first-degree murder. When the Supreme Court rejected that argument, Rudner was left lobbying for a pardon from the governor, or hoping for parole. For good behavior, he was transferred to Ohio's prison farm in London, an hour's drive southwest of Columbus. It was from there that he wrote James Aungst in the prosecutor's office in 1941, "Are you adverse to seeing me released?" Early in 1949, George Gordon Battle, eighty-one and only months away from death, wrote the Ohio parole board to plead for Rudner's release for medical reasons. But Ben remained in prison, and at 4:00 P.M. on August 11, 1949, he collapsed and died of a massive heart attack while working in the prison farm garage. He was fifty-one years old. His family buried him in Canton. At the time Ben Rudner had served a longer sentence for second-degree murder than any other man in Ohio criminal history.[12]

Floyd Streitenberger, once so completely broken by incarceration, was also transferred to the prison farm. He returned to his roots there, working quietly as a gardener. He died in late November 1962 at the age of seventy. Perhaps his most honest statement of his part in the Mellett murder, Streitenberger gave up all thoughts of release from prison and dropped all appeals.[13]

Louis Mazer was released from prison after serving only five years, a term deemed too short by most people in Canton. As prosecutors often do, they traded with the devil for his cooperation. He subsequently kept a low profile and was rumored to have quietly run a bar or poolroom for several years. He died in Cincinnati in 1951.[14]

While Canton might have wished to forget Patrick McDermott, he wasn't about to serve his life in prison quietly. During the first twenty-five years of his imprisonment, he was considered "a thoroughly bad actor" by state corrections officials. He escaped the Ohio Penitentiary in 1929 by climbing over a roof near the front wall of the prison. He was recaptured the next day. During the disastrous 1930 fire that killed hundreds of inmates, Pat was one of the prisoners who threw rocks at National Guardsmen attempting to restore order. He tried to hang himself at least once. In 1936 Pat contracted tuberculosis, which was endemic in the damp, poorly ventilated prison, and was sent to the London farm to recuperate. When he recovered he was deemed too dangerous to stay at the prison farm and was sent back to Columbus. He was assigned to work in the prison's medical laboratory, and it was there that he gave a small glimpse of what might have been. Assigned to test sputum samples in the lab for TB, Pat developed a shortcut that reduced the testing time from days to hours. Because of his aptitude for lab work, he was also placed in charge of blood typing all new inmates. In 1947 it was noted that his reputation as a triggerman enabled him to serve as a moderating influence for other tough lifers in the lockup.[15]

McDermott's and Streitenberger's cases came up jointly before the parole board in 1948. The board could have reduced their sentences to second-degree murder and made them eligible for parole. Instead, the board scathingly wrote of the pair, "They are not deserving of clemency, and were lucky to have escaped the electric chair."[16]

Pat McDermott, age fifty-six, donned a suit, topcoat, and hat in November 1954 and, in the company of an attractive red-haired woman, calmly walked past guards and out of the Ohio Penitentiary to a waiting Oldsmobile. A short time later, he robbed a cab driver at gun point. Pat had been working as a nurse in the prison's honor dormitory, where private visits were permitted for trusted prisoners. The embarrassed warden admitted that his men "should have recognized him" as he exited. A nationwide manhunt was launched, which landed Pat on the FBI's Ten-Most-Wanted list. Rumors had Pat headed for Mexico.[17]

In July 1955, an alert New York City policeman thought that an ambulance attendant he rode with to the Jewish Memorial Hospital looked familiar. Returning to the station, the patrolman checked the wanted posters and went back for his man. At first claiming to be "Steve Garish," McDermott, police noted, had the same tattoos and missing fingertip as Garish. Pat admitted his identity. He had been living in New York since December with a clueless woman named Rose Bern and using the medical knowledge he gained in prison to land the hospital job. A clever and lucky Pat had been arrested several times in New York for minor offenses, but he'd never been recognized.[18] He was eventually returned to Columbus. Pat was transferred to Lima, Ohio, to the prison hospital in June 1970, where he died on January 1, 1972, at the age of seventy-four, the last of the conspirators.[19]

. . .

A plaque in the journalism building at Indiana University commemorates Donald R. Mellett as one "who gave up his life rather than lower his high ideals of the editor's duty to his community." Among many posthumous honors, in addition to the Pulitzer Prize, Mellett was inducted into the Ohio and Indiana journalism halls of fame. Also, in 1931 the Don R. Mellett Memorial Fund Lectures in Journalism was established at New York University. For thirty years, the privately funded lecture series featured prominent members of the press until its demise in the 1960s.[20]

For Florence Mellett, Don's death took on religious overtones. In 1930 she told *Editor and Publisher*, "His heart and soul were in his work and he gave his life that others might live as truly as Jesus did." A widow can be forgiven for canonizing her husband. Yet Don Mellett was human. In Canton he at times stretched the ethics of journalism and the tenants of good reporting to suit his point of view and sell newspapers. Of course, as a newspaper publisher in the 1920s, he was not alone in this.

Was Canton a better place to live because of Don Mellett? The municipal police department improved visibly, first under the capable leadership of John "Jiggs" Wise, who succeeded Lengel. When Wise died tragically in an automobile accident in September 1927, Earl Hexamer replaced him and served, perhaps tellingly, until he had a breakdown in 1934. Statistics are scarce, but overall arrests in Canton fell 25 percent from 1924 to 1929, and liquor-related arrests declined by a third.[21] The *Canton Repository*, looking back in April 1976 at the city since the Mellett era, observed, "His [Mellett's] constant attacks on crime and corruption and his death resulted in a massive cleanup in Canton. Eternal vigilance is the price a city must pay to keep crime and corruption to a minimum, and Canton has had to undertake one or two additional cleanups since the Mellett era. But later inroads by the underworld here, bad as they were, never saw the city plummet to the depths it reached in the years before Mellett's murder."

The *Canton Daily News* without Don Mellett returned to being the newspaper it had been before the crusading editor took charge. James Cox installed his right-hand man, Charles Morris, as the new editor and spent freely on a new building and printing plant. The paper's circulation peaked in the summer of 1926, thereafter slowly declining back to pre-Mellett levels. Profits evaporated, as did Cox's interest. Admitting that he was not very keen on his Canton investment, even though it had won a Pulitzer Prize, Cox declared that Canton could not properly support two daily newspapers. He accepted a "handsome offer" from the owners of the rival *Evening Repository*, and on July 3, 1930, the *Daily News* changed ownership again. The management at the *Repository* promptly closed the *Daily News* and made Canton a one-newspaper town.[22]

By the 1930s Don Mellett, his murder, and his message were well on the way to being forgotten. Many respectable Canton residents saw the murder as a black eye on the city. It was bad for business, a public relations nightmare to be buried and forgotten as quickly as possible. Former *Daily News* owner James Cox consigned the entire episode to the dustbin of history when he devoted just two paragraphs of his 447-page autobiography to his Canton experience. Worse yet, he wrote just half of one sentence about his slain employee, whom he never mentioned by name: "Gangsters organized and carried out the murder of our editor." John Barlow Martin, writing for *Harper's Magazine* in September 1946, on the twentieth anniversary of the murder, found Canton an easy place once again to find gambling, prostitution, and illegal liquor. He wrote unflatteringly, "It looks cheap, dirty; the low buildings are old and grimy or have flashy false fronts." He concluded by quoting an unidentified source: "Canton is still Canton." In 1982 an elderly madam recalled in an *Akron Beacon Journal* story that Canton was a wide-open town until a crackdown in the 1950s. The attitude on Cherry Street in the 1920s and 1930s, she said, was one of live and let live.[23]

Eighty years later, Canton has been rehabilitated, but the Mellett name is gone. And the *Daily News* can only be found on microfilm in the county library. The jail and workhouse logbooks for 1926–27 are missing. The Tuscarawas Avenue murder scene is now an unremarkable gas station in a declining part of town. Only a plaque dedicated in 1976 in the McKinley memorial serves as a reminder that Don Mellett was ever in Canton. Its citation memorializes Donald Ring Mellett as "a martyr in the fight for a free and crusading press."

The slaying of Donald Ring Mellett in the summer of 1926 roused America's free press in a way few events do. Mellett was a crusading editor, not always a popular role in any community. But his brief time in Canton demonstrated the power that a brave journalist can wield. His friend Walter Vail recalled that Mellett "did just what he thought." He absolutely believed he was right, and he believed in the power of the press to make change. As the Mellett brothers wrote in an editorial on May 12, 1926, "The Constitution of the United States guarantees the freedom of the press because the press is expected to guarantee the freedom of the people."[24]

Notes

PREFACE

1. *Editor and Publisher,* July 31, 1926.
2. Kimberly Kenny, *Canton: A Journey Through Time* (Chicago: Arcadia, 2003), 119.
3. William Dean Krahling, "Don R. Mellett of the *Canton Daily News,*" (M.A. thesis, University of Iowa, 1967), 6.
4. *Editor and Publisher,* July 24, 1926.
5. *Cleveland Plain Dealer,* Dec. 5, 1926.

1. THE NEWSPAPERMAN

1. Franklin Miller Jr., *The Mellett and Hickman Families of Henry County, Indiana* (Gambier, Ohio: Privately published, 1976), 48–50.
2. Unless otherwise noted, most of the material that forms the basis for this chapter is drawn from Krahling, "Don R. Mellett," 1–25; and Glenn Himebaugh, "Donald Ring Mellett, Journalist: The Shaping of a Martyr" (Ph.D. diss., Southern Illinois University, 1978), 74–152.
3. Krahling, "Don R. Mellett," 14.
4. Himebaugh, "The Shaping of a Martyr," 110–11.
5. Ibid., 117.
6. Ibid., 147.
7. Krahling, "Don R. Mellett," 17.

8. Elizabeth Jane Greiner, "Saxton Street: Reconstruction of a Red Light Community 1906–1913" (M.A. thesis, Ohio State University, 1987), 1.
9. William S. Couch. "Canton: A Lurid City." In *An Ohio Reader: Reconstruction to the Present*, ed. Thomas H. Smith (Grand Rapids, Mich: Eerdmans, 1975).
10. Mark Thorton, "Alcohol Prohibition Was a Failure," Cato Policy Analysis No. 157 (July 19, 1999), accessed Aug. 29, 2005, from http://www.cato.org/pubs/pas/pa-157.html.
11. Ibid.
12. Edward Behr, *Prohibition: Thirteen Years That Changed America* (New York: Arcade, 1996), 103.
13. Greiner, "Saxton Street," 3–27.
14. The 1926 transcript of S. A. Lengel's hearing is found in the Day, Ketterer File, William McKinley Presidential Library and Archives, Canton, Ohio.
15. "Stench" *Time*, Aug. 2, 1926.
16. H. C. Pontius letter to Governor Vic Donahey, Nov. 5, 1926, Day, Ketterer File.
17. Greiner, "Saxton Street," 25–27.
18. Gary Brown, "The District May Be Gone, but Not the Profession," *Canton Repository*, June 15, 1985.
19. E. T. Heald, *The Stark County Story*, 4 vols. (Canton, Ohio: Stark County Historical Society, 1949–59), 4:801–2.
20. Greiner, "Saxton Street," 63, 111, 270, 278.
21. James M. Cox, *Journey Through My Years* (New York: Simon and Schuster, 1946), 220.
22. Jerry L. Updegraff, "A Study of the Circumstances Surrounding the Murder of Don R. Mellett in 1926" (M.A. thesis, Ohio University, 1974), 15–18.
23. Ibid.
24. Heald, *The Stark County Story*, 4:801–2.
25. James E. Cebula, *James M. Cox, Journalist and Politician* (New York: Garland, 1985), 19–27.
26. Cox, *Journey Through My Years*, 49.
27. Paul F. Bollar, *Presidential Campaigns* (New York: Oxford University Press, 1984), 212–13.
28. Cox, *Journey Through My Years*, 323.
29. Ibid.
30. Cebula, *James M. Cox*, 130.
31. Himebaugh, "The Shaping of a Martyr," 151–52.
32. Krahling, "Don R. Mellett," 25.

2. MELLETT IN CANTON

1. Unless otherwise noted, most of the material that forms the basis of this chapter is drawn from Krahling, "Don R. Mellett," 16–24, 48–235; and Himebaugh, "The Shaping of a Martyr," 42–46, 64, 163.
2. Krahling, "Don R. Mellett," 51–52.
3. Michael Schudson, *Discovering the News: A Social History of American Newspapers* (New York: Basic Books, 1978) 144–45, 158, 161.
4. Krahling, "Don R. Mellett," 43.
5. Himebaugh, "The Shaping of a Martyr," 163–65.
6. Krahling, "Don R. Mellett," 7.
7. Deposition of D. R. Mellett, Mar. 1, 1926, Day, Ketterer File.
8. Krahling, "Don R. Mellett," 28.
9. Statement of Lloyd Mellett, July 27, 1926, Day, Ketterer File.
10. Krahling, "Don R. Mellett," 55–56.
11. *Canton Daily News*, Nov. 1, 1926.
12. Judge H. C. Pontius, "Notes on Ben Clarke," n.d., Day, Ketterer File.
13. Updegraff, "A Study of the Circumstances," 18.
14. Statement of Lloyd Mellett, July 27, 1926, Day, Ketterer File.
15. Updegraff, "A Study of the Circumstances," 20.
16. Himebaugh, "The Shaping of a Martyr," 44.
17. Statement of Lloyd Mellett, July 27, 1926, Day, Ketterer File.
18. Krahling, "Don R. Mellett," 87–90.
19. Ibid., 90.
20. Kenny, *Canton*, 120.
21. Himebaugh, "The Shaping of a Martyr," 42–43.
22. John Barlow Martin, "Murder of a Journalist," *Harper's Magazine*, Sept. 1946, 275.
23. Statement of Leo Schumacher, July 28, 1926, Day, Ketterer File.
24. Updegraff, "A Study of the Circumstances," 22.
25. Martin, "Murder of a Journalist," 275.
26. Krahling, "Don R. Mellett," 109.
27. Ibid., 95, 105.
28. Deaths in Canton's black community during the Prohibition era were regularly attributed to consumption of poisonous wood alcohol. Krahling, "Don R. Mellett," 106–8.
29. Affidavit of J. E. Wing, n.d., Day, Ketterer File.
30. Himebaugh, "The Shaping of a Martyr," 49.
31. *Canton Daily News*, Dec. 21, 1925.
32. *Canton Repository*, Apr. 21, 1976.
33. Ibid.
34. Krahling, "Don R. Mellett," 128–31.
35. Ibid., 128.
36. Ibid., 134.

37. Ibid., 137–38.
38. *Canton Daily News*, Jan. 31, 1926.
39. Statement of Floyd Streitenberger, May 20, 1927, Day, Ketterer File.
40. Krahling, "Don R. Mellett," 147.
41. Ibid., 144.
42. Deposition of D. R. Mellett, Mar. 1, 1926, Day, Ketterer File.
43. *Canton Daily News*, Mar. 1, 1926.
44. Krahling, "Don R. Mellett," 158–59.
45. *Cleveland Plain Dealer*, May 17, 1927.
46. *Canton Evening Repository*, Mar. 17, 1926.
47. Ibid., Mar. 26, 1926.
48. Krahling, "Don R. Mellett," 160–65.
49. *State of Ohio vs. Louis Mazer*, Sworn Statement, May 5, 1927, Stark County Library District, Main Branch, Canton, Ohio.
50. Statement of Floyd Streitenberger, May 20, 1927, Day, Ketterer File.
51. *Youngstown Vindicator*, Mar. 10, 1928.
52. Krahling, "Don R. Mellett," 164–79.
53. Updegraff, "A Study of the Circumstances," 63.
54. Krahling, "Don R. Mellett," 188.
55. Statement of Lloyd Mellett, July 27, 1926, Day, Ketterer File.
56. Krahling, "Don R. Mellett," 169.
57. James Cox letter to H. C. Pontius, Apr. 2, 1926, Day, Ketterer File.
58. Krahling, "Don R. Mellett," 234.
59. Ibid., 216–19.
60. *Canton Evening Repository*, July 13, 1926.
61. Krahling, "Don R. Mellett," 231–32, 235.
62. Statement of Lloyd Mellett, July 27, 1926, Day, Ketterer File.
63. Krahling, "Don R. Mellett," 235.
64. Ibid., 246–48.
65. *Canton Evening Repository*, July 16, 1926.

3. THE MURDER

1. Krahling, "Don R. Mellett," 240–41.
2. Ibid., 233.
3. Himebaugh, "The Shaping of a Martyr," 65.
4. *Canton Evening Repository*, Feb. 18, 1915.
5. *Canton Daily News*, Aug. 11, 1921.
6. Krahling, "Don R. Mellett," 232–33.
7. The *Canton Daily News*, *Canton Evening Repository*, and *Cleveland Plain Dealer* provide the most detailed contemporary accounts of the murder of Don Mellett. Much of the material in this chapter is drawn from articles appearing in the July and December 1926 and February and May 1927 editions.
8. *Canton Daily News*, July 15, 1926.

9. Krahling, "Don R. Mellett," 240.

10. *Canton Daily News*, July 16, 1926.

11. Krahling, "Don R. Mellett," 248.

12. Himebaugh, "The Shaping of a Martyr," 179.

13. Krahling, "Don R. Mellett," 248.

14. This often-repeated excuse for Don's lateness is part of the Mellett mythology that cannot be verified.

15. Krahling, "Don R. Mellet," 40–42.

16. Martin, "Murder of a Journalist," 271.

17. Ibid.

18. *Cleveland Plain Dealer*, May 13, 1927.

19. Statement of Walter Vail, July 26, 1926, Day, Ketterer File.

20. *Canton Repository*, Apr. 18, 1976.

21. WWI Draft Registration and Stark County, Ohio, Census 1920, both accessed Feb. 5, 2006, at www.Ancestry.com.

22. Statement of Lloyd Mellett, July 27, 1926, Day, Ketterer File.

23. *Cleveland Plain Dealer*, Dec. 14, 1926.

24. Transcript of S. A. Lengel Civil Service Hearing, Sept. 8, 1926, Day, Ketterer File.

25. Statement of Lloyd Mellett, July 27, 1926, Day, Ketterer File.

26. *Canton Evening Repository*, Dec. 18, 1926.

27. Statement of Leo Schumacher, July 28, 1926, Day, Ketterer File.

28. Statement of Florence Mellett, July 27, 1926, Day, Ketterer File.

29. *Canton Evening Repository*, Dec. 13, 1926.

30. Heald, *The Stark County Story*, 4:51.

31. H. C. Pontius, "Notes on Ben Clarke," n.d., Day, Ketterer File.

32. *Salem News*, May 9, 1927.

33. *Cleveland Plain Dealer*, Feb. 2, 1927.

34. Statement of Bessie Zimmer, July 28, 1926, Day, Ketterer File.

35. Hutchinson and Smith Detective Bureau notes, n.d., Day, Ketterer File.

36. Statement of Bessie Zimmer, July 28, 1926, Day, Ketterer File.

37. Statement of Florence Mellett, July 27, 1926, Day, Ketterer File.

38. *Cleveland Plain Dealer*, Feb. 19. 1927.

39. Hutchinson and Smith Detective Bureau notes, Day, Ketterer File.

40. Statement of Lloyd Mellett, July 27, 1926, Day, Ketterer File.

41. *Canton Repository*, Apr. 18, 1976.

42. Merchant policemen were private security guards.

43. *Canton Daily News*, Feb. 11, 1927.

44. Himebaugh, "The Shaping of a Martyr," 79.

45. *Canton Evening Repository*, July 16, 1926.

46. Ora Slater, "How I Trapped the Don Mellett Slayers," *True Detective Mysteries*, May 1931, 50.

47. Updegraff, "A Study of the Circumstances," 39.

48. *Canton Daily News*, July 16, 1926.

49. Krahling, "Don R. Mellett," 253–55.
50. *Editor and Publisher*, July 24, 1926.
51. Himebaugh, "The Shaping of a Martyr," 9.
52. James M. Cox letter, July 17, 1926, Day, Ketterer File.
53. James M. Cox letter, July 17, 1926, Day, Ketterer File.
54. Himebaugh, "The Shaping of a Martyr," 179.
55. Ibid., 8–9.
56. *Canton Daily News*, July 16, 1926.
57. *Editor and Publisher*, July 31, 1926.
58. Himebaugh, "The Shaping of a Martyr," 179.
59. Martin, "Murder of a Journalist," 271–72.

4. UNRAVELING THE CONSPIRACY

1. *Canton Daily News*, Aug. 15, 1926.
2. Himebaugh, "The Shaping of a Martyr," 8–9.
3. Martin, "Murder of a Journalist," 227.
4. *Cleveland Plain Dealer*, Dec. 21, 1926. The story behind the murder investigation became public and available to the press during the trial of Patrick McDermott. This chapter relies on articles in the *Cleveland Plain Dealer* and the *Canton Evening Repository* from December 1926. The only account of the murder investigation by a participant was Ora Slater's as told to Karl Pauly, "How I Trapped the Don Mellett Slayers," *True Detective Mysteries*, May 1931, 48–53, 95–102.
5. Krahling, "Don R. Mellett," 117–18.
6. *Canton Daily News*, July 18, 1926.
7. H. C. Pontius, "Notes on Ben Clarke," n.d. Day, Ketterer File.
8. *Cleveland Plain Dealer*, July 17, 1926.
9. Krahling, "Don R. Mellett," 5.
10. Martin, "Murder of a Journalist," 278.
11. *Salem News*, Aug. 8, 1926.
12. *Cleveland Plain Dealer*, May 16, 1927.
13. Krahling, "Don R. Mellett," 5.
14. Hutchinson and Smith Detective Bureau notes, Day, Ketterer File.
15. WWI Draft Registration, Ora Major Slater, Sept. 1918.
16. *Lawrenceburg Register*, Feb. 8, 1945.
17. Slater, "How I Trapped," 52.
18. Kenny, *Canton*, 35.
19. *Cleveland Plain Dealer*, Dec. 5, 1926.
20. *Canton Sunday Repository*, July 18, 1926.
21. *Canton Daily News*, May 18, 1927; Slater, "How I Trapped," 95. It appears that initially, like many people in Canton, the Bitzlers found Slater underwhelming for so famous a detective.
22. Slater, "How I Trapped," 95.

23. *Canton Daily News*, Feb. 11, 1927.
24. Ibid., May 18, 1927.
25. Ibid., May 12, 1927.
26. *Canton Evening Repository*, Dec. 7, 1926.
27. Ibid., Dec. 15, 1926.
28. Updegraff, "A Study of the Circumstances," 39.
29. Ibid., 41.
30. *Time*, July 26, 1926.
31. Martin, "Murder of a Journalist," 276.
32. Ibid., 278.
33. Updegraff, "A Study of the Circumstances," 39.
34. *Canton Daily News*, Feb. 18, 1926.
35. Martin, "Murder of a Journalist," 271.
36. Transcript of the Lengel Civil Service Hearing, Sept. 8, 1926, Day, Ketterer File.
37. Updegraff, "A Study of the Circumstances," 44.
38. Future guests at the New Barnett Hotel included "Pretty Boy" Floyd and "Machine Gun" Kelly. *Canton Repository*, Apr. 18, 1976.
39. *Cleveland Plain Dealer*, Dec. 16, 1926.
40. *Canton Evening Repository*, Dec. 15, 1926.
41. Slater, "How I Trapped," 97.
42. Ibid.
43. *Canton Evening Repository*, Dec. 16, 1926.

5. THE GANG OF THREE

1. *Canton Daily News*, Feb. 18, 1927.
2. Ibid.
3. The story behind the murder investigation became public during the trial of Pat McDermott. Newspapers reported this information as it became available through trial testimony. This chapter relies on articles in the *Cleveland Plain Dealer* and the *Canton Evening Repository* for December 1926. *Cleveland Plain Dealer*, Feb. 18, 1927.
4. *Canton Daily News*, May 12, 1927.
5. *Salem News*, Aug. 18, 1926.
6. Slater, "How I Trapped," 99.
7. *Canton Daily News*, May 12, 1927.
8. Ohio Military Men, 1917–18, Louis Mazer, accessed Mar. 2, 2005, from www.ancestry.com.
9. Greiner, "Saxton Street," 283–84.
10. Slater, "How I Trapped," 99–100.
11. *Editor and Publisher*, Jan. 1, 1927.
12. H. C. Pontius letter, Oct. 8, 1926. Day, Ketterer File. Roach was from Indiana, and it is likely the Melletts and Wendell Willkie had some part

in retaining him. Still, it is unlikely Roach would have gone to Canton if Henry Timkin had not given him a retainer of $10,000.

13. *Salem News*, Aug. 14, 1926.
14. Ibid., Aug. 12, 1926.
15. Ibid., Aug. 14, 1926.
16. Slater, "How I Trapped," 99–100.
17. *Salem News*, Aug. 17, 1926.
18. Ibid., Aug. 18, 1926.
19. *Cleveland Plain Dealer*, Dec. 10, 1926.
20. Ibid., Dec. 4, 1926.
21. Martin, "Murder of a Journalist," 279.
22. Telegram from Clement Curry to William Tugman, Aug. 19, 1926, Day, Ketterer File. It has often been reported, but never verified, that Streitenberger was in Buffalo for a marksmanship contest.
23. *Cleveland Plain Dealer*, May 16, 1927.
24. Telegram from Clement Curry to William Tugman, Aug. 19, 1926, Day, Ketterer File.
25. Himebaugh, "The Shaping of a Martyr," 179.
26. Martin, "Murder of a Journalist," 279.
27. *Salem News*, Aug. 18, 1926.
28. Studer, who was in reality broke, was eventually convicted on state charges of perjury and keeping a house of ill repute. When he was sentenced, he wept and asked to be assigned to the prison chaplain. *Canton Evening Repository*, Sept. 3, 1926.
29. Ibid., Dec. 11, 1926.
30. According to Mrs. Mellett, the purpose of the lawsuit was not money but as another means of getting at the conspirators and securing "vigorous prosecution of the murders." *Canton Evening Repository*, Sept. 3, 1926.
31. *Salem News*, Aug. 24, 1926.
32. *Editor and Publisher*, Jan. 1, 1927.
33. *Canton Evening Repository*, Sept. 3, 1926.
34. Krahling, "Don R. Mellett," 261.
35. *Canton Daily News*, May 14, 1927.
36. Slater did not mention it when writing in 1931, but it is possible that Tugman was also there, as he had been an unofficial mediator between Slater and the McDermott kin.
37. Miscellaneous newspaper clippings, n.d., McDermott Family File, Nanty Glo Historical Society, Nanty Glo, Pa.
38. Ora Slater letter to Reward Committee, July 16, 1927, Day, Ketterer File.
39. *Cleveland Plain Dealer*, Feb. 17, 1927.

6. THE SLUGGER GOES ON TRIAL

1. The only written accounts of the trial of Patrick Eugene McDermott are contemporary press reports and the trial transcript of *State of Ohio vs. Patrick Eugene McDermott*. This chapter draws from the transcript and on articles in the *Canton Daily News*, *Canton Evening Repository*, *Cleveland Plain Dealer*, and *New York Times* for December 1926.

2. Updegraff, "A Study of the Circumstances," 39.

3. *Canton Evening Repository*, Dec. 3, 1926.

4. WWI Draft Registration, Louis Mazer, accessed Feb. 10, 2005, from www.Ancestry.com.

5. The same day the three defendants were entertaining reporters at police headquarters, the Ohio State Industrial Commission awarded Florence Mellett $6,500 in workmen's compensation for her husband's untimely death. The Industrial Commission ruled that newspapermen were always subject to hazard, even at home, and that Mellett's death was "in the line of duty." *Canton Daily News*, Dec 3, 1926.

6. Heald, *The Stark County Story*, 25.

7. *Cleveland Plain Dealer*, Dec. 18, 1926.

8. *Cleveland Plain Dealer*, Dec. 8, 1926.

9. *Canton Evening Repository*, Dec. 12, 1926.

10. Ibid., Dec. 10, 1926.

11. Ibid.

12. *Cleveland Plain Dealer*, Dec. 12, 1926.

13. Ibid., Dec. 5, 1926.

14. All trial testimony is derived from the official transcript and contemporary newspaper accounts.

15. *Canton Evening Repository*, Dec. 13, 1926.

16. *Cleveland Plain Dealer*, Dec. 14, 1926.

17. Ibid.

18. Ibid.

19. Ibid.

20. Ibid., Dec. 15, 1926.

21. Ibid. Durand later complained to reporters about having to read Steve's love letters, "Did you ever hear of a man having a tougher job than reading a lot of illiterate love letters?" *Canton Evening Repository*, Dec. 15, 1926.

22. *Cleveland Plain Dealer* and *Canton Evening Repository*, Dec. 15, 1926.

23. Ibid.

24. *Canton Evening Repository*, Dec. 8, 15, 1926.

25. *Cleveland Plain Dealer*, Dec. 12, 1926.

26. Ibid.

27. *Canton Evening Repository*, Dec. 15, 1926.

28. Ibid., Dec. 19, 1926.

29. *Cleveland Plain Dealer*, Dec. 19, 1926; *Canton Evening Repository*, Dec. 18, 1926.
30. *Cleveland Plain Dealer*, Dec. 19, 1926.
31. Ibid.
32. *Canton Evening Repository*, Dec. 20, 1926.
33. *Cleveland Plain Dealer*, Dec. 21, 25, 1926.
34. Ibid., Dec. 21, 1926.
35. Ibid.
36. *Canton Evening Repository*, Dec. 22, 1926.
37. *Cleveland Plain Dealer*, Dec. 21, 1926.
38. *Canton Evening Repository*, Dec. 21, 1926.
39. *Cleveland Plain Dealer*, Dec. 22, 1926.
40. *Canton Evening Repository*, Dec. 23, 1926. Pat was variously described by the courtroom reporters as earnest, nonchalant, suave, and debonair. They likened him to a young clerk or businessman. The defendant and his attorneys seemed to be auditioning different attire and attitudes as they searched for those that placed Pat in the most favorable light. It proved to be a challenge remaking a shiftless career criminal into someone other than what he was.
41. *Canton Evening Repository*, Dec. 24, 1926.
42. Ibid., Dec. 22, 1926.
43. *Cleveland Plain Dealer*, Dec. 23, 1926.
44. Ibid., Dec. 24, 1926.
45. Ibid.; *Canton Evening Repository*, Dec. 24, 1926.
46. *Canton Evening Repository*, Dec. 23, 1926; *Cleveland Plain Dealer*, Dec. 24, 1926.
47. *Canton Evening Repository*, Dec. 24, 1926.
48. *Cleveland Plain Dealer*, Dec. 24, 1926.
49. *Canton Repository*, Apr. 18, 1976.
50. *Canton Evening Repository*, Dec. 24, 1926.
51. Ibid.
52. *Cleveland Plain Dealer*, Dec. 25, 1926; *Canton Evening Repository*, Dec. 24, 1926.
53. *Cleveland Plain Dealer*, Dec. 25, 1926.
54. *New York Times*, Dec. 25, 1926.
55. Ibid.
56. *Cleveland Plain Dealer*, Dec. 25, 1926.
57. Ibid.
58. Ibid.
59. Ibid., Dec. 31, 1926.
60. Ibid., Dec. 25, 1926; *Canton Repository*, Apr. 18, 1976.
61. *Canton Evening Repository*, Dec. 25, 1926.
62. *Cleveland Plain Dealer*, Dec. 29, 1926.

63. The ever-frugal prosecutor McClintock urged that McDermott be sent to prison in Columbus as soon as possible as the extra guards were costing the county $50 a day. *Cleveland Plain Dealer*, Dec. 31, 1926.
64. Ibid.
65. Ibid., Dec. 25, 1926.

7. THE RICH MAN FACES A JURY

1. The only contemporary accounts of the *State of Ohio vs. Ben Rudner* are found in press reports of the trial. Much of the material in this chapter is derived from articles in the *Canton Daily News, Canton Evening Repository*, and *Cleveland Plain Dealer* for February 1927. Once in Columbus, Pat McDermott was assigned by Warden P. E. Thomas, who stated flatly that Pat's jail loafing days were over, to collect garbage in the 3,200-inmate prison. *Canton Daily News*, Feb. 4, 1927.
2. *Canton Daily News*, Jan. 20, 1927.
3. *Canton Evening Repository*, Nov. 18, 1929.
4. *Cleveland Plain Dealer*, Feb. 8, 1927.
5. Greiner, "Saxton Street," 220.
6. The prosecution wanted jurors unafraid to impose the death penalty. The defense asked two standard questions: "Do you read the *Canton Daily News?*" and "Do you belong to any organization?" One potential juror, Jacob Boughman of Alliance, was ordered by the court to answer when he balked, "Well, I belong to the Ku Klux Klan." This brought a ripple of laughter in the courtroom. Boughman quickly added, "But our principles are as good as any other organization." The anti-Semitic klansman wasn't seated. *Cleveland Plain Dealer*, Feb. 9, 1927.
7. On March 21, 1927, Nadel, free pending appeal of his conviction for hiding Pat McDermott, was gunned down in East Cleveland. He was shot fourteen times. A stunned McDermott said Nadel was "big hearted." *Cleveland Plain Dealer*, Mar. 22, 1927.
8. *Cleveland Plain Dealer*, Feb. 11, 1927.
9. Reporters continued to note Florence Mellett's girlish appearance, something unusual, they agreed, for a woman with four children. The *Cleveland Plain Dealer* commented, "Although she has four children, the oldest of whom is twelve, she looked to be a mere girl as she stepped to the witness stand" (Feb. 11, 1927).
10. *Canton Daily News*, Feb. 11, 1927.
11. Ibid.
12. *Canton Daily News*, Feb. 11, 1927.
13. *Cleveland Plain Dealer*, Feb. 15, 1926.
14. Ibid.
15. *Cleveland Plain Dealer*, Feb. 16, 1927.
16. *Canton Daily News*, Feb. 16, 1927.

17. Ibid., Feb. 19, 1927.
18. *Cleveland Plain Dealer*, Feb. 19, 1927.
19. Ibid., Feb. 20, 1927.
20. *Canton Daily News*, Feb. 21, 1927.
21. *Cleveland Plain Dealer*, Feb. 22, 1927.
22. Ibid.
23. *Canton Daily News*, Feb. 22, 1927.
24. *Cleveland Plain Dealer*, Feb. 23, 1927.
25. Ibid., Feb. 24, 1927.
26. *Canton Daily News*, Feb. 24, 1927.
27. *Canton Daily News* and *Cleveland Plain Dealer*, Feb. 25, 1927.
28. *Canton Daily News*, Feb. 28, 1927.

8. MAZER CONFESSES

1. *Cleveland Plain Dealer*, May 8, 1927.
2. *Canton Daily News*, Feb. 11, 1927.
3. Much of the material in this chapter is derived from two primary sources: the transcript of Louis Mazer's confession on March 5, 1927, and Mazer's testimony during the trial of Floyd Streitenberger, May 7–18, 1927, which can be found in press reports in the *Canton Daily News, Canton Evening Repository,* and *Cleveland Plain Dealer.*
4. *State of Ohio vs. Louis Mazer*, Mar. 5, 1927.
5. *Cleveland Plain Dealer*, May 12, 1927.
6. Ibid.
7. *Canton Daily News*, May 11, 1927.
8. *State of Ohio vs. Louis Mazer*, Mar. 5, 1927.
9. *Canton Daily News*, May 11, 1927.
10. Ibid.
11. Ibid.
12. H. C. Pontius notes on Louis Mazer confession, n.d., Day, Ketterer File.
13. *Canton Daily News*, May 11, 1927.
14. Ibid., May 27, 1927.
15. *State of Ohio vs. Louis Mazer*, Mar. 5, 1927.
16. *State of Ohio vs. Louis Mazer*, Mar. 5, 1927.
17. H. C. Pontius notes on Louis Mazer confession, n.d., Day, Ketterer File.
18. *Cleveland Plain Dealer*, May 12, 1927.
19. *State of Ohio vs. Louis Mazer*, Mar. 5, 1927.
20. *Canton Daily News*, May 11, 1927.

9. THE DETECTIVE'S DAY IN COURT

1. Helen Bloom, "Editor Don Mellett's 'Classic Martyrdom' Reexamined at Scene 39 Years Later," *News Workshop* (New York University), Jan. 1965, 1.

2. *New York Times*, May 3, 1927.

3. Ibid.

4. *Canton Daily News*, May 14, 1927. The only written accounts of the *State of Ohio vs. Floyd Streitenberger* are contemporary press reports; no trial transcript has been located. Most of the material in this chapter is derived from articles in the *Canton Daily News*, *Canton Evening Repository*, and *Cleveland Plain Dealer* from May 1927.

5. *Wilmington Daily News Journal*, souvenir ed., 1929.

6. *Wilmington Daily News Journal*, Feb. 19, 1949.

7. Ben Clarke, in the company of Chief Wise, arrived at a New Year's Eve party, and while checking his coat, Clarke accidentally dropped his service revolver. The weapon discharged, the bullet striking Clarke near the spine. The wound left Clarke with a partial disability for which the Canton police department spent years trying to dismiss him. In later years, Clarke's sister would claim that her brother was actually a Mellett supporter. *Canton Evening Repository*, Jan. 2, 1927.

8. *Salem News*, May 9, 1927.

9. *Cleveland Plain Dealer*, May 10, 1927.

10. Ibid., May 12, 1927. The *Cleveland Plain Dealer* reported that Mazer decided to drop his $50,000 libel lawsuit against the *Canton Daily News* (May 12, 1927).

11. *Canton Daily News*, May 14, 1927.

12. H. C. Pontius letter to L. G. Nutt, Nov. 9, 1926, Day, Ketterer File.

13. *Cleveland Plain Dealer*, May 14, 1927.

14. *Canton Daily News*, May 14, 1927.

15. *Cleveland Plain Dealer*, May 15, 1927.

16. Ibid.

17. *Canton Daily News*, May 18, 1927.

18. To its credit, the *New York Times* ran seventy-one stories on the Mellett murder and its aftermath from July 1926 to March 1928. *Canton Repository*, Apr. 18, 1976.

19. *Cleveland Plain Dealer*, May 19, 1927.

20. Transcript of Floyd Streitenberger interrogation, May 20, 1927, Day, Ketterer File; and *Canton Evening Repository*, May 21, 1927. The five spent shell casings recovered by Slater were from two ammunition manufacturers. This concurred with Mazer's earlier recollection that he received a handful of mismatched cartridges when he purchased the revolver. The recovery of only five casings for a six-shot revolver is explained by the

standard practice of leaving the chamber under the revolver's hammer empty to avoid accidental discharge.

21. Ibid.
22. H. C. Pontius, "Notes on Ben Clarke," n.d., Day, Ketterer File.
23. Transcript of Floyd Streitenberger interrogation, May 20, 1927, Day, Ketterer File. The same day Streitenberger talked to investigators, Lengel went to the jail to see his former protégé at the suggestion of a deputy. But Streitenberger had changed his mind now that he was talking to investigators and refused to see Lengel.
24. Transcript of Floyd Streitenberger interrogation, May 20, 1927, Day, Ketterer File.
25. *Cleveland Plain Dealer,* May 24, 1927.
26. Ibid., May 22, 1927.

10. THE DUTCH BAKER DEFENDS HIMSELF

1. *Canton Daily News,* July 17, 1927. The only contemporary accounts of Lengel's trials are press reports. Much of the material in this chapter is derived from articles in the *Canton Daily News, Canton Evening Repository, Cleveland Plain Dealer,* and *Salem News* for July 1927 and February 1928.
2. Ibid., July 13, 1927.
3. *Canton Evening Repository,* Jan. 8, 1941.
4. Krahling, "Don R. Mellett," 46–48.
5. *Cleveland Plain Dealer,* July 12, 1927.
6. *Canton Daily News,* July 13, 1927.
7. *Cleveland Plain Dealer,* July 14, 1927.
8. *Canton Daily News,* July 13, 1927.
9. *Cleveland Plain Dealer,* July 14, 1927.
10. *Canton Daily News,* July 14, 1927.
11. Ibid., July 6, 1927.
12. Ibid., July 14, 1927.
13. *Cleveland Plain Dealer,* July 14, 1927.
14. Ibid.
15. Ibid.
16. Ibid.
17. *Canton Daily News,* July 15, 1927.
18. *Cleveland Plain Dealer,* July 16, 1927.
19. Ibid.
20. *Canton Daily News,* July 15, 1927.
21. *Cleveland Plain Dealer,* July 15, 1927.
22. Ibid.
23. Ibid., July 17, 1927.

24. Ibid.

25. *New York Times*, July 17, 1927.

26. *Canton Daily News*, July 17, 1927.

27. *Cleveland Plain Dealer*, July 17, 1927.

28. *New York Times*, July 17, 1927.

29. *Cleveland Plain Dealer*, July 17, 1927.

30. Ibid., July 18, 1927.

31. *Canton Daily News*, Feb. 19, 1928.

32. *Salem News*, Nov. 4, 1927.

33. Ibid., Dec. 28, 1927.

34. *Canton Daily News*, Feb. 13, 1928.

35. *Salem News*, Feb. 11, 1928.

36. Ibid., Feb. 13, 15, 16, 1928.

37. *Canton Daily News* and *Salem News*, Feb. 13–16, 1928.

38. Transcript of James M. Aungst interview on WCMW Radio, Aug. 11, 1956, William Dean Krahling Archive, William McKinley Presidential Library and Museum, Canton, Ohio.

39. *Canton Daily News*, Feb. 14, 1928.

40. *Salem News*, Feb. 18, 1928.

41. *Canton Daily News*, Feb. 17, 1928.

42. *Salem News*, Feb. 18, 20, 1928.

43. Ibid., Feb. 21, 1928.

44. *New York Times*, Feb. 22, 1928.

45. *Salem News*, Feb. 21, 22, 1928. The deal that Lengel was really seeking was not that unreasonable. He would be reinstated as chief of police for the two weeks he needed to qualify for a pension, and then he would retire. This would allow him to restore his honor and gain the financial security he desired for retirement. Unfortunately for Lengel, the same C. C. Curtis, whose safety director brother Ed Lengel had helped send to prison, was now mayor again. Mayor Curtis was not inclined to help the former chief.

46. *New York Times*, Feb. 22, 1928.

47. *Canton Daily News*, Feb. 22, 1928.

48. *Canton Repository*, July 8, 1971.

11. MCDERMOTT HAS THE LAST WORD

1. *Canton Daily News*, Feb. 4, 1927.

2. Ella Kerber (Resch) Perrin letter to William Dean Krahling, Oct. 10, 1965, Krahling Archive.

3. *Youngstown Vindicator*, Mar. 10, 1928. The conversation between McDermott and Resch was personally overseen by Warden Thomas. Most of the material in this chapter is taken from the interview published in the *Vindicator.*

4. Martin, "Murder of a Journalist," 277.
5. *Youngstown Vindicator*, Mar. 10, 1928.
6. *Canton Daily News*, Mar. 14, 1928.
7. *Youngstown Vindicator*, Mar. 1, 1928.
8. Ibid., Mar. 11, 1928.
9. *Canton Daily News*, Mar. 14, 22, 1928.

12. UNANSWERED QUESTIONS

1. Slater, "How I Trapped," 96.
2. Martin, "Murder of a Journalist," 273; Bloom, "Editor Don Mellett's 'Classic Martyrdom'"; Updegraff, "A Study of the Circumstances," 71–72; Himebaugh, "The Shaping of a Martyr," 190.
3. *Canton Repository*, Apr. 18, 1976.
4. Ibid.; Krahling, "Don R. Mellett," 275.

13. THE AFTERMATH

1. *Canton Daily News*, Mar. 15, 1928.
2. Ibid., Mar. 26, 1928. One small glitch had arisen in the fall of 1927 when Mrs. Steve Kascholk, who was suing for divorce in Cleveland, attempted to get an injunction to stop Steve from receiving his share of the reward. But while the Cleveland court readily granted Mrs. Kascholk a divorce on the grounds of abandonment, the judge denied her requested injunction. Steve's case was aided by Charles McClintock who testified for his star witness in divorce court. Mrs. Kascholk's appearance for the defense in the McDermott trial was not forgotten in Canton. Ibid., Dec. 4, 1927.
3. Defense attorney Everett Mills later claimed that he never received a penny from the McDermott family for defending Pat. Ibid., Mar. 26, 1928.
4. Ibid.
5. *Lawrenceburg Press*, Oct. 3, 1941; *Lawrenceburg Register*, Feb. 8, 1945.
6. *Canton Repository*, Feb. 2, 1965.
7. Ibid., Nov. 23, 1949.
8. Himebaugh, "The Shaping of a Martyr," 52; *Canton Repository*, Sept. 21, 1971; Indianapolis, Indiana, 1930 United States Census, William Lloyd Mellett, accessed Nov. 20, 2008, from www.AncestryLibrary.com; Miller, *The Mellett and Hickman Families*, 404.
9. *Canton Daily News*, Nov. 30, 1927.
10. *Canton Evening Repository*, Jan. 8, 1941.
11. Cleveland, Ohio 1930 U. S. Census, AncestryLibrary.com, Jan. 20, 2005.
12. *Canton Daily News*, Dec. 28, 1927; Himebaugh, "The Shaping of a Martyr," 55; *Canton Repository*, Aug. 11, 1949.
13. Himebaugh, "The Shaping of a Martyr," 55.
14. *Cleveland Plain Dealer*, Dec. 3, 1954.

15. *Canton Repository*, Nov. 29, 1954.

16. Ibid.

17. Ibid.

18. Ibid., July 20, 1955.

19. Updegraff, "A Study of the Circumstances," 56. No one from the Mc-Dermott family claimed Pat's remains. As was the custom at the time, his body was given to the Ohio State University medical school for research.

20. Don R. Mellett Memorial Lecture Series File, William Dean Krahling Archive.

21. Canton City Police Department Annual Report, 1929, William McKinley Library and Museum, Canton, Ohio.

22. Cebula, *James M. Cox*, 130–31.

23. Cox, *Journey Through My Years*, 323; Martin, "Murder of a Journalist," 282; *Akron Beacon Journal*, Oct. 14, 1982.

24. *Canton Daily News*, May 12, 1926.

Bibliography

PRIMARY SOURCES

Day, Ketterer File. William McKinley Presidential Library and Museum, Canton, Ohio.

William D. Krahling Archive. William McKinley Presidential Library and Museum, Canton, Ohio.

Mellett Murder File. Stark County Library District, Main Branch, Canton, Ohio.

McDermott Family File. Nanty Glo Historical Society, Nanty Glo, Pennsylvania.

Canton City Police Department Annual Report, 1929. William McKinley Presidential Library and Museum, Canton, Ohio.

State of Ohio vs. Louis Mazer. Sworn Statement. Stark County Library District, Main Branch, Canton, Ohio.

State of Ohio vs. Patrick Eugene McDermott. Trial Transcript. University Archives, Polsky Building, University of Akron, Akron, Ohio.

SECONDARY SOURCES

Behr, Edward. *Prohibition: Thirteen Years That Changed America.* New York: Arcade, 1996.

Bloom, Helen. "Editor Don Mellett's 'Classic Martyrdom' Reexamined at Scene 39 Years Later." *News Workshop* (New York University), January 1965.

Bollar, Paul F. *Presidential Campaigns.* New York: Oxford University Press, 1984.

Cebula, James E. *James M. Cox, Journalist and Politician.* New York: Garland, 1985.

"Corruption." *Time,* July 26, 1926.

Cox, James M. *Journey Through My Years.* New York: Simon and Schuster, 1946.

Crouch, William S. "Canton: A Lurid City." In Smith, ed., *An Ohio Reader: Reconstruction to the Present.* Vol. 2, 1975. 127-29.

Daniels, Jonathan. *They Will Be Heard: America's Crusading Newspaper Editors.* New York: McGraw Hill, 1965.

Greiner, Elizabeth Jane. "Saxton Street: The Reconstruction of a Red Light Community 1906–1913." M.A. thesis, Ohio State University, 1987.

Heald, E. T. *The Stark County Story.* 4 vols. Canton, Ohio: Stark County Historical Society, 1949–59.

Himebaugh, Glenn A. "Donald Ring Mellett, Journalist: The Shaping of a Martyr." Ph.D. dissertation, Southern Illinois University, 1978.

Kenny, Kimberly. *Canton: A Journey Through Time.* Chicago: Arcadia, 2003.

Kobler, John. *Ardent Spirits: The Rise and Fall of Prohibition.* New York: DeCapo, 1973.

Krahling, William D. "Don R. Mellett of the *Canton Daily News.*" M.A. thesis, University of Iowa, 1967.

Leeke, Jim. "Who Killed Harry Beasley?" *Timeline,* October–December 2004.

Martin, John Barlow. "Murder of a Journalist." *Harper's Magazine,* September 1946.

McDonald, B. F. "Fifth Annual Report of the Prohibition Commission." In Smith, ed., *An Ohio Reader: Reconstruction to the Present.* Vol. 2, 1975. 146-48.

Miller, Franklin, Jr. *The Mellett and Hickman Families of Henry County, Indiana.* Gambier, Ohio: Privately published, 1976.

Osinski, Bill. "Wages of Sin Aren't Enough, Madam Says." *Akron Beacon Journal,* October, 14, 1982.

Plummer, Elizabeth L. "Tourism at the Ohio Penitentiary." *Timeline,* January–February 2004.

Reppetts, Thomas. *American Mafia.* New York: Henry Holt, 2004.

Roseboom, Eugene H., and Francis P. Weisenberger. *A History of Ohio.* Columbus: Ohio Historical Society, 1988.

Schudson, Michael. *Discovering the News: A Social History of American Newspapers.* New York: Basic Books, 1978.

Slater, Ora, as told to Karl Pauly. "How I Trapped the Don Mellett Slayers." *True Detective Mysteries,* May 1931.

Smith, Thomas H., ed. *An Ohio Reader: Reconstruction to the Present.* Grand Rapids, Mich.: Eerdmans, 1975.

"Stench." *Time,* August 2, 1926.

Sullivan, Robert, ed. *The Most Notorious Crimes in American History.* New York: Time, Inc., 2007.

Thorton, Mark. "Alcohol Prohibition Was a Failure." *Cato Policy Analysis* No. 157 (July 17, 1999). Accessed August 29, 2005, from http://www.cato.org/pubs/pas/pa-157.html.

Updegraff, Jerry L. "A Study of the Circumstances Surrounding the Murder of Don R. Mellett in 1926." M.A. thesis, Ohio University, 1974.

Warner, Landon. "James M. Cox." Ohio Fundamental Documents Searchable Database. http://www.ohiohistory.org/onlinedoc/ohgovernment/governors/coxjames.

Williams, Michael W. "Profits from Prohibition: Walter Kidder and the Hayner Distillery." *Timeline*, March–April 1999.

NEWSPAPERS

Akron Beacon Journal
Canton Daily News
Canton Evening Repository
Canton Repository
Canton Sunday Repository
Cleveland Plain Dealer
Detroit News
Editor and Publisher
The Journal (Nanty Glo, Pennsylvania)
Lawrenceburg (Indiana) Press
Lawrenceburg (Indiana) Register
New York Times
Salem (Ohio) News
Youngstown Vindicator

Index